# A Long-Term Vision for an Ecologically Sound Platte River

Zea Books
Lincoln, Nebraska
26 September 2022

ISBN: 978-1-60962-258-9   paperback
ISBN: 978-1-60962-259-6   ebook
DOI: 10.32873/unl.dc.zea.1331

Zea Books are published by
the University of Nebraska–Lincoln Libraries.

Electronic (pdf) edition available online at
https://digitalcommons.unl.edu/zeabook/

Nebraska
UNIVERSITY OF
Lincoln

# AUTHORSHIP

Andrew J. Caven[1,2,*], Melissa M. Mosier[3], Kristal J. Stoner[3], Bill Taddicken[3], Brice Krohn[1], Ashley Gramza[4], Craig R. Allen[5], Mike Carter[4], Michelle Koch[6], Kirk D. Schroeder[7], Sarah Bailey[8], Rich Walters[9], Brian C. Chaffin[10], Erica Gnuse[11], Amy Jones[8], and Kate Bird[5]

1) Platte River Whooping Crane Maintenance Trust, 6611 W. Whooping Crane Drive, Wood River, NE 68883, USA [DBA "Crane Trust"]

2) International Crane Foundation, E11376 Shady Lane Rd, Baraboo, WI 53913, USA

3) Audubon Nebraska, 3310 Holdrege Street, 407 Hardin Hall, Lincoln, NE 68583, USA

4) Playa Lakes Joint Venture, 2675 Northpark Drive, Suite 208, Lafayette, CO 80026, USA

5) Center for Resilience in Agricultural Working Landscapes (CRAWL), University of Nebraska-Lincoln, 1825 N. 38th Street, Lincoln, NE 68583, USA

6) Nebraska Game and Parks Commission, 2200 N. 33rd Street, Lincoln, NE 68503, USA

7) Partners for Fish and Wildlife – Nebraska, U.S. Fish and Wildlife Service, 9325 S. Alda Road, Wood River, NE 68883, USA

8) Prairie Plains Resource Institute, 1307 L St, Aurora, NE 68818, USA

9) The Nature Conservancy in Nebraska, 1007 Leavenworth Street, Omaha, NE 68102, USA

10) W.A. Franke College of Forestry & Conservation, University of Montana, 32 Campus Drive, Missoula, MT 59812, USA

11) Nebraska Ducks Unlimited, 2121 N. Webb Road, Suite 309, Grand Island, NE 68803, USA

*Correspondence: acaven@savingcranes.org, +1-(605)-252-8007

# Table of Contents

# EXECUTIVE SUMMARY

The Platte River extends about 310 mi (499 km) from North Platte, Nebraska, to its terminus at the Missouri River confluence near Plattsmouth, Nebraska. The Platte River Valley is a continentally significant ecosystem that serves as a major stopover for migratory waterbirds in the Central Flyway including the endangered Whooping Crane (*Grus americana*) and >1 million Sandhill Cranes (*Antigone canadensis*) at the peak of spring migration. However, the Platte River Valley also supports a great diversity of avifauna including grassland breeding birds, native stream fish, vascular plants, herpetofauna, mammals, pollinators, and aquatic macroinvertebrates. Despite ongoing conservation efforts since the mid-1970s the ecosystem remains largely conservation dependent and an increasing number of species across taxa are being considered at risk of regional extirpation or outright extinction. However, given the attention provided to conservation in the Platte River Valley and the need to maintain ecologically functional stopover sites in the Central Flyway, there is a great opportunity to create a resilient refugium for biodiversity conservation in the central Great Plains. To that end we convened a working group of $\geq$18 individuals representing $\geq$9 organizations including representatives from non-profit conservation organizations, universities, and state and federal natural resource agencies to develop a long-term vision for an ecologically sound Platte River Valley (PRV). We met in groups of varying size for >170 hours throughout a more than 3-year period and developed conservation priorities and objectives using a landscape design process. Landscape design is an interdisciplinary conservation planning process that incorporates components of landscape ecology and social dimensions of natural resources with the explicit intention of improving conservation implementation.

Our working group defined broad "future desired conditions" associated with hydrology and habitat conservation including increasing the extent, connectivity, and resilience of seasonal and temporary wetlands, warm-water slough wetlands, lowland tallgrass prairies, and ecologically functional braided river habitats as well as improving water quality and hydrological functionality within the riparian ecosystem. We clearly defined "processes" that maintain ecological diversity within the PRV landscape (e.g., elevated spring flows that maintain shallow groundwater levels that subirrigate wet meadows) as well as "drivers" which are human influences that impede desirable ecological processes (e.g., suburban sprawl that displaces native habitats). We also proposed "needed actions" to mitigate the undesirable drivers as well as related "quantitative goals." Goals generally fell into the following categories including flow and habitat conservation targets, engineering solutions, research objectives, management aims, funding targets, outreach plans, or a combination. We specified ≥40 groups as "key audiences" to engage with to achieve our conservation goals, including several community-based organizations. We used the best available science to set our goals, but reasonable uncertainty often remained as to the ultimate impacts of achieving our goals, highlighting the need for continued regional research regarding a diversity of taxa and ecosystem processes. For example, a key goal is to restore ≥30% of the land within 800 m of the main channel of the Platte River to wetland and/or grassland habitat within each ~12 km (~8 mi)-reach of the Platte River via cooperation with willing private and public landowners. Research indicates that achieving this goal would reduce flooding impacts on human communities and increase habitat connectivity for dispersal-limited species, but more research will be needed to test the approach's effectiveness. The discussion section of this document provides the rationale for quantitative goals using the scientific literature.

Our vision document concentrates on conservation priorities in the mainstem Platte River including the Central Platte River Valley (CPRV) and the Lower Platte River Valley (LPRV), but we plan to expand this work throughout the Platte River watershed. Conservation efforts that are ecosystem- rather than species-centric will likely improve long-term outcomes. Additionally, if conservation efforts focus on promoting ecological functionality as compared to meeting minimum suitability thresholds, improvements in ecosystem condition may be more resilient to future stressors. Restoring hydro-geomorphological processes and improving habitat connectivity are essential to advancing ecosystem function. Finally, sustainable conservation efforts will need to consider the desires of the human community and actively engage partners whose interests align with conservation aims. Success on the Platte River is a litmus test for conservation in the Great Plains and across highly transformed landscapes with intensive developmental, industrial, and agricultural pressures. Success in this river system could indicate a path forward for ecosystems facing similar challenges. Continuing to restore ecological connectivity, functionality, and resilience within the PRV can safeguard the ecosystem's role as a refugium for a diversity of taxa for many generations to come.

# INTRODUCTION

## Ecological & Social Significance of the Platte River Valley

The Platte River is formed at the confluence of the North and South Platte Rivers and extends about 310 mi (499 km) from North Platte, Nebraska, to its terminus at the confluence of the Missouri River near Plattsmouth, Nebraska (Eschner et al. 1981, 1983; Figure 1). However, measured from its furthest direct source at the beginning of the North Platte River, the system flows for about 990 mi. (1,593 km) from the Rocky Mountains on the east side of the Continental Divide to its terminus (Eschner et al. 1981, 1983). The Platte River Basin encompasses the North Platte, South Platte, Loup, and Elkhorn Rivers as well as their tributaries and drains about 86,000 mi.$^2$ (222,740 km$^2$) of the eastern Rocky Mountains and Great Plains making the Platte River one of the most important tributaries to the Missouri River (Eschner et al. 1981, 1983; Figure 1). The Platte River and its major tributaries comprise one of the most reliable sources of fresh water traversing the arid central Great Plains and for that reason it has been extremely important to human communities including indigenous peoples such as the Pawnee as well as early European settlers for many centuries (Kinbacher et al. 2012). The west to east flowing river system was similarly important to wildlife populations migrating across the arid Great Plains such as Plains Bison (*Bison bison bison*) and Whooping Cranes (*Grus americana*) (Allen 1952, Hart 2001).

The Platte River Valley is a continentally significant and well-studied ecosystem, supporting expanses of braided river, lowland tallgrass prairie, wet meadow, shallow marsh, and riparian woodland that provide habitat for a range of species of conservation concern (Currier 1982, Henszey et al. 2004, Kaul et al. 2006, Caven et al. 2019b). It serves as the "pinch in the hourglass" of the Central Flyway for several species of waterbirds, including over 1 million

Sandhill Cranes that stage there during the spring, millions of geese and ducks, a diversity of shorebirds, and is designated as critical habitat for the endangered Whooping Crane (USFWS 1978, 1981, Vrtiska and Sullivan 2009, Brown and Johnsgard 2013, Caven et al. 2020a, 2020b). Additional species of concern that utilize the Platte River Valley (PRV) include the federally-listed Piping Plover (*Charadrius melodus*) and Pallid Sturgeon (*Scaphirhynchus albus*), as well as the state-listed Interior Least Tern (*Sterna antillarum athalassos*), Henslow's Sparrow (*Ammodramus henslowii*), Plains Topminnow (*Fundulus sciadicus*), Regal Fritillary (*Speyeria idalia*), Platte River Caddisfly (*Ironoquia plattensis*), Plains Pocket Mouse (*Perognathus flavescens*), Red-bellied Snake (*Storeria occipitomaculata*), Cardinal Flower (*Lobelia cardinalis*), and several others (Kim 2005, Roche et al. 2016, Caven et al. 2017a, 2017b, Johnson and Geluso 2017, Tye et al. 2017, Schneider et al. 2018). Despite the diversity this river valley supports, and the prominent role it plays in the migration of many bird species, its ecological and hydrological functionality continues to be threatened by the development of land and water resources (Krapu et al. 1982, Simons and Associates 2000, Pauley et al. 2018, Caven et al. 2019a, SPROWG 2020).

Crossing three states, a myriad of counties, municipalities, and other political subdivisions, the human communities along the Platte River are relatively heterogeneous - which means that the human drivers influencing ecological processes along the river vary across the basin as well. To some degree following the river continuum concept (Vannote et al. 1980), rural communities line the river from headwaters in eastern Colorado and Wyoming through the agriculturally rich but relatively rural western and central Nebraska, toward the more urban centers of Lincoln and Omaha at the lower reaches of the river as it empties into the Missouri

(Figure 1). The exceptions to this assessment are the rapidly growing urban communities of the front range of Colorado.

This paper will outline specific recommendations for working toward a more ecologically sound Platte River, successes of past conservation efforts and goals still to be attained, and the importance of studying how communities within the watershed influence and are influenced by the Platte River and its environs. The direct and indirect interactions, dependencies, pressures, and services that connect humans and the Platte River define its riverscape; and the current condition of the Platte River riverscape and all of the ecological processes it supports reflect the legacy of values held by humans who have stewarded it for hundreds of years (Dunham et al. 2017). The ecological goals outlined below are presented in order to achieve certain desired conditions along the riverscape that reflect the value we now hold for resilience to be supported at multiple scales in order to adapt to future disturbances, increasing natural resource use, a changing climate, and other stressors (Birge et al. 2014). The pressures placed on the Platte "riverscape" will continue to be complex, dynamic, ever changing, and are likely to increase in scale and will therefore require conservation efforts coordinated at broader geographic, ecological, social, and temporal scales than previously attempted.

**Pre-Development Conditions and Change**

We have a much better picture of the pre-development Platte River ecosystem than we do of many other river systems because of its prominent location along multiple paths of westward expansions including the Oregon Trail, Mormon Trail, and the Union Pacific Railway (Williams 1978, Eschner et al. 1983, Currier and Davis 2000). Measurements from between 1800 and 1860 indicated that the river was generally 1 to 2 miles wide (~ 3 miles wide in some locations at flood stage), with peak flows reaching 45,000 cfs in the Central Platte River Valley (CPRV; Eschner et al. 1983, Currier and O'Brien 1987, Simons and Associates 2000). The annual hydrograph was typified by high flow events in the late spring and a gradual decline to low flows by the late summer, with persistent moderate flows generally the rest of the year (Eschner et al. 1983, Currier and O'Brien 1987, Simons and Associates 2000). It was also a shallow river with depths varying little across low and high flows (< 2 m), as its tendency with additional discharge was to spread laterally rather than increase in depth (Eschner et a. 1983, Simons and Associates 2000, Piégay et al. 2006). This broad river valley was dominated by wetland and grassland habitats with aggregations of Plains Cottonwood (*Populus deltoides*) and Peachleaf Willow (*Salix amygdaloides*) woodland (Currier and Davis 2000, Simons and Associates 2000).

These expansive wetlands and generally shallow waters made the CPRV an important stopover site for Whooping Cranes during their migration (Allen 1952, USFWS 1981). Historic records (1722 – 1948) indicate that more Whooping Cranes were killed along the Platte River than in almost any other portion of their range (13% of kill records were from Nebraska and concentrated along the Platte River; Allen 1952). Over 370 species of birds have been recorded using the PRV making it one of the most species-rich sites in the central Great Plains (Bomberger Brown and Johnsgard 2013). However, this habitat, which likely hosted significant Whooping Crane concentrations per kill records, was changed drastically by human development including widespread damming, diversion, and constriction of the Platte River beginning in earnest in the late 1800s (Krapu et al. 1982, Sidle et al. 1989, Currier and Henszey 1996, Eisel and Aiken 1997, Nemec et al. 2014).

The majority of the diversion structures, canals, and storage reservoirs were built along the North and South Platte Rivers as well as the western portion of the CPRV, primarily for the purposes of storing water for irrigation, hydropower, and coal-fired powerplant cooling systems (Figure 1; Simons and Associates 2000). By the 1970s river flows (-70%), sediment transportation (-87%), and channel width (-60 to -90%) had been drastically reduced, and the river's character significantly changed (Williams 1978, Eschner et al. 1983, Sidle et al. 1989, Simons and Associates 2000). The once wide, shallow, prairie, braided river had transitioned to a much narrower, wooded, incised, and meandering channel, with negative consequences for wildlife (USFWS 1981, Krapu et al. 1982, Currier 1982, O'Brien and Currier 1987, Johnson 1994, Horn et al. 2012). The Platte River west of Overton, Nebraska, had been largely abandoned by Sandhill and Whooping Cranes from the 1940s to the 1980s (Walkinshaw 1956, USFWS 1981, Krapu et al. 1982, Faanes and LeValley 1993). Furthermore, much of the prairie and meadow habitats that provided important sources of protein and nutrients to crane species, as well as other birds, and habitat for additional native plants and wildlife had been lost by the late 1970s (-70 to -80%; Currier et al. 1985, Sidle et al. 1989).

**Early Platte River Valley Conservation Efforts – 1970s to 1990s**

Conservationists began to focus substantial attention on the PRV beginning in the 1970s with the passage of the Endangered Species Act (ESA; NRC 2005). Several avian research efforts focused on Whooping Cranes, Sandhill Cranes, Bald Eagles, and waterfowl were conducted to assess the status of those species on the Platte River (Firth 1974, Aronson and Ellis 1979, Ferguson et al. 1979, USFWS 1981, Krapu et al. 1982). Whooping Cranes, with under 80 individuals left in the last wild flock in the 1970s, and Bald Eagles, with less than 420 breeding pairs estimated to be remaining within the lower 48 states in the 1960s, were seen as particularly at risk of extinction or regional extirpation (Sprunt 1963, Miller et al. 1974). Additionally, the continued threat of habitat loss resulted in the National Audubon Society and The Nature Conservancy protecting land along the Platte River in the 1970s, and ultimately the formation of the Crane Trust in 1978 as a mitigation to the loss of Whooping Crane habitat expected from the construction of Greyrocks Dam in Wyoming (VanDerwalker 1982). Subsequent decades saw coordination regarding research and management of the Platte River between conservation organizations, state and federal agencies (e.g., USFWS, USGS, EPA), and regional universities, with particular attention on the CPRV (e.g., Currier 1994, Nagel and Kolstad 1987, Lingle 2001, NRC 2005, Caven et al. 2019c). During this time period several techniques were developed and evaluated for restoring braided river and wet meadow habitats in the CPRV to meet the needs of at-risk species, such as the disking of stabilized islands and methods for wet meadow flora establishment (Currier 1994, Pfeiffer 1999, Pfeiffer and Currier 2005, Kinzel et al. 2006, Kinzel 2009). The mid-1980s saw the listing of the Piping Plover and Interior Least Tern to the ESA and subsequently increased attention to their conservation on the Platte River as well (Faanes 1983, Lingle 1993, Kirsch 1996, NRC 2005). Efforts such as the *Platte River Basin Ecosystem Symposium* were important to disseminating information and promoting shared conservation goals for the Platte River through the 1990s and beyond (Lingle 2001, Caven et al. 2019c).

Concurrent to on-the-ground conservation efforts in the PRV a complicated policy conflict was developing regarding the ESA and water development interests in the river valley and its tributaries (Aiken 1989, Eisel and Aiken 1997, Echeverria 2001). The U.S. Bureau of Reclamation (USBR) had proposed the development of a one-million-acre-foot capacity dam along the South Platte River (The Narrows Unit) for irrigation purposes and the U.S. Fish and Wildlife Service (USFWS) had issued a jeopardy opinion in 1983 suggesting that additional reductions in flow could negatively impact critical Whooping Crane habitat (Aiken 1989, Eisel and Aiken 1997, Echeverria 2001). This impasse led the USFWS and the USBR to form the Platte River Management Joint Study (PRMJS), which could further clarify the needs of species of concern in the PRV and subsequently recommend alternative strategies for conservation that could allow water development to continue (PRMJS Biology Workgroup 1990, Eisel and Aiken 1997, Echeverria 2001). The PRMJS continued from 1984 to 1993 and ultimately failed to create an agreed upon set of management objectives and alternative conservation strategies for the PRV that would have allowed the continued development of water resources while maintaining compliance with the ESA (Eisel and Aiken 1997, Echeverria 2001). The need to relicense Kingsley Dam in 1997 eventually spurred additional coordination efforts between the states of Colorado, Wyoming, and Nebraska to ensure compliance with the ESA and ultimately led to the creation of the Platte River Recovery Implementation Program, which officially began in January 2007 (PRRIP; Freeman 2008, Smith 2011, Birge et al. 2014).

**The Platte River Recovery Implementation Program – 2000s to 2022**

PRRIP is a cooperative effort including participation from the U.S. Department of the Interior, the states of Colorado, Wyoming, and Nebraska, water users, and environmental organizations intended to maintain ESA compliance for current and future water developments by benefiting target species (Whooping Crane, Least Tern, Piping Plover, and Pallid Sturgeon) and their habitats through increases and management of river flows and land protection (USFWS and USBR 2006, Smith 2011). PRRIP included targeted land and water management objectives that were to be achieved within a 13-year period (2007-2019; USFWS and USBR 2006). These included reducing annual deficits to target flows developed for the CPRV by the USFWS to meet the demands of federally-listed species and their habitats by 130,000–150,000 acre-feet per year;

15

as well as the restoration and maintenance of ≥10,000 acres of wet meadow and riverine habitat in multiple complexes; and the cooperative protection of ≥29,000 acres including the efforts of additional regional entities (e.g., environmental organizations; USFWS and USBR 2006, Smith 2011). PRRIP met the objectives of their land plan but failed to meet the objectives of the water plan and therefore requested, and were granted, an additional 13-year extension in 2019 to make further progress in meeting the water plan objectives (USDOI 2019).

PRRIP applies an adaptive management framework to evaluate and refine land and water management actions to most efficiently meet conservation objectives associated with target species (USFWS and USBR 2006, Smith 2011). These efforts have improved our knowledge regarding metrics associated with target species habitat selection (e.g., Baasch et al. 2019a) and ecosystem function (e.g., Farnsworth et al. 2018), as well as some measurable habitat improvements throughout the CPRV (PRRIP 2018). In addition, Nemec (2014) noted a substantial increase in social resilience and a small improvement in ecological resilience of the Platte River social-ecological system (SES) following the initiation of PRRIP, indicating an increased capacity for stakeholder coordination, but a relatively limited scale of habitat improvement.

Historic data broadly indicates that PRRIP represents a continuation and intensification of ecological restoration efforts as opposed to a qualitative shift (i.e., not a paradigm shift; Currier and Lingle 1996, Crane Trust 1998, Whitney 1999). For instance, Krapu et al. (2014) found large increases in lowland grassland (i.e., lowland tallgrass prairie and wet meadow) landcover from 1982 to 1998 following large-scale restorations on conservation-owned properties in the eastern half of the CPRV. Similarly, Caven et al. (2019b) noted improvements in channel widths and lowland grassland landcovers across most of the CPRV from 1998 to

2016, with some of those improvements likely coming before the initiation of PRRIP in 2007,

some resulting from PRRIP, and some from the continued work of conservation organizations in

partnership with state and federal agencies (e.g., Crane Trust 1998, Panella 2020).

**Limitations of the Current Conservation Paradigm**

While acknowledging the benefits of PRRIP, it is also helpful to reflect on some of its

limitations as they relate to ecosystem restoration and long-term species recovery. First, PRRIP

represents a species-centric recovery program focused on only four currently or formerly

federally threatened or endangered species and lacks the programmatic flexibility to address the

needs of a host of other species of conservation concern (USFWS and USBR 2006, Smith 2011).

For example, data indicates the Regal Fritillary (Regal) has experienced strong declines in recent

decades, and one of the most robust metapopulations within the state of Nebraska persists in the

PRV (Currier and Henszey 1996, Swengel and Swengel 2016). Despite the importance of the

PRV to this state-listed species and the fact the Regal is currently being considered for listing

under the federal ESA, PRRIP is not obligated to consider its needs when making decisions

(Selby 2007, Caven et al. 2017b). For example, in recent years PRRIP has sold tracts of land that

constitute appropriate Regal habitat without easement protections as their Whooping Crane

habitat selection models indicated these properties were of limited value (e.g., "North Binfield"

property; Wiese et al. 2019). A growing body of literature contends that ecosystem approaches to

endangered species recovery ultimately result in more sustainable conservation outcomes than

species-centric models (Schwartz 1999, Carignan and Villard 2002, Roemer and Wayne 2003,

Hintz and Garvey 2012). For example, Roemer and Wayne (2003) demonstrated how species-

centered management focused on recovering the critically endangered San Clemente Loggerhead

Shrike (*Lanius ludovicianus mearnsi*) fostered declines in another species of concern, the San Clemente Island Fox (*Urocyon littoralis clementae*).

Another constraint of PRRIP is that its land, water, and species management objectives are narrowly target-based, which research indicates may occasionally result in inflexibility and counterproductive outcomes (Soulé and Sanjayan 1998, Cawardine et al. 2009). For example, what is the purpose of continuing to improve conditions if minimum recovery objectives have already been met (Soulé and Sanjayan 1998)? The species-centric and narrowly target-based features of PRRIP are clearly observable in the execution of Least Tern and Piping Plover recovery efforts. PRRIP found that the most economically efficient way to increase Least Tern and Piping Plover production was through the creation of artificial island habitats within off-channel sand and gravel mining pits, rather than directing resources to restoration of in-channel or shoreline habitat (Baasch et al. 2017). This strategy has clearly increased populations and production in the PRV, but it represents a highly intervention-dependent recovery and conservation strategy (Carroll et al. 2015, Farrell et al. 2018, Jorgensen et al. 2021). In short, the approach works *around* rather than *with* the river. We support these efforts and recognize that off-channel habitat is an integral component of sustainable Piping Plover and Least Tern metapopulation management within a highly altered river system (Kirsch 1996, Catlin et al. 2016, Jorgensen et al. 2021). However, substantially restoring sediment loads and streamflow regimes that replicate historic processes would also improve Least Tern and Piping Plover production, albeit potentially to a lesser degree depending on the scale of intervention (Kirsch 1996, Simons and Associates 2000, Kinzel et al. 2009, Alexander et al. 2013).

Importantly, efforts to restore historic sediment loads and streamflow regimes would also improve the ecological function and resilience of the Platte River, thereby reducing the ecosystem's long-term dependence on human intervention (Piégay et al. 2006, Wohl et al. 2015, Alexander et al. 2020). PRRIP does engage in efforts to improve riverine function, such as sediment augmentation, but its current approaches are similarly narrowly focused, require repeat intervention, and are arguably insufficient in scale in most years (e.g., pumping, or bulldozing ≥50,000 tons of sediment into the river from local excavations; The Flatwater Group, Inc. 2010, 2014). Sediment starvation of rivers resultant from deposition behind reservoir and diversion dams is a global problem, and several creative engineering solutions already exist that have the capability to sustainably mobilize sediment loads and build resilience in rivers (e.g., sediment bypass systems; Sumi and Hirose 2009, Kondolf et al. 2014). However, holistic approaches would likely exceed minimum restoration targets and certainly initial (but not necessarily ultimate) project costs.

It is important to note that the PRRIP has been additive to ongoing conservation efforts in the PRV. It is also essential to mention that conservation organizations and state and federal agencies have not been able to restore robust ecological functionality and resilience to the PRV ecosystem as a loosely integrated consortium of individual actors. For example, despite operating for over 40 years with partner support, the Crane Trust has not yet achieved its goal of restoring 2,640-acre (1,070 ha) habitat complexes, including ≥2 mi. (3.2 km) of open braided river channel and ≥2,400 acres (970 ha) of lowland prairie and wet meadow, within each of the 11 major reaches of the CPRV (Crane Trust 1998). The solutions individual organizations can offer rarely rise to the scale of the problem. In this way, cooperation fostered by the PRRIP has been helpful. However, to truly restore ecological resilience and functionality to the PRV and to cement its status as a biodiversity refugium in the central Great Plains we will need to consider the needs of a broader swath of species and ecosystem processes. We will also need to reach out to several actors not party to the PRRIP including community interests within the socio-ecological riverscape and a wider variety of economic interests. Finally, we will need to work closely together toward a shared set of goals to ensure our efforts are targeted and efficient.

**Pursuing a Vision for an Ecologically Sound Platte River (VESPR)**

We have made substantial strides toward the protection and restoration of the PRV over the last 50 years. However, the ecosystem largely remains dependent on intensive human intervention to maintain its historic character and important processes (Strange et al. 1999, Pfeiffer and Currier 2005, Hobbs et al. 2006, Nemec et al. 2014, Caven et al. 2019b). This situation becomes even more dire looking into the future as we face climate change, which may reduce snowpack in the Rocky Mountain headwaters of the Platte River, alter the typical annual hydrograph, and change the movement and activity patterns of native wildlife (Acharya et al. 2012, Harner et al. 2015, Fassnacht et al. 2018, Caven et al. 2019b). Our progress is similarly threatened by the continued conversion of native grassland and wetland habitats to agricultural and suburban landscapes, as well as increased water demands to support a growing human population (Samson et al. 2004, Wright and Wimberly 2013, Wright et al. 2017, Caven et al. 2019a, SPROWG 2020). Given these challenges, it is imperative to reimagine conservation in the PRV, and throughout the entire Platte River Basin watershed, through consideration of future threats and opportunities in the contexts of social and ecological resilience (Palmer et al. 2005, Birgé et al. 2014, Parsons and Thoms 2018). To enhance ecological resilience in the PRV over the coming decades we will need to take an ecosystem-based, watershed-wide, conservation approach that promotes ecological functionality, considers the needs of a broad complement of species and their diverse habitats as well as those of regional human communities (Strange et al.

1999, Palmer et al. 2005, White and Stromberg 2011, Birgé et al. 2014). As Palmer et al. (2005) notes, successful riverine restorations should result in ecosystems being more self-sustaining, resilient to disruption, and ultimately require limited post-restoration maintenance. Similarly, we will have to build social resilience by integrating the interests of a diversity of stakeholders including agricultural producers (e.g., ranchers and irrigators), state and federal agencies (e.g., state and federal departments of transportation, wildlife agencies, etc.), municipalities, and local landowners to succeed in our conservation efforts (Birgé et al. 2014, Allen et al. 2018). To this end, we formed an initial working group composed of representatives from nonprofit conservation organizations, state and federal natural resource agencies, and regional universities to develop a long-term vision for an ecologically sound Platte River (VESPR). As the scope and scale of the VESPR project expands throughout the Platte River watershed, additional stakeholders will be sought out in order to bring diverse perspectives and data from other portions of the riverscape into subsequent phases of this conservation planning process. This manuscript details the initial working group's goals, reflections, and objectives following approximately three years of cooperative planning.

## METHODS

### Conservation Planning – Landscape Design

Our working group was convened May 2019 by Audubon Nebraska to promote cooperative action and resource sharing to improve conservation throughout the Platte River watershed, starting with a focus on the PRV in central and eastern Nebraska. Our initial coalition included 18 individuals engaged in conservation and/or natural resources management in the PRV from eight regional organizations as well as a facilitator experienced in the landscape design process (Bartuszevige et al. 2016). Participating organizations included Audubon Nebraska, the Crane Trust, The Nature Conservancy, Ducks Unlimited, Prairie Plains Resource Institute, the State of Nebraska, the U.S. Fish and Wildlife Service, the University of Nebraska-Lincoln, and others. Additionally, the Playa Lakes Joint Venture provided technical support for this effort. We conducted 26 interactive in-person or virtual (Zoom, San Jose, CA) workshops with the majority of participants between 3 May 2019 and 7 June 2022 for a cumulative duration >100 hours. Additionally, smaller groups (2-8 persons) gathered to address specific matters in more detail for a minimum of >70 hrs.

Landscape design is an interdisciplinary conservation planning process that incorporates components of landscape ecology and social dimensions of natural resources with the explicit intention of improving conservation implementation compared to traditional planning approaches (Nassauer and Opdam 2008, Bartuszevige et al. 2016). Landscape design is a data-driven process that integrates quantitative assessments of landscape patterns, the establishment of measurable goals, forecasting potential future conditions, and monitoring landscape change during implementation (Cushman and McGarigal 2008, Bartuszevige et al. 2016). Like adaptive management, landscape design is an iterative process in which quantitative goals are revisited and adjusted as necessary to effectively meet conservation objectives (Cushman and McGarigal 2008, Opdam et al. 2008, Bartuszevige et al. 2016). Landscape design processes typically incorporate a number of important conceptual components rooted in landscape ecology that frame conservation planning efforts (Turner et al. 2001, Cushman and McGarigal 2008, Nassauer and Opdam 2008, Bartuszevige et al. 2016). We describe those used for our case study below:

1) *Desired conditions*: contexts we hope to observe in the future as a result of effective conservation efforts.

2) *Processes*: biotic or abiotic mechanisms that create landscape patterns (e.g., high river flow events).

3) *Drivers*: human influence on (or alteration of) a process (e.g., fire suppression) and the resulting landscape pattern (e.g., woody encroachment).

4) *Key Audiences*: stakeholders with a vested interest in the management of a relevant resource that are essential to engage in further conservation efforts.

5) *Needed actions*: measures aimed at achieving a desired outcome via promotion of a "process" or mitigation of a "driver" based on best available science.

6) *Quantitative goals*: achievable plan (i.e., considers social needs and values) that is based on objective measures (e.g., landcover of an at-risk habitat type) that will lead to real benefits to ecosystem services based on the best available science.

7) *Confidence*: Level of certainty that meeting the "quantitative goal" would achieve the "desired condition." This helps frame key areas for research and monitoring efforts. This represents an addition to the landscape design process detailed by Bartuszevige et al. (2016). The measure was cooperatively scored by all participants on a 5-point scale from low (1) to high (5) certainty.

We populated the conceptual components of our plan for the PRV based on the best available data and expert opinion. For example, a *desired condition* was an increased extent of functional braided river habitat, a corresponding *process* was summer base flows that prevent seedling establishment, a related *driver* was extensive groundwater extraction that ultimately reduces growing season flows and subsequently promotes an undesirable landscape pattern (e.g., woody encroachment within the active channel bed), and so forth.

**Priority Species**

Our ultimate goal is ecosystem-centric [as opposed to species-centric]: to maintain biodiversity and enhance ecological resilience in the PRV. Nonetheless, a diverse set of priority species can serve as valuable indicators of ecosystem function and provide direction to our conservation planning process (Schwartz 1999, Carignan and Villard 2002, Schwenk and Donovan 2011). First, we considered species listed as tier-1 and tier-2 "at-risk" by the Nebraska Game and Park Commission and those listed as "threatened" or "endangered" under the ESA (NRC 2005, Schneider et al. 2018). We also considered native species present in the PRV that are in decline throughout a significant portion of their range, as well as those that depend on spatially limited habitats in the PRV (Goldowitz and Whiles 1999, Baker and Hill 2003, Frey and Malaney 2009, Rondeau et al. 2011, Adams et al. 2013, SD GFP 2014, Reeder and Clymer 2015, Rohweder 2015, Rosenberg et al. 2016, USFWS 2019, Wilsey et al. 2019). Efforts that maintain regionally stable populations of otherwise declining species can promote species resilience to anthropogenic and natural disturbances across a larger range, scaling-up the benefits of our actions beyond the target area (Monsarrat et al. 2019). We selected priority species representing a broad range of taxa that regularly spend a biologically meaningful portion of their lifecycle in the PRV, and for which basic habitat requirements and/or dispersal abilities are generally recognized (Carignan and Villard 2002, Opdam et al. 2008, Lechner et al. 2017). These choices were intended to maximize the applicability of our plan and enable quantitative monitoring of species outcomes throughout the implementation process (Carignan and Villard 2002, Opdam et al. 2008, Lechner et al. 2017). This priority species list (Appendix 1) represents an initial effort, and the habitat requirements of additional species can be added to expand our quantitative goals as new information becomes available. The priority species list currently includes 88 species including 4 amphibians, 39 birds, 9 mammals, 2 mollusks, 13 ray-finned fishes, 7 reptiles, and 3 vascular plants (Appendix 1).

**Priority Habitats**

Our priority habitats for protection, restoration, and maintenance in the PRV include those that have been reduced significantly in scale over pre-development conditions (e.g., Sidle et al. 1989). This includes functional braided river, lowland tallgrass prairie, seasonal and temporary wetlands including wet meadow, shallow marsh, and deep marsh habitats, as well as perennial and semipermanent warm-water (open-water) slough wetlands (Williams 1978, Currier et al. 1985, Currier and Henszey 1996, Horn et al. 2012, Caven et al. 2019). Several of our priority habitats have not only declined regionally, but throughout the Great Plains (Samson et al. 2004, Wright and Wimberly 2013). Additionally, we considered natural habitats that maintain significant biodiversity in the current ecosystem but exist across a larger spatial scale than historically, during our planning efforts (e.g., riparian woodland; Davis 2005a, 2005b, Scharf et al. 2008).

Braided rivers tend to carry high sediment loads, display wide seasonal variation in discharge, include steeper channel gradients than most other river forms, and are relatively unconfined by distinctive banks within alluvial valleys (O'Brien and Currier 1987, Simons and Associates 2000, Piégay et al. 2006). They are characterized by an interwoven and migrating pattern of channels and sandbars (O'Brien and Currier 1987, Piégay et al. 2006). Braided river provides important roosting, foraging, and nesting habitat for a range of waterbirds including wading birds, shorebirds, and waterfowl as well as essential habitat for ray-finned fishes (Currier and Eisel 1984, Faanes et al. 1992, Kirsch 1996, Zuerlein et al. 2001, Brown and Johnsgard 2013; Appendix 1). The Platte River is highly integrated with and drives variation in shallow groundwater (i.e., hyporheic) levels that sustain a distinctive regional herbaceous ecosystem (Nagel and Kolstad 1987, Henszey and Wesche 1993, Chen 2007, Caven and Wiese 2022). Small elevation gradients across herbaceous riparian habitats result in a mosaic of interconnected wetlands and grasslands in the PRV (Currier 1989, Henszey et al. 2004).

Seasonal and semi-permanent wetlands become inundated through endosaturation (from below ground) when groundwater levels are high, often in response to increased river discharge (Henszey and Wesche 1993, Brinley Buckley et al. 2021a). Wet meadows exist topographically and hydrologically between lowland tallgrass prairies, which are not wetlands but productive subirrigated herbaceous habitats, and shallow marshes, which have longer duration hydroperiods that extend throughout much of the growing season in normal years (Kantrud et al. 1989, Rolfsmeier and Steinauer 2010, Tiner 2016). Characteristic PRV wet meadow plants include *Carex emoryi* (Emory's sedge), *C. pellita* (Woolly *Sedge*), and *Symphyotrichum lanceolatum* (White Panicle Aster); lowland tallgrass prairies are typified by *Andropogon gerardii* (Big Bluestem), *Sorghastrum nutans* (Indiangrass), and *Helianthus maximiliani* (Maximillian Sunflower); while common shallow marsh plants include *Sparganium eurycarpum* (Broadfruit Bur-reed*)*, *Typha latifolia* (Broadleaf Cattail), and *Persicaria coccinea* (Scarlet Smartweed; Kantrud et al. 1989, Currier 1989, Henszey et al. 2004, Rolfsmeier and Steinauer 2010). Moisture provided by shallow groundwater in the Platte and North Platte River Valleys extends lowland tallgrass prairie habitat west of its typical rainfall-dependent range and some of the largest relict tracts of this habitat remain in river valleys west of the tallgrass prairie ecoregion

26

within Nebraska (Noss et al. 1995, Ratcliffe and Hammond 2002, Kaul et al. 2006). The mosaic of herbaceous wetland and grassland habitats in the PRV provides important foraging and nesting habitat for a number of avifauna, herpetofauna, and insect species of conservation concern (Lingle and Hay 1982, Geluso and Harner 2013, Caven et al. 2017b; Appendix 1).

The PRV is often described as having a "ridge and swale topography" and linear wetland swales are commonly referred to a "sloughs" (Henszey et al. 2004, Meyer and Whiles 2008, Harner and Whited 2011). In this way, "slough" is in part a topographic distinction and does not represent a specific vascular plant or soil-based wetland classification (Goldowitz and Whiles 1999, Tiner 2016). Those with shorter hydroperiods may support wet meadow habitat and those with near permanent hydroperiods often represent open-water palustrine wetlands (Kantrud et al. 1989, Henszey et al. 2004). For the purposes of this planning process, we refer to warm-water slough wetlands as those with semipermanent or permanent hydroregimes that resist freezing during the winter as a result of the differential between shallow groundwater and ambient temperatures (Whiles and Goldowitz 2001, Vivian et al. 2013). These distinctive linear wetlands often support deep marsh or open-water palustrine habitat and are important for late fall and early spring migrating as well as wintering waterfowl, amphibians, and aquatic-emergent insects (Goldowitz and Whiles 1999, Conly 2001, Whiles and Goldowitz 2001, Ducks Unlimited 2011, Harner and Whited 2011, Vivian et al. 2013; Appendix 1).

Riparian woodlands provide some important habitat for neotropical breeding (e.g., Baltimore Oriole - *Icterus galbula*) and migrant birds (e.g., Black-and-White Warbler - *Mniotilta varia*), movement corridors for large carnivores (e.g., Mountain Lions - *Felis concolor*), and habitat for aquatic mammals (e.g., American Beaver - *Castor canadensis*) as well as regionally rare herpetofauna (e.g., Red-bellied Snake; Baker and Hill 2003, Davis 2005a, 2005b, LaRue and

27

Nielsen 2008, Scharf et al. 2008, Tye et al. 2017). Though we did not target this habitat type for direct protection considering its significant expansion over the last century, it is one we must reflect upon while implementing our conservation strategies (Scharf et al. 2008, Caven et al. 2019b). Data indicates Plains Cottonwood woodlands will increasingly be replaced by Eastern Redcedar (*Juniperus virginiana*) and Siberian Elm (*Ulmus pumila*) forests in unmanaged reaches of the PRV through ecological succession (Currier 1982, Caven and Wiese 2020), which will reduce the value of these habitats for neotropical migrants (Davis et al. 2005a, Scharf et al. 2008). Caven (2019b) suggested that tree clearing for grassland, wetland, and riverine restorations could be concentrated along the main channel of the Platte River to maximize the benefits for cranes and grassland breeding birds, while focusing peripheral channel restorations on the removal of invasive tree species (e.g. Russian Olive - *Elaeagnus angustifolia*, Eastern Redcedar, and Siberian Elm) and the maintenance of native broadleaf woodlands and savannas (Plains Cottonwood, Common Hackberry, Green Ash - *Fraxinus pennsylvanica*) for the benefit of neotropical migrants and tree-roosting bats (e.g.. Eastern Red Bat - *Lasiurus borealis*; Johnson and Geluso 2017).

**Target Flows**

Based on recorded discharge at Grand Island, Nebraska, several target flows have been developed to meet the needs of species of concern and the ecosystem within the PRV (Zuerlein et al. 2001, Anderson and Rodney 2006, USFWS and USBR 2006, Smith 2011). However, our conservation planning efforts discussed here are focused on meeting the needs of the mainstem Platte River as a whole. Therefore, we used discharge records at Grand Island, Nebraska, to predict values for target flows upstream at Overton, Nebraska, and downstream at Duncan,

Nebraska. We first assessed the relationships between river discharge via U.S. Geological

Survey (USGS) National Water Information System gauge stations at Overton (no. 06768000),

Grand Island (no. 06770500), and Duncan (no. 06774000), Nebraska, using sample cross

correlation functions employing the "astsa" package for time series analysis in the open-source

statistical software program R (R Core Team 2019, Stoffer 2020). Based on this assessment we

ran bivariate linear regression models including time lags indicated by the cross-correlation

functions holding the y-intercept at 0 (i.e., regression through the origin (RTO)) to estimate

appropriate target flows at Overton and Duncan based on recommendations for wildlife and

ecosystem services at Grand Island, NE (Zuerlein et al. 2001, Eisenhauer 2003, Anderson and

Rodney 2006, USFWS and USBR 2006, Smith 2011). We used RTO due to stochastic localized

variation across sites during low flow periods, and it improved model performance via $R^2$ values

compared to ordinary least squares (OLS) regression models with a traditional intercept

(Eisenhauer 2003). We did not extend this flow model downstream of Duncan, Nebraska, as it

does not account for flow contributions from the Loup and Elkhorn Rivers. We also calculated

mean and maximum daily discharges for the period of record from USGS gauge stations near

Overton, Grand Island, and Duncan, Nebraska, and plotted that data with our proposed flow

recommendations to understand how they corresponded to the typical hydrograph.


**RESULTS**

**Conservation Planning – Landscape Design**

Our working group defined five broad "future desired conditions" associated with

hydrology and habitat conservation. Habitat goals related to increasing the extent and resilience

of seasonal and temporary wetlands (e.g., wet meadows and shallow marshes), semi-permanent and perennial warm-water slough wetlands, lowland tallgrass prairies, and ecologically functional braided river habitats (Appendix 2). Goals related to improvement of water quality and hydrological functionality within these riparian ecosystems were also included. We expect that many of our target species would benefit significantly from the achievement of these desired conditions (Appendix 1, 2). We defined 15 "processes" that maintain ecological diversity within the PRV landscape, though several were closely related (e.g., flows that inundate sloughs compared to those that subirrigate lowland tallgrass prairies). The processes identified can largely be grouped into those related to hydrological as well as habitat dynamics. Hydrological processes included infrequent but relatively high peak flows that facilitate nutrient exchange and sustain sediment mobility, as well as more regular and moderate target flows that maintain shallow groundwater levels which subirrigate priority habitats (e.g., wet meadows), prevent woody encroachment within the active channel, and meet the immediate needs of wildlife. Habitat processes included preserving priority habitats at an appropriate scale considering species resource needs (e.g., area sensitivity, home range sizes, etc.), maintaining interconnectedness considering behavioral patterns (e.g., dispersal capabilities, edge avoidance, etc.), and implementing management that simulates natural disturbances including controlled burning, grazing, haying, and rest.

We identified 35 "drivers" in the PRV, which are defined herein as human influences that negatively impact or impede desirable ecological processes (Appendix 2). The drivers we identified were thematically diverse, but some general patterns were apparent. Several were "practices" such as fire suppression, intensive agricultural techniques (e.g., regular tilling), severe and repetitive management (e.g., chronic overgrazing), and misapplications of herbicide (e.g., spraying all forbs). Other drivers were "structural" in nature such as suburban sprawl and exurban development that displaces native habitats, dams that trap sediment, and diversions that siphon flows from the Platte River. Finally, other drivers represented largely unintentional human "alterations" to the natural world such as exotic/invasive species and climate change. We determined an equal number (35) of "needed actions" to mitigate the undesirable drivers (Appendix 2). These, again, were diverse but fell into larger themes. Several needed actions focused on outreach and education efforts, such as providing information regarding at-risk species and conservation easement programs to ranchers. Others focused primarily on capacity building, including efforts to cooperatively fund and operate exotic/invasive species management programs. Additional "needed actions" represented integrated approaches employing several components such as habitat protection (e.g., conserve wetlands through land acquisition), management (e.g., river disking), engineering solutions (e.g., sediment bypass systems), and research (e.g., identify point sources of pollution; Appendix 2).

We developed 35 "quantitative goals" generally representing further specification and operationalization of "needed actions", and though we made efforts to create quantifiable targets, some are simply clarified objectives. Goals generally fell into the following categories including flow and habitat conservation targets, engineering solutions, research objectives, management aims, funding goals, outreach targets, or a combination. Specific habitat conservation goals included restoring ≥30% of the land within 800 m of the Platte River to wetland and/or grassland habitat via tree clearing and crop ground restoration, prioritizing the protection and restoration of contiguous habitats >575 ha (1,420 acres) and neighboring patches >80 ha (~200 acres) within 2 km, while protecting or restoring smaller habitat patches if they are high quality, relict, facilitate connectivity, or represent unproductive cropland. River discharge targets include ≥20-day peak flows of ≥12,000 cfs (340 cms) occurring on at least a 3-year interval at Grand Island, Nebraska, to maintain braided river habitat. Flow targets also include year-round base flows of ≥1,160 cfs (33 cms) at Grand Island to maintain fish communities. Engineering solutions include restoring 400,000 tons of appropriately sized sediment (<0.90 mm diameter) to the Platte River annually between Lexington and Grand Island, Nebraska, through sediment augmentation as well as the installation of a sediment bypass system or other augmentation at the Tri-County Canal Diversion Dam near North Platte, Nebraska. Research goals include estimating the area of remnant warm-water slough habitat in various reaches of the PRV, and management aims include maintaining a ≤5-year burn interval on all appropriate (e.g., grasslands, wetlands, etc.) state, federal, and conservation organization owned lands. Outreach goals were often associated with promoting efficiency in resource use, such as reaching ≥90% water meter use on agricultural irrigation wells in the PRV within the next 20 years (Appendix 2).

Though we used our interpretation of the best available science to inform our quantitative goals, their efficacy occasionally remained uncertain. Our working group had a moderate level of confidence that our goals would effectively achieve future desired conditions. Confidence levels averaged 3.2 ($sd = 0.9$) on the 5-point scale, with confidence in individual goals ranging from 1 (i.e., low) to 5 (i.e., high). Confidence was generally higher than average concerning habitat conservation and flow targets, and lower than average regarding the efficacy of outreach and education goals. Achieving our quantitative goals is a task well beyond the capacity of this working group alone, and therefore will require engagement with a broad swath of interest groups, organizations, and local communities throughout the PRV and upstream. In our plan we specify over 40 groups as "key audiences" (Appendix 2). This includes a diversity of federal agencies such as the Natural Resources Conservation Service, several branches of state government including the Nebraska Department of Natural Resources, and interest groups like the Nebraska Grazing Lands Coalition. It also entails engaging community-based organizations such as regional Prescribed Burn Associations and local elected officials such as the Hall County Weed Board.

**Target Flows**

Our models indicated that flows at Overton preceded flows at Grand Island by two days, while flows at Duncan lagged Grand Island by one day based on maximized values for sample cross correlation functions ($r = 0.941$, +2 days, and $r = 0.944$, -1 day, respectively). Regression models suggested that a 1 cfs increase in flows at Grand Island would predict a $0.95\pm0.001$ increase two days previously at Overton and a $1.14\pm0.001$ cfs increase one day later at Duncan, Nebraska. Models demonstrated an excellent fit to the data ($R^2 = 0.93$ and 0.96, respectively). From 1930 to 2020 median flows at Overton were 1,150 cfs (33 cms; $\bar{x}\pm sd = 1,570\pm1,805$ cfs; range = 0–29,400 cfs), from 1934 to 2020 median flows at Grand Island were 1,090 cfs (31 cms; $\bar{x}\pm sd = 1,556\pm1,857$ cfs; range = 0–23,500 cfs), and from 1895 to 2020 median flows at Duncan were 1,220 cfs (35 cms; $\bar{x}\pm sd = 2,016\pm2,815$ cfs; range = 0–42,300 cfs). The differing periods of record clearly influenced discharge summary statistics as models indicated that flows typically gained moving from Overton to Grand Island and eventually Duncan, Nebraska. However, summary statistics indicated slightly higher median and maximum discharge values at Overton where the period of flow record was slightly longer than at Grand Island, Nebraska. Similarly, maximum flows at Duncan were much higher than those observed at Grand Island or Overton because records included a period of the late 1800s and early 1900s the other sites did not.

Our recommendations for peak flows in early May generally fall within the first (late spring) peak visible in the daily maximum hydrograph for Duncan, and what is the period of more modest spring high flows preceding occasional larger summer peak flows at Grand Island and Overton, Nebraska (Figure 2). The decision to advance the timing of peak flow recommendations into May was related to several factors including water availability, climate change, and a desire to promote in-channel Least Tern and Piping Plover nesting in the lower Platte. Our base flow recommendations, intended primarily to support fish communities, were very close to median flows at all three sites across the period of record (i.e., Overton, Grand Island, Duncan, Nebraska). However, the daily average hydrograph drops below base flow recommendations at all three sites to varying degrees from mid-July to late-September. Flow recommendations for Sandhill Crane roosting habitat were generally below mean daily discharge levels in the early spring while Whooping Crane flow recommendations were just above daily mean discharge levels at Grand Island and Overton, but near daily averages at Duncan, Nebraska. Wet meadow maintenance flows were similarly above daily mean discharge levels at Grand Island and Overton, but comparable to mean daily flows at Duncan. Germination prevention flows were near daily average discharges in the early summer at Overton and Grand Island, but below mean discharge levels for Duncan, Nebraska. In short, our flow recommendations appear relatively conservative considering the hydrographs for Overton, Grand Island, and Duncan, Nebraska. In the discussion we describe the reasons for our quantitative goals, highlight uncertainties, and suggest future directions for research and monitoring to ensure effectiveness.

## DISCUSSION

Our workshop results highlight the importance of addressing several key problems to improving the resilience and function of the PRV ecosystem. Our quantitative goals attempt to address the disruption of natural hydrogeomorphological processes, the limited connectivity and extent of priority habitats, and inadequate community engagement. This report represents an initial plan and attempts to describe the information upon which our goals were based, as well as highlight remaining uncertainties to guide future research.

**Hydrogeomorphology**

*Maintaining a Braided River*

*Peak Flows* – Vegetation establishment within the active river channel is regulated by several concurrent hydrogeomorphic processes including ice jams, sediment availability, growing season base flows, and spring peak flow magnitude and duration (O'Brien and Currier 1987, Johnson et al. 1994, Currier 1997, Simons and Associates 2000, Farnsworth et al. 2018). Historically, annual peak flows averaged about 16,000 cfs (453 cms) per year in the CPRV, regularly exceeded 20,000 cfs (566 cms), and occasionally reached 45,000 cfs (1,274 cms). However, beginning in the 1930s peak flows were drastically reduced in the North Platte and mainstem Platte Rivers as a result of damming, diversion, and drought (Eschner et al. 1983, Simons and Associates 2000). The removal of peak flows from the hydrograph as well as reductions in summer base flows and sediment loads resulted in conditions that promoted widespread tree establishment over the maintenance of a wide braided river (Williams 1978, Currier 1982, 1987, Johnson 1994, Simons and Associates 2000). Peak flows mobilize sediment, flatten the channel bed resulting in increased inundation under lower discharges, and paradoxically build sandbar heights (Smith 1971, O'Brien and Currier 1987, Simons and Associates 2000, Alexander et al. 2013, 2020). Several recommendations for peak flows have been made to maintain unvegetated channel widths and build sandbars for avian species of concern, but the variation in outcomes associated with a range of peak flow magnitudes, durations, and frequencies remains inadequately understood (Simons and Associates 2000, Farnsworth et al. 2011, 2018).

Faanes and Bowman (1992) suggested that annual peak flows of 8,000 cfs (227 cms) sustained for 5 days could maintain channel widths over time. However, Currier (1997) alternatively found that most seedlings under two years of age were removed by 16,000 cfs (453 cms) floods in 1995, but seedlings 3-5 years of age were merely thinned. Johnson (1994) noted that flows of 24,500 cfs (700 cms) effectively scoured the riverbed of woody vegetation in 1983. Similarly, Johnson (1997) indicated that the 16,000 cfs flood in 1995 resulted in significant Plains Cottonwood and Willow (*Salix* spp.) mortality on sandbars to seedlings under four years of age. O'Brien and Currier (1987) suggested, using equations from Ferguson (1984), that peak flows of >7,800 cfs (221 cms) at ≤2-year intervals could maintain braided channels in the central Platte River given historic channel bed sediment sizes (90th percentile = 1.00 mm), but that >16,900 cfs (479 cms) was necessary to maintain a braided river following widespread damming and water development because of significant increases in channel bed sediment sizes (90th percentile = 3.84 mm). However, data from Kinzel and Runge (2010) indicate that the majority of sediments in the Platte River are actually <2.0 mm in diameter, particularly east of Overton, Nebraska. Therefore, the magnitudes and frequencies of peak flows needed to maintain a braided river may be lower than O'Brien and Currier (1987) suggested. Simons and Associates (2000) noted that peak (i.e., "pulse") flow recommendations developed in 1994 by an expert working group contended 16,000 cfs at an interval of <5 years or 12,000 cfs at an interval of <2.5 years for a duration of 5 days preceded by a 10–12-day gradual increase and followed by a similar decline would maintain a braided river (25-29 total days of elevated flows). Farnsworth et al.

(2018) similarly found peak flow was a top predictor of total and maximum unobstructed channel widths, but that 40-day mean values of peak discharge were the best hydrologic predictor of channel widths (1, 3, 5, 10, 20, 30, 40, 50, and 60-day mean peak discharges were evaluated).

Data from Farnsworth et al. (2018) indicated that the 40-day mean peak discharge in 2015 of 12,501 cfs (354 cms), with a 1-day mean peak discharge during this event at 16,000 cfs (453 cms), resulted in a significant increase in channel widths throughout the CPRV. Currier (1997) and Johnson (1997) did not explicitly report on the duration of the 1995 peak flow they assessed, however, data from USGS (2020, station no. 06770500) indicates that flows exceeded 10,000 cfs (283 cms) for 26 consecutive days from 11 June to 6 July, which included 23 days above 12,000 cfs (340 cms). The 20-day mean peak discharge for this period was 13,942 cfs (395 cms) and the 40-day mean peak discharge was 11,604 cfs (329 cms). This peak flow was preceded by more than 2 weeks of gradual flow increase and followed by a month-long decline to relatively "normal" flows (USGS 2020).

Johnson (1994) found that the rate of seedling establishment within the active channel bed was best predicted by the maximum discharge (i.e., peak flow) observed between 15 May and 15 July, the logged value of mean June flows, and estimated icing of the river during the winter months, with all variables demonstrating an inverse relationship to seedling establishment. Interestingly, Johnson (1994) did not find peak flow duration an important predictor of seedling establishment. However, Johnson (1994, 1996) did indicate that the peak flows in 1983 and 1995 were capable of removing establishing woodlands, including young trees up to 5 years of age. USGS data from the Grand Island gauge station (2020, station no. 06770500) indicates that flows exceeded 10,000 cfs for 42 days from 4 June to 15 July 1983, including 38 days over 12,000 cfs. The 20-day mean peak discharge was 20,025 cfs (567 cms) and the 40-day mean peak discharge was 17,775 cfs (503 cms).

Though uncertainty remains, largely as a result of infrequent high flows during the period of scientific record, we hypothesize that sustained flows ($\geq$20 days) of $\geq$12,000 cfs (340 cms) at an interval of $\leq$3 years at Grand Island, Nebraska, will maintain functional braided river habitat. Based on our equations, this would be about $\geq$11,400 cfs (323 cms) at Overton and $\geq$13,700 cfs (388 cms) at Duncan, Nebraska.

*Vegetation Suppression* – An alternative strategy for preserving braided river habitat is the prevention of widespread germination of exotic and woody species by maintaining sufficient flows to inundate the majority of the active channel bed from spring to mid-summer (Johnson 1994). Currier (1997) documented significant (-4 to -41%; median = 26%) declines in channel width as a result of woody encroachment over only a 6-year period as a result of low summer base flows as well as a lack of significant spring flooding or winter ice jam activity. Currier (1997) recommended mid-summer base flows of 810 to 990 cfs (23 to 28 cms) in the CPRV in combination with annual peak flows from 2,650 to 7,950 cfs (75 to 225 cms) and 3-year peak flows from 12,000 to 15,900 cfs (340 to 450 cms) to maintain braided river habitat. Johnson (1994, 1997) indicated that Plains Cottonwood seedlings established predominantly from mid-May to early July and that discharges of approximately 2,650 cfs (75 cms) to 3,000 cfs (85 cms) can inundate the majority of the channel bed and prevent this germination. Simons and Associates (2000) similarly suggested that discharges between 2,500 (71 cms) to 3,000 cfs (85 cms) through the mid-summer could prevent widespread germination of Willows and Plains Cottonwoods within the active channel bed. However, Karlinger et al. (1981) estimated that flows of 3,800 cfs (108 cms) for a period of about 16 days during the seedling germination period would be necessary to maintain a 500 ft (152 m) wide channel near Overton, Nebraska, using equations considering bed sediment sizes, discharge, and channel slope. Interestingly, Farnsworth et al. (2018) found that mean June flows were not predictive of unvegetated channel widths.

The problem of island stabilization as a result of vegetation establishment during low-flow periods has only been further complicated by increased invasion of Common Reed (*Phragmites australis*; Galatowitsch et al. 2016, Caven et al. 2019a). Galatowitsch et al. (2016) suggests that controlled flooding of the active channel has a limited capacity to fully manage *P. australis* invasion. Galatowitsch et al. (2016) found that *P. australis* germinates best under conditions of fully saturated substrate, but that germination is reduced by further submerging seed. The most effective controlled-flooding technique evaluated for suppressing germination (~ 25 % survival) included submerging 2-week-old seedlings for a period of two weeks under 4 cm of water (Galatowitsch et al. 2016). It is notable that Galatowitsch et al. (2016) only evaluated the impacts of +4 cm, 0 cm, and -4 cm water levels relative to *P. australis* seedling establishment rates, and it is possible the greater submersion depths or distances to hyporheic moisture could further reduce germination or survival rates. However, to fully control *P. australis* it is likely necessary to employ chemical and mechanical (removal of inflorescence) treatments at a river-wide scale on a regular basis (Galatowitsch et al. 2016). This underscores the importance of building cooperative capacity to mechanically and chemically control *P. australis* invasion within the active channel as well as additional exotic species (e.g., Purple loosestrife - *Lythrum salicaria*) that threaten priority habitats (e.g., wet meadows; Caven et al. 2019a, Caven and Wiese 2022).

Questions related to the amount of flow needed to suppress the germination of invasive and woody species within the active channel bed requires additional investigation. This question is further confounded by variation in the topography of the active channel bed across reaches and years as a result of previous flows and management actions (Johnson 1997, Galatowitsch et al. 2016, Farnsworth et al. 2018). Generally, target flows for the late spring and early summer period are much lower than those hypothesized to prevent widespread seedling germination (USFWS and USBR 2006). It is also unclear, given variations in channel geomorphology, that flows as high as 3,000 cfs are necessary to prevent seedling establishment, particularly when coupled with regular (≤3-year interval) peak flows (≥12,000 cfs) that flatten the channel bed (O'Brien and Currier 1987, Currier 1997). Given that water is an expensive and limited resource, it will be essential to establish reach-specific thresholds that consider channel characteristics (bed elevations, channel width, median sediment size, etc.) when determining flows necessary to prevent tree seedling germination (Johnson 1997, Farnsworth et al. 2018). For instance, what would be the percentage of the main channel that is inundated by flows of 1,200 cfs (34 cms), 1,600 cfs (45 cms), 2,000 cfs (57 cms), and 2,400 cfs (68 cms) in various reaches of the PRV? What aggregate level of seedling germination would occur under each of these growing-season hydrological scenarios?

*Sediment Transport* – Braided rivers tend to be sediment positive, which allows them to maintain a low depth to width ratio (i.e., spreading out vs. increasing in depth with additional discharge), including significant hydrologic roughness that facilitates bedload mobilization (i.e., sandbar migration/erosion; Smith 1971, Eschner et al. 1983, Piégay et al. 2006). Randle and Samad (2003) indicate that the North Platte River historically provided 3-6 times more sediment to the mainstem Platte River than the South Platte River. However, as a result of more extensive damming, as well as the distribution of those dams (i.e., further downstream), the South Platte

River now provides the majority of sediment to the mainstem Platte River (Simons and

Associates 2000, Randle and Samad 2003, Murphy et al. 2004). Widespread damming and

diversion of the Platte River resulted in a significant reduction in sediment loads and an increase

in median sediment sizes, which contributed to channel narrowing, island stabilization, and

changes in river character (i.e., reaches shifting from a braided to an anabraching or meandering

river; O'Brien and Currier 1987, Simons and Associated 2000, Horn et al. 2012).

Simon and Associates (2000) estimated that Platte River sediment loads have decreased

87% from pre-development estimates. Similarly, Randle and Samad (2003) estimated that

sediment loads decreased 4-5-fold comparing estimates from 1895-1909 and 1970-1990.

Estimates of sediment load previous to major damming of the Platte and its tributaries (pre-

Pathfinder Dam 1909) ranged from 1,040,000 to 1,680,000 tons per year (tpy) at Grand Island,

Nebraska, while recent estimates range from 347,000 to 845,000 tpy depending on the model

equations and assumptions employed (Karlinger et al. 1981, Kircher 1983, Simon and Associates

2000, Randle and Samad 2003, Murphy et al. 2004). However, declines in sediment load over

time have not been spatially homogenous; deficits are more pronounced downstream of Lake

McConaughey (i.e., Kingsley Dam) on the North Platte River as well as in the western portion of

the mainstem Platte River (e.g., below the Johnson-2 return from the Tri-County Canal), than

further downstream (i.e., below the Loup-Platte River confluence; Columbus, Nebraska; Chen et

al. 1999, Murphy et al. 2004, 2006).

Sediment loads have been diminished through two related processes; first, a reduction in

discharge that effectively limits the amount of sediment that can be mobilized, and secondly, the

trapping of sediment behind dams, particularly in reservoirs (Kircher 1983, Simons and

Associates 2000, Murphy et al. 2004, 2006). Simons and Associates (2000) estimates that 4.25 million tons of sediment are trapped behind reservoirs annually within the Platte River and its tributaries. Additionally, data indicates that a significant amount of sediment can be trapped behind diversion dams. For instance, Boyd (1995) found that about 100,000 tons of sediment is trapped behind the Tri-County Canal Diversion Dam below North Platte, Nebraska, annually.

Sediment sizes have also increased significantly over time, which has resulted in larger magnitude flows being necessary to achieve sufficient sediment mobility and maintain a braided river ecosystem (Karlinger et al. 1981, Eschner et al. 1983, O'Brien and Currier 1987, Murphy et al. 2004, Kinzel and Runge 2010). Simons and Associates (2000) estimated from multiple sources that the median sediment size has increased from about 0.41 to about 0.86 mm diameter in the CPRV over the last century. Historically, median sediment sizes were relatively homogenous throughout the central and lower Platte River (0.32- 0.52 mm; Kinzel and Runge 2010). However, sediment sizes have coarsened in the western portion of the CPRV from Gothenburg to Grand Island, Nebraska, by a factor of 2-6 based on recent measurements (Simons and Associates 2000, Kinzel and Runge 2010).

The amount of suspended sediment carried by a river is a factor of both discharge and the distribution of sediment sizes within the active channel bed (O'Brien and Currier 1987, Murphy et al. 2004, 2006). Smaller sediments are the most easily suspended and therefore become mobilized under lower discharges (Smith 1971, O'Brien and Currier 1987). However, once these suspended sediment loads reach large reservoirs without flow, they tend to drop to the bottom of the reservoir, resulting in a loss of reservoir capacity as well as changes to downstream river geomorphology (Sumi and Hirose 2009, Kondolf et al. 2014). Clear water released below dams and from diversion returns tends to be comparatively devoid of suspended sediment and thus tends to accumulate sediment from those reaches (i.e., "sediment negative"; Randle and Samad 2003, Murphy et al. 2004, 2006, Kinzel and Runge 2010). This has resulted in significant levels of channel erosion and sediment coarsening below dams and in other locations where "hungry water" is returned to Platte River and its tributaries (Randle and Samad 2003, Murphy et al. 2004, 2006, Kinzel and Runge 2010).

Randle and Samad (2003) noted about 6 ft. (1.8 m) of channel erosion within just a 14-year period below the Johnson-2 diversion return upstream of Overton, Nebraska. This sediment deficit, associated patterns of channel erosion, and sediment coarsening continues downstream and varies somewhat in extent between years depending on hydrological conditions (O'Brien and Currier 1987, Simons and Associates 2000, Murphy et al. 2004, 2006). Murphy et al. (2004, 2006) indicated that the sediment deficit often persists east to Kearney, Nebraska, while the reach from Wood River to Chapman, Nebraska, remains relatively sediment neutral. However, research indicates that the sediment deficit continues to migrate east through the CPRV, and hydrogeomorphic models extrapolating data forward indicate that the sediment deficit may be as far east as Grand Island in a 60-year period given current trends (Murphy et al. 2004, 2006). However, additional data indicates that there may already be a significant trend of channel degradation (-0.044 m/decade) east to Grand Island, Nebraska (Chen et al. 1999, Mussetter 2019).

PRRIP is currently trying to mitigate trends in channel degradation by augmenting sediment deficits via bulldozing and/or pumping 50,000 – 150,000 tons of sediment into the river per year from local excavations, using sediments of similar size to historic values (median diameter = 0.5 mm) as well as coarser sediments (diameter = 1.2 mm; The Flatwater Group, Inc. 2010, 2014). PRRIP sediment augmentation objectives were derived from the estimated sediment deficit between Lexington and Odessa, Nebraska, based on a 12.5-year study (1 October 1989 – 1 April 2002; The Flatwater Group, Inc. 2010, 2014). However, 150,000 tons of sediment likely represents the minimum amount of sediment augmentation needed to halt the eastern progression of channel bed degradation (Murphy et al. 2004). Sediment transport rates indicate the deficit in the CPRV is closer to 400,000 tons per year (Randle and Samad 2004, Murphy et al. 2004, Mussetter 2019). Furthermore, as Murphy et al. (2004, 2006) notes, smaller median sediment sizes (0.25-0.5 mm) result in wider channel width equilibriums than coarser substrates (0.5-1.0 mm), indicating that PRRIP's use of comparatively large sediments for augmentation likely fails to maximize the benefits of sediment deficit mitigation efforts. Another criticism of PRRIP's current approach is that it requires repeat intervention and does not build long-term ecological resilience.

Kondolf et al. (2014) describes sustainable options employed throughout the world to preserve sediment transportation in rivers while simultaneously maintaining storage capacity in reservoirs. Sediment bypass systems generally divert high flows that suspend large volumes of sediment around reservoirs from the upstream end using a diversion weir that directs flows to below a dam via a large capacity tunnel (Sumi et al. 2004, Kondolf et al. 2014). As high flow events recede, river discharge is then redirected back into the reservoir or other distribution systems (i.e., canal, etc.), which helps maintain storage capacity as low-moderate flows carry significantly lower volumes of sediment (Sumi et al. 2004, Sumi and Hirose 2009, Kondolf et al. 2014). Sediment bypass systems have been regularly employed in east Asia (e.g., Japan) as well as Europe (e.g., Switzerland), have been operative for over 100 years, and are functionally applied at a range of spatial scales (sediment diversion tunnels regularly extend several kilometers in length; Sumi et al. 2004, Kondolf et al. 2014). Kondolf et al. (2014) also highlighted additional approaches to sediment management in reservoirs/regulated rivers including "sluicing" (i.e., drawdown routing), which includes lowering reservoirs before anticipated high flow events and then almost entirely opening discharge gates with the hope of maintaining some flow and thus sediment transportation through the reservoir. We have identified Kingsley Dam and the Tri-County Canal Diversion Dam as sites where exploratory research should assess the feasibility of alternative sediment management strategies. Modifications associated with the Tri-County Diversion Dam will likely provide the best opportunity to deliver additional sediment (~100,000 tpy) to the PRV in the short term, and thus it may be prudent to focus our initial efforts at that location.

It is worth noting that the mainstem Platte River and its major tributaries (North and South Platte Rivers) represent one of the most regulated river systems in the Great Plains, including thousands of diversion canals dating back well over a century and more than 65 reservoirs with moderate storage capacities ($\geq$5,000-acre feet; Simons and Associates 2000; Figure 1). There are many diversion canals and small dams that are no longer functional along the Platte River and its tributaries, and working to decommission these structures, regardless of size, could provide a valuable contribution to both river flows and sediment availability if achieved at a reasonably significant scale (Tonitto and Riha 2016). Restoration actions that improve hydrological connectivity and sediment conveyance within the Platte River Basin will also improve ecological functionality by increasing population connectivity (e.g., fish), facilitating nutrient exchange across terrestrial and aquatic habitats, enhancing riparian wetland dynamism, increasing seed dispersal, and more (Junk et al. 1989, 2004, Poff 1997, 2018). Measures of "channel complexity" may provide a useful approach to monitoring the ecological condition of the Platte River and assessing its responses to changes in sediment availability and discharge patterns (O'Neill and Thorp 2011).

*North Platte Chokepoint* – The "North Platte Chokepoint" represents a reach of the North Platte River, just west of its confluence with the South Platte River, north of the City of North Platte, Nebraska, where channel capacity has been consistently decreasing (Turner 2021). This is restricting the ability of water managers to increase streamflows to the biologically important mainstem of the Platte River for the benefit of wildlife and their habitats without flooding communities in the North Platte area (Simon and Associates 2000, NRC 2005, Murphy et al. 2006, NeDNR 2013). However, the degree of flooding risk to the City of North Platte at various river discharges, the future trajectory of channel capacity, the major factors contributing to a loss of capacity, and potential solutions remain unclear.

The "North Platte Chokepoint" represents one of the few areas of consistent bed aggregation in the North Platte and Central Platte River Valleys (Chen et al. 1999). This area stretches west of the City of North Platte along the North Platte River for >7 miles, and flow capacity in this reach has declined from approximately 10,000 cfs in 1938 to about 1,600 cfs today (Turner 2021). Reduced channel conveyance capacity has also likely increased the risk of extensive flooding near North Platte due to significant precipitation events downstream of Lake McConaughey (NRC 2005, NeDNR 2013). Currently about 100,000 tons of sediment is dredged per year at the Tri-County Canal Diversion Dam (41.113844°N, -100.675896°W), which removes water from near the confluence of the South and North Platte Rivers, predominantly for irrigation purposes (Boyd 1995). As a result of localized bed aggregation (i.e., increased channel bed elevation), potentially channel constriction via bridges (e.g., Union Pacific railroad bridge,

41.141697°N, -100.722176°W; US Highway 83, 41.154232°N, -100.759185°W), and vegetation encroachment, flow conveyance (as well as sediment mobility) is limited.

The Executive Director's office of the Platte River Recovery Implementation Program (PRRIP) has examined a number of potential mitigations to this problem and determined most of them insufficient to increase channel capacity to 3,000 cfs and/or prohibitively costly (PRRIP 2021). However, limited evaluations of the root causes of this problem have been conducted and most solutions evaluated by the PRRIP have focused on the temporary removal of sediment and/or increasing flow capacity via control structures (e.g., berms), but solutions to increase the natural outflow of sediment from the choke reach that could improve ecosystem resilience have not been thoroughly evaluated. To that end the VESPR working group has pooled resources to commission a scoping study using available data to provide a road map for future conservation actions and research regarding the North Platte Chokepoint. This study asks three major questions: 1) What are the major factors contributing to a loss of channel capacity at the North Platte Chokepoint?; 2) What potential actions could increase capacity through the North Platte Chokepoint?; and 3) What is the flooding risk to the city of North Platte under various high flow conditions?

*Sustaining Ecological Processes and Wildlife Habitat*

*Whooping Crane Roosting Flows* – A long-term objective of water management in the PRV has been to sustain sufficient flows to maintain habitat for a variety of wetland birds including Bald Eagles, Least Terns, Piping Plovers, Sandhill Cranes, Whooping Cranes, and other waterbirds (PRMJS 1990, Crane Trust 1998, NRC 2005, USFWS and USBR 2006). The overarching focus of this effort has been to maintain riverine roosting habitat for Whooping

Cranes and to a lesser degree Sandhill Cranes (Farmer et al. 2005, Pearse et al. 2017a). Both Sandhill Cranes and Whooping Cranes prefer wide unobstructed channel widths, open views, a lack of human disturbances (e.g., roads) or endangerments (e.g., powerlines), proximity to foraging habitats (e.g., wet meadows, harvested corn fields, etc.), and shallow roosting depths (Reinecke and Krapu 1986, Faanes et al. 1992, Austin and Richert 2001, 2005, Davis 2003, Farmer et al. 2005, Pearse et al. 2017a, 2017b, Baasch et al. 2019a, 2019b, Caven et al. 2019b).

Faanes and Bowman (1992) found that from 1912 to 1987 flows ranged from 838 cfs (24 cms) to 5,150 cfs (146 cms) during Whooping Crane stopovers on the Platte River with 10th percentile value of about 1,200 cfs (34 cms) and a mean of 2,683 cfs (76 cms), and suggested based on this data that 2,000 cfs (57 cms) would be an appropriate target flow to maintain roosting habitat. Flows above 5,000 cfs (142 cms) have been associated with Whooping Cranes roosting in off-channel riverine wetlands while discharges above 3,550 cfs (101 cms) in combination with high winds were associated with Sandhill Cranes behaving similarly (PRMJS 1990, Baasch et al. 2019b). Using Sandhill Cranes as a surrogate, Baasch et al. (2019b) found that roosting habitat availability was maximized for medium (501-5,000) and large (>5,000) Sandhill Crane groups in 275 m wide channels when flows were near 1,400 cfs (40 cms). Similarly, Kinzel et al. (2005) estimated that available roosting habitat in 250 m-wide channels was maximized between flows of 1,200 cfs (34 cms) and 1,400 cfs. In contrast, Currier and Eisel (1984) argued that Whooping Crane roosting habitat was maximized at flows >2,013 cfs (57 cms). It is important to note that although Sandhill Cranes can serve as an acceptable surrogate for Whooping Cranes in cases where data availability is limited, the two species demonstrate some notable differences in habitat selection (Baasch et al. 2019b).

Whooping Cranes are broadly more wetland and less grassland dependent than Sandhill Cranes (Reinecke and Krapu 1986, Baasch et al. 2019c, Caven et al. 2019d). Moreover, they are significantly taller and therefore may tolerate deeper roosting depths (Johnsgard 1983, Krapu et al. 2011). Norling et al. (1992) found that Sandhill Cranes used water depths ranging from 1-13 cm above availability, while depths of 14-19 cm were used in proportion to their availability, and depths of 0 cm or >20 cm were generally avoided in the PRV. Folk and Tacha (1990) similarly found that depths of ≤21 cm were preferred by Sandhill Cranes in the NPRV, but that use was recorded to depths of ≤35.5 cm.

Whooping Cranes are most frequently observed both roosting and foraging in water depths between 14 and 20 cm (Faanes et al. 1992, Austin and Richert 2005, Pearse et al. 2017). Research indicates that 30-32 cm water depth may represent a suitability threshold for roosting (Armbruster 1990, Pearse et al. 2017b). Interestingly, Caven et al. (*In Press*) found that migration stopover duration decreased an estimated 0.7 days as the maximum water depth of utilized wetlands increased from 5 cm to 60 cm, indicating that though deeper wetland habitats may be usable, they are likely not preferred. Flow management strategies that maximize the channel area at depths of >1 cm and ≤30 cm in relatively wide conservation-managed channels (≥250 m) likely provide robust roosting conditions for both species (Kinzel et al. 2005, Baasch et al. 2019b). Flows that sustain these ideal depths in conservation-managed channels likely range from 1,200 cfs (34 cms) to 2,700 cfs (77 cms) depending on local channel conditions, and we posit that current target flows of 1,800 cfs (51 cms) for Sandhill Cranes and 2,400 cfs (68 cms) for Whooping Cranes likely generate a sufficient amount of roosting habitat for both species (Faanes and Bowman 1992, Kinzel et al. 2005, USFWS and USBR 2006, Baasch et al. 2019b).

*Least Tern and Piping Plover Nesting Flows* – The relationship between streamflow and habitat needs of the Least Tern and Piping Plover is complex and unfolding it requires consideration of the Platte River's annual hydrograph, the fluvial geomorphologic processes at different reaches of the river, as well as the breeding phenology and nesting behavior of the Least Tern and Piping Plover (Kirsch and Lingle 1993, Alexander 2013, Alexander et al. 2018). Nesting generally occurs for both species from spring (late-April) through summer (early August), timing and location of nest sites can vary depending on environmental conditions, and both species have been found to renest within a breeding season if the first nest was unsuccessful (Farnsworth et al. 2017, Alexander et al. 2018, Silcock and Jorgensen 2022a, 2022b). Least Tern and Piping Plover nests occur on sandbars in the channel of the Platte River and also on off-channel sandpits that were formed by sand and gravel mining operations (Kirsch 1996, Baasch et al. 2017, Farrell et al. 2018). The sandpit sites created and maintained on the banks of the Platte River are important pieces to the conservation goals for the Least Tern and Piping Plover but rely on continuous human investment and management (Alexander et al. 2018, Jorgensen et al. 2021).

Although the majority of nests initiated by both species are now found on off-channel sandpits, historical records indicate that when the river carried more streamflow and sediment, nesting regularly occurred on sandbars within the channel (Jenniges and Plettner 2008, Roche et al. 2016, Alexander et al. 2018, Silcock and Jorgensen 2022a, 2022b). Abundance of preferred in-channel nesting habitat has decreased in the PRV due to the diversion and damming of streamflows that scoured vegetation and carried sandbar-building sediment; but along the lower Platte River, downstream of the Platte River's confluence with the Loup and Elkhorn rivers, enough hydrologic and geomorphologic processes remain to provide more abundant suitable in-channel habitat (Kirsch and Lingle 1993, Kirsch 1996, Alexander 2013).

Preferred in-channel nesting habitat occurs on un-vegetated, sandy islands of high enough elevation to prevent inundation or flooding of nests (Kirsch 1996, Alexander et al. 2018). Streamflows required to create and maintain these nesting habitat conditions include moderate flows in the spring and summer to prevent vegetation germination and establishment as well as periodic, shorter duration but larger-discharge flows, which are the main processes responsible for the formation of higher-elevation sandbars (Alexander 2013). Generally, the authors' streamflow recommendations in the "Maintaining a Braided River" section align with the streamflow recommendations to create and maintain nesting habitat for Least Tern and Piping Plover.

The timing of managed releases of water to provide or supplement moderate to large discharge streamflows in the PRV in the spring and early summer should be considered in relation to the timing of Least Tern and Piping Plover nest initiation in order to reduce the threat of nest flooding along high in-channel sandbars. An analysis by Alexander et al. (2018) overlayed historic annual instantaneous peak flows in the PRV with the timing of nest initiation and found that 50% of the peak flows occurred between February and the end of May – prior to or at the beginning of Least Tern and Piping Plover nesting season. Therefore, recommended managed releases of peak flows for maintenance of in-channel nesting habitat for Least Terns and Piping Plovers should occur by mid-May or earlier.

*Native Fish Flows* – Significant range contractions and population declines have been observed in native Great Plains stream fish (Hoagstrom et al. 2011, Perkin et al. 2015, Worthington et al. 2016). Native stream fish communities represent an important part of the

51

ecosystem occupying multiple trophic levels within the food web, including as food sources for several avian species of concern including Whooping Cranes and Least Terns (Tibbs and Galat 1998, Caven et al. 2019d, Caven et al. 2021, Sherfy et al. 2021). This is predominantly a result of large-scale anthropogenic changes to riverine ecosystem structure and function including decreased discharge, habitat fragmentation, reductions in geomorphic complexity and hydrological variability, pollution, and exotic species (Hoagstrom et al. 2011, Perkin et al. 2015, Worthington et al. 2016, Poff 2018). As Perkin et al. (2015) notes, diverse fish communities, including species that reproduce in pelagic environments, endure where habitat connectivity remains and streamflow is persistent, but homogenous benthic guilds predominate where considerable habitat fragmentation exists, and stream desiccation regularly occurs. Hoagstrom et al. (2011) found that 84% of the 49 Great Plains endemic fish they assessed were either extinct or declining in abundance. Habitat characteristics (e.g., depth ranges, substrate sizes, velocities), water quality parameters (e.g., turbidity, salinity, temperature, dissolved oxygen), and aquatic food webs (e.g., macroinvertebrates communities) have all been altered as a result of anthropogenic activities (Ward and Stanford 1995, Perkin et al. 2015, Poff 2018).

Extreme environmental conditions that exceed the tolerance thresholds (e.g., salinity >20 parts per thousand (ppt), temperature >35 °C, etc.) of individual species are more likely to occur in highly regulated rivers (Sutton 2005, Perkin et al. 2015, Worthington et al. 2016). For instance, within dewatered river reaches water temperatures often increase beyond the physiological limits of many species (Dinan 1992, Goldowitz 1996, Sutton 2005, Worthington et al. 2016). Fish kill events of various scales were documented in the CPRV during 57% of years between 1974 and 1996, predominantly as a result of elevated water temperatures associated with low flow events (Goldowitz 1996, Zuerlein et al. 2001, Sutton 2005). It is extremely challenging to restore natural flow regimes to highly regulated rivers and therefore it is generally necessary to simulate ecological processes important to species of concern through artificial flow manipulation (Strange et al. 1999, Poff 2018). The Crane Trust (1998) recommended minimum flows (i.e., base flows) of 1,100 cfs (31 cms) throughout the year (including the late summer and early fall) regardless of prevailing climatic conditions (i.e., drought) to maintain fish communities in the CPRV. Zuerlein et al. (2001) indicated that base flows of 1,000 cfs (28 cms) at Grand Island, 1,800 cfs (51 cms) below the confluence with the Loup River, and 3,700 cfs (105 cms) below the confluence with the Elkhorn River would effectively maintain fish communities in the PRV.

Current summer to early fall target flows range from 1,000-1,200 cfs (28-34 cms) during normal and wet years but range from only 600-800 cfs (17-23 cms) during dry years (USFWS and USBR 2006). Additional data sources suggest that the dry year target flows are insufficient to prevent fish kill events (Dinan 1992, Zuerlein et al. 2001, Sutton 2005, Worthington et al. 2016). Sutton (2005) indicates there is a 29%, 11%, and 4% chance of exceeding critical water temperature thresholds of 32 °C, 33.5 °C, and 35 °C respectively at flows ranging from 1,100-1,499 cfs (31-42 cms). However, those probabilities of exceedance increase to 42% (32 °C), 23% (33.5 °C), 13% (35 °C) at flows from 500-699 cfs (14-20 cms; Sutton 2005). Moreover, these probabilities of exceedance are expected to increase with climate change, which will likely imperil more Great Plains stream fishes (Matthews and Zimmerman 1990). Higher flows create a broader range of thermal refugia within the active channel that can help sustain Great Plains fishes through temporary warm periods (Schaefer et al. 2003). Data indicates that the Plains Minnow (*Hybognathus placitus*) loses its righting response (LRR; i.e., natural vertical orientation) at 28.4 °C and experiences the onset of pre-mortality muscular spasms (OS) at 31.8

°C, emerald shiner (*Notropis atherinoides*) experience LRR at 30.1 °C and OS at 34.1 °C, and channel catfish (*Ictalurus punctatus*) experience LRR at 31.3 °C and OS at 33.3 °C (Lutterschmidt and Hutchinson 1997). Brinley Buckley (2016) recorded a maximum temperature of 31°C in the Platte River across the summers of 2013 and 2014 as flows dropped below recommended target levels (<500 cfs), which highlights the probability that fish species experience extreme physical stress or mortality as a result of very high water temperatures during low river discharge periods.

In short, we broadly agree with the assessments of the Crane Trust (1998) and Zuerlein et al. (2001) that flows of 1,100 cfs (31 cms) should be maintained throughout the CPRV even in dry years to avoid frequent fish kill events during periods of high ambient temperatures. Our model indicates that flows of 1,100 cfs (28 cms) at Overton would equate to discharges of 1,160 cfs (33 cms) at Grand Island and 1,320 cfs (37 cms) at Duncan, Nebraska. Zuerlein et al. (2001) estimates of 1,800 cfs (51 cms; downstream of the Loup confluence) and 3,700 cfs (105 cms; downstream of the Elkhorn confluence) for respective reaches of the LPRV are likely sufficient for local fish communities. Achieving these target flows will be important to maintain fish communities, however, it will also be important to improve fish population connectivity. The removal or alteration (i.e., addition of fish passage infrastructure) of small dams (<10 m height) could significantly improve fish population connectivity, as well as increase flows and sediment transportation in the PRV (Perkin et al. 2015, Tonitto and Riha 2016). Perkin et al. (2015) indicates that of five basins evaluated (Platte, Kansas, Arkansas, Canadian, and Red River) the Platte had one of the highest potentials for fishery restoration based on the removal small dams.

*Wet Meadow Flows* – Wet meadows are herbaceous palustrine wetlands with temporary seasonal hydroregimes (Tiner 2016, Brinley Buckley et al. 2021a). They provide valuable habitat for a number of migratory and breeding birds in the PRV including Whooping Cranes, Sandhill Cranes, Bobolinks (*Dolichonyx oryzivorus*), as well as small mammals (e.g., Meadow Jumping Mouse – *Zapus hudsonius*), herpetofauna (e.g., Boreal Chorus Frog – *Pseudacris maculata*), insects (e.g., Two-spotted Skipper – *Euphyes bimacula illinois*), and plants (e.g., Western Prairie Fringed Orchid – *Platanthera praeclara*; Lingle and Hay 1982, Silvia 1995, Currier and Henszey 1996, Schneider et al. 2018, Brinley Buckley et al. 2021b). The majority of wet meadows have been lost from the PRV due to agricultural conversion, human development (e.g., roads), woody encroachment, and loss of hydrologic functionality (Currier et al. 1985, Sidle et al. 1989, Currier and Henszey 1996). Channel bed erosion, particularly in the NPRV and the western portion of the PRV, has resulted in shallow groundwater levels dropping below elevational thresholds necessary to maintain wet meadows and other endosaturated wetlands (e.g., shallow marsh; Murphy et al. 2004, McKee 2006, Simons and Associates 2000, Tiner 2016).

In the PRV wet meadows are typically inundated or saturated from late winter through early spring, with wide annual variation in late spring (Henszey and Wesche 1993, Wesche et al. 1994, Goldowitz and Whiles 1999, Whiles and Goldowitz 2001, Brinley Buckley et al. 2021a). Inundation is largely driven by interactions of river discharge, river stage, and groundwater level, but factors such as evapotranspiration and precipitation can be influential in the late spring and summer (Henszey and Wesche 1993, Wesche et al. 1994, Brinley Buckley et al. 2021a). At a relict PRV wet meadow on Mormon Island, Hall County, Nebraska, median groundwater level was 0.15 m (0.5 ft) below surface elevation from February through April and 0.63 m (2.1 ft) below the surface from June to September across a 7-year period, with water levels periodically reaching or exceeding surface elevation (Brinley Buckley et al. 2021a). McKee (2006) similarly suggested that groundwater levels were within <0.91 m (3.0 ft) of surface elevation at CPRV wet meadows throughout the growing season, with full soil saturation generally occurring for a period in the spring. USFWS and USBR (2006) indicated that wet meadows are sustained by full soil saturation and/or water inundation for a minimum of $\geq 5\%$ of the growing season. Brinley Buckley et al. (2021a) found that mean inundation extent at an archetypal wet meadow was higher in the early spring ($\bar{x} = 22\%$; 21 February – 6 April) than in the late spring ($\bar{x} = 12\%$; 7 April – 6 June), with maximum observed extents occurring during the late spring period (max. = 50%). This individual site reflected estimates for the whole of Mormon Island made by Currier (1989), which indicated that 10-35% of the island may be inundated in the spring as a result of several interrelated factors (groundwater levels, snow melt, precipitation, river discharge, etc.). Interestingly, McKee (2006) found that ~35% of the soils in floodplain grasslands (i.e., herbaceous habitats) in the CPRV exhibited hydric features, with the remainder exhibiting categorically upland soils.

High water events during the growing season are probably more important to the maintenance of distinctive wet meadow vegetation communities than mean or median water levels (Currier et al. 1989, Henszey et al. 2004). Henszey et al. (2004) found that 7-day moving average high-water levels were a top predictor of plant community composition across years with values ranging from -30 cm to +20 cm during the growing season in wet meadows (i.e., sedge meadows). Wet meadow plant communities can expand their cover following sustained periods of high groundwater, but they tend to largely return to pre-flood conditions within a few years (Currier 1989). Davis et al. (2006) demonstrated that soil macroinvertebrate communities varied markedly from year-to-year in association with changes in river flows and contended that more efforts need to be made to link biotic processes in wet meadows to fluctuations in discharge over time. Though these wetland systems demonstrate significant interannual variation, it is imperative that they experience inundation and/or soil saturation regularly enough to maintain

wetland plant communities (e.g., facultative wetland plants) and soil characteristics (e.g., high

organic content; Henszey et al. 2004, Tiner et al. 2016). Despite our basic understanding of

these wetland habitats, uncertainty remains regarding the duration, magnitude, frequency, and

timing of flows necessary to maintain wet meadow function in the PRV.

Murphy et al. (2006) found that an increase in discharge from 6,000 cfs (170 cms) to

10,000 cfs (283 cms) would have a measurable effect on groundwater levels within 500 ft (152.4

m) of the Platte River. Brinley Buckley et al. (2021a) demonstrated that groundwater levels

needed to be within ≤0.38 m (≤1.25 ft) of surface elevation at Mormon Island for sustained

inundation to occur and that groundwater depth's influence on inundation stabilized at 0.18 m

(0.59 ft) below ground. Soils may be fully saturated at groundwater depths of ~0.18 m (0.59 ft),

particularly during the growing season as plant communities create hydrologic lift that brings

moisture toward the surface (Chen 2007, Brinley Buckley et al. 2021a). Brinley Buckley et al.

(2021a) found that the relationship between river discharge and wet meadow inundation varied

by season, with larger flows being necessary to elicit similar inundation responses in the summer

and early fall compared to the winter and spring as a result of lower groundwater levels

associated in part with intensive agricultural pumping.

Brinley Buckley et al. (2021a) outlined a number of pulse flow events that highlighted

inundation dynamics at a Mormon Island wet meadow site about 600 m (1,970 ft) south of the

middle channel and 1,000 m (3,280 ft) north of the main (south) channel of the Platte River. In

mid-January 2015, river discharge increased from 880 cfs (25 cms) to 3,720 cfs (105 cms),

groundwater elevation increased by 0.25 m (0.82 ft), and wet meadow inundation increased by

19% following a 6-day time lag. In mid-February 2014, discharge increased from 885 cfs (25 cms) to 2,280 cfs (65 cms) resulting in a 20% increase in wet meadow inundation following a 2-day lag, during a period of full soil saturation. A 4-day peak flow reaching 9,260 cfs (262 cms) increased groundwater levels by 0.7 m (2.3 ft) and water inundation by 17% for a period of 5 days following a 5-6-day lag in late September 2013 (Brinley Buckley et al. 2021a).

Brinley Buckley et al. (2021a) predicted that 17% wet meadow inundation would occur (~3$^{rd}$ quartile value) in the late spring at flows of 2,470 cfs (70 cms) holding groundwater at the seasonal mean elevation of 0.27 m (0.89 ft) below ground. It is of note that the wet meadow site on Mormon Island was relatively similar in elevation to the nearby channels; it may take significantly larger flow magnitudes to inundate higher elevation wet meadow sites in the CPRV (Brinley Buckley et al. 2021a). Zuerlein et al. (2001) recommended flows of 2,700 cfs (77 cms) in February, 3,200 cfs (91 cms) in March, and 5,900 cfs (167 cms) from May to June annually to support wet meadow inundation and function throughout the PRV. Following the recommendations made by Zuerlein et al. (2001), we would expect about 18% inundation in February, 29% inundation in March, and 17% inundation in May at the aforementioned Mormon Island site based on models developed by Brinley Buckley et al. (2021a). The Crane Trust (1998) recommended flows of at least 2,000 cfs (57 cms) from 15 February to 10 May to recharge and sustain wet meadows. This would equate to an estimated 25% inundation in the early spring (21 February – 6 April) and 14% in the late spring (7 April – 6 June) at Mormon Island based on Brinley Buckley et al. (2021a).

Davis et al. (2006) suggests that emulating the historic hydrograph, which includes elevated spring flows, is likely the most effective way to maintain wet meadow communities in the long term. Similarly, Currier and Henszey (1996) suggested targeted flow management was the most robust approach to restoring wet meadows on a large scale. Interestingly, Brinley

Buckley et al. (2021a) indicated that the impact of river discharge on wet meadow inundation at Mormon Island was relatively stable from 2,650 cfs (75 cms) to 10,595 cfs (300 cms) during the late spring period (7 April to 6 June). These results imply that groundwater may be fully saturated locally at flows of 2,650 cfs (75 cms) during this time (i.e., after evapotranspiration begins but before widespread agricultural pumping starts), with increases in inundation above 10,595 cfs (300 cms) likely resulting from overbank flooding (Brinley Buckley et al. 2021a). There are some key caveats with these results. First, Mormon Island represents the largest and not coincidentally the wettest tract of contiguous herbaceous habitat remaining in the CPRV (Nagel and Kolstad 1987, Sidle et al. 1989, Krapu et al. 2014). Much of the island was too wet to be effectively drained and farmed previous to its protection in the late 1970s (Currier 1982, Currier and Henszey 1996). Furthermore, channel erosion within the Mormon Island reach of the Platte River has also remained limited, leaving the river and associated riparian wetlands relatively well connected hydrologically (Chen et al. 1999, Chen 2007, Murphy et al. 2004, 2006, Mussetter 2019). Additionally, considering Mormon Island's comparatively low elevation relative to the adjacent channel beds, flows of ~2,650 cfs (75 cms) at Grand Island likely represent the minimum discharge for promoting soil saturation critical to the maintenance of wet meadows throughout the PRV (Wesche et al. 1994, Zuerlein et al. 2001, Murphy et al. 2006).

Future research should investigate the extent of wet meadow inundation/saturation resulting from variations in late spring (i.e., ~May) high flow magnitudes and durations. Assessment priorities should include current target flows (USFWS and USBR 2006) for 20–26 May during "wet" (4,900 cfs; 139 cms) and "normal" (3,400 cfs; 96 cms) years at Grand Island Nebraska, as well as those recommendations made by Zuerlein et al. (2001; e.g., 5,900 cfs) over a ≥1-week duration. Additional research should identify sites that retain wet meadow vegetation,

59

soil, invertebrate, and wildlife communities and examine the flow regimes that lead to soil saturation and/or inundation (groundwater depths of $\leq 0.18$ m (0.59 ft) in these areas (Brinley Buckley et al. 2021a).

Flows should exceed 2,650 cfs (75 cms) throughout the month of May at Grand Island and include a week-long pulse flow of between 3,400 cfs (96 cms) and 5,900 cfs (167 cms) in normal and wet years, depending on future research results, for the maintenance of wet meadows in the PRV (Zuerlein et al. 2001, Henszey et al. 2004, USFWS and USBR 2006, Murphy et al. 2006, Brinley Buckley et al. 2021a). This would equate to continued May flows of 2,520 cfs (71 cms) at Overton and 3,020 cfs (86 cms) at Duncan, Nebraska. We feel that soil saturation should be achieved in May to promote wet meadow function even in dry years, and current targets for such years, of as low as 800 cfs (23 cms), are inadequate (Zuerlein et al. 2001, Henszey et al. 2004, Chen 2007, Brinley Buckley et al. 2021a). Median seasonal inundation levels in dry years can be achieved in the late spring at Mormon Island with flows of about 1,400 cfs (40 cms) at Grand Island (1,330 cfs/38 cms at Overton; 1,600 cfs/45 cms at Duncan) following Brinley Buckley et al. (2021a), which may serve as an acceptable minimum flow until models are further refined to assess a wider swath of the PRV.

**Water Quality**

Water quantity and timing are important to ecosystem function, but so is water quality. Clean water is paramount to the food web as aquatic ecosystems overloaded with nutrients and other contaminants from point source and non-point source pollution can become eutrophic and biologically denuded (Rabalais 2002, Yamamuro et al. 2019). Macroinvertebrates, fish, and native hydrophytes (i.e., aquatic plants) depend on certain conditions including reasonably high levels of dissolved oxygen, appropriate nutrient loading, moderate temperatures, and minimal pesticide contamination (Rabalais 2002, Yamamuro et al. 2019). Extreme values regarding any of the aforementioned water quality parameters can result in reduced reproductive success, fitness, or survival for aquatic flora and fauna, and even aquatic ecosystem collapse with only the most tolerant taxa surviving (Lutterschmidt and Hutchinson 1997, Rabalais 2002, Yamamuro et al. 2019).

Water quality in wetlands can also become reduced when wildlife site use becomes too intensive (Blanchong et al. 2006, Moser et al. 2014). Research demonstrates that *E. coli*, *Enterococcus* spp., *Giardia* spp., and other pathogens increase in abundance in the Platte River and neighboring wetlands when millions of waterbirds including geese and ducks (Anatidae spp.) as well as Sandhill Cranes stage in the region during their spring migration (Blanchong et al. 2006, Moser et al. 2014). Localized overcrowding of wetlands by waterbirds is often a consequence of limited habitat availability in the Great Plains as a large proportion of wetlands have been lost in the region directly to agricultural conversion or related sedimentation (Currier et al. 1985, Sidle et al. 1989, Caven et al. 2019b, 2020b). For instance, Caven et al. (2019b) indicates that Sandhill Crane densities have increased where conservation organizations have implemented habitat improvement projects and decreased in undermanaged reaches of the PRV. Mortality risks to overcrowded waterbirds are posed by several communicable diseases including Avian Cholera (*Pasteurella multocida*), highly pathogenic avian influenza viruses (HPAI; e.g., H5N1), and others (Blanchong et al. 2006, Wille and Barr 2022).

The Platte River provides many environmental services to human communities as well including providing water for irrigation (Hoffman and Zellmer 2013) as well as human consumption (Blum et al. 1993, Nguyen and Gilliland 1998). The alluvial Platte River valley can be categorized as a hyporheic system where surface and groundwater levels are highly integrated

(Chen 2007, Brinley Buckley et al. 2021a). Therefore, groundwater, when high, can contribute to surface water levels and in turn be recharged by river flows when groundwater levels are low (Chen 2007, Brinley Buckley et al. 2021a). Several cities and townships use groundwater well fields adjacent to the Platte River to supply drinking water to their municipalities, including Grand Island and Lincoln, Nebraska (Blum et al. 1993, Nguyen and Gilliland 1998). However, contaminants such as nitrates, ammonia, coliform bacteria, and atrazine can percolate into the groundwater supplies that support municipalities and individual wells in rural communities, often during low river flow periods (Blum et al. 1993, McMahon et al. 1994, Emmons 1996, Nguyen and Gilliland 1998, Gosselin et al. 2009). These trends suggest that maintaining flows in the PRV does not just benefit wildlife but human communities. Contaminants can result from both point and non-point sources including intensive industrial agricultural production, concentrated animal feeding operations (CAFOs), stormwater runoff, and poor sewage maintenance or industrial disposal (Olson et al. 1973, Rabalais 2002, Powers et al. 2010, Brinley Buckley 2016). The PRV regularly has nitrate concentrations in groundwater that exceed standards for human consumption and also has one of the highest rates of pesticide occurrence in groundwater wells within Nebraska, particularly atrazine (Gosselin et al. 2009, Ferguson 2015). Few studies have assessed neonicotinoid concentrations in aquatic ecosystems in the region, but research indicates that high concentrations can result in massive impacts to the aquatic food web (Yamamuro et al. 2019, Schepker et al. 2020). Nevertheless, there are approaches that can improve water quality in the region and some progress has already been made.

Research indicates that moving from flood irrigation to center pivot irrigation may have played a large part in reducing or at least maintaining contaminant levels in the water supply despite increases in agricultural production across recent decades in the PRV (Olson et al. 1973,

Ferguson 2015). Technological advances in farming practices may provide additional opportunities to reduce environmental impacts moving forward. Precision agriculture is an emerging field of research and practice where geospatial technologies have allowed more efficient use of water, fertilizers, and pesticides while maintaining or increasing yields and ultimately increasing profitability for farmers (Kent Shannon et al. 2018). Promoting such practices in the PRV through partnerships with universities and private landowners may offer significant long-term benefits. A preliminary goal in this effort is to achieve >90% water meter use on agricultural irrigation wells in the PRV in the next 20 years via landowner outreach, grant funding, and policy advocacy.

Landcover influences groundwater supplies, with natural landscapes (e.g., herbaceous wetlands, forests, etc.) generally demonstrating better groundwater quality than agricultural (e.g., monocultural production) or urbanized landscapes (Vymazal 2010, Bawa and Dwivedi 2019, He et al. 2020). Research indicates that wetlands generally filter out contaminants as water passes through them horizontally (i.e., surface flow) or vertically (i.e., percolation downward; Johnston 1991, Vymazal 2010). However, it remains less clear how islands in relatively natural condition influence downstream water quality? Quantification of such impacts could help us better evaluate the environmental services provided by riparian conservation lands in the PRV. Research indicates that vegetation-based water treatment systems, which approximate the structure of natural herbaceous wetlands but are sealed off from groundwater, can be very effective at reducing nutrient pollution from CAFOs (Mariappan 2001, Powers et al. 2010). However, they should be structured for long-term durability, or they could negatively impact local groundwater resources (Mariappan 2001).

Vegetation buffers around wetlands or along riparian corridors provide another useful tool for protecting water quality and ecosystem function (McElfish et al. 2008, Riens et al. 2013, Haukos et al. 2016). Natural upland vegetation can buffer wetlands from sedimentation, nutrient and pesticide contamination, and moderate water temperatures as well as provide wildlife habitat (Castelle et al. 1994, Haukos et al. 2016, Schepker et al. 2020). Vegetative buffers tend to deliver increasing benefits with increased width and continuity around wetlands or along streams (Castelle et al. 1994, McElfish et al. 2008, Wang et al. 2020). For instance, relatively narrow buffers (~30 m) may effectively reduce sediment loads, but wider buffers are required to remove contaminants (~50-90 m) or to provide wildlife habitat ($\geq$100 m; Castelle et al. 1994, McElfish et al. 2008, Haukos et al. 2016). Moreover, buffer effectiveness is moderated by the scale and intensity of neighboring land use (i.e., rate of contaminant input), buffer quality (e.g., herbaceous vs. woody, percent cover, etc.), and the slope of the banks surrounding the wetlands (i.e., steeper slopes require wider buffers; Castelle et al. 1994, Wenger 1999, McElfish et al. 2008). Therefore, we suggest that wherever possible we work with private landowners, conservation partners, and state and federal agencies to promote vegetative buffers of $\geq$100 m (328 ft) in width around restored and remnant wetlands such as open-water sloughs as well as along river channels in the PRV. We also recommend that $\geq$100 m buffers be implemented around existing CAFOs and associated vegetation-based water treatment systems and that new CAFO development within the 100-year Platte River floodplain be avoided.

**Habitat Conservation**

*Metapopulation Connectivity*

Species not only depend on the availability of appropriate habitat for the completion of

various stages of their lifecycle (e.g., roosting, foraging, and young rearing habitat) but also

sufficient extent and connectivity of that habitat to maintain viable and sustainable populations

(Herkert 1994, Carroll et al. 2015, Lechner et al. 2017). Therefore, effective habitat conservation

is a question of scale and configuration as well as quality, and needs can vary widely across taxa

(Helzer and Jelinski 1999, Schwartz 1999, Ricketts 2001, Cushman and McGarigal 2008). The

distributions of species of conservation concern or special interest in the PRV are limited

primarily as a factor of inadequate connectivity between metapopulations and insufficient extent

of appropriate habitat (Helzer and Jelinski 1999, Vivian et al. 2013, Caven et al. 2017b). For

instance, a number of species have relatively limited space use (e.g., home range) requirements

and therefore can utilize comparatively small patches of appropriate habitat (i.e., prairie) (Klug et

al. 2011, Trainor et al. 2012, Wright and Frey 2015, Brazeau and Hecnar 2018). However, these

same species are often limited in their dispersal abilities and for this reason they are subject to

declines as a result of genetic isolation and other factors (Keyghobadi et al. 2006, Vivian et al.

2013, Carroll et al. 2015, Keinath et al. 2017). The risk of genetic isolation is particularly

pronounced for habitat specialists that are less likely to disperse across or maintain a

metapopulation within subprime or marginal habitats (Keyghobadi et al. 2006, Joshi et al. 2006,

Sacerdote- Velat et al. 2014, Perkin et al. 2015, Keinath et al. 2017). Furthermore, species with

limited dispersal abilities can face extirpation from isolated habitats as a result of blanket

applications of unsuitable management, as these species do not have areas to disperse to or local refugia from which to repopulate remote patches (Ballinger and Watts 1995, Swengel et al. 2011).

Keinath et al. (2017) contends that habitat specialization increases sensitivity to fragmentation. The Regal Fritillary is an instructive example, as it is constrained by connectivity as well as space needs (e.g., area sensitivity), and has relatively narrow habitat requirements (Mason 2001, Swengel et al. 2011, Caven et al. 2017b). This species prefers large tracts of relict tallgrass prairie with well drained soils, abundant floral resources, ample larval host plants, and limited shrub encroachment (Mason 2001, Caven et al. 2017b). Moreover, Regal Fritillary larvae are regularly killed by controlled burns, and therefore if this treatment is applied to a pasture at large during the larval life stage, small, isolated populations can become extirpated, and given the Regal Fritillary's limited dispersal abilities, the area may never be recolonized (Ries and Debinski 2001, Ferster and Vulinec 2010, Swengel et al. 2011, Caven et al. 2017b). For instance, Ferster and Vulinec (2010) noted that only about 6% of recaptured Regal Fritillaries dispersed over 1.25 km (0.78 mi). Similarly, Keyghobadi et al. (2006) found that Regal Fritillaries were genetically similar across two sites 2.6 km (1.6 mi) apart but were less similar across sites 6.9 km (4.3 mi) and 9.5 km (5.9 mi) apart, respectively. Additional research indicates that habitat connectivity is further constrained by woodland, which Regal Fritillaries are less likely to traverse than other barriers (e.g., agricultural fields) separating appropriate grassland habitats (Ries and Debinski 2001, Caven et al. 2017b).

The Platte River Caddisfly is similarly a habitat specialist that exhibits sensitivity to land management regimes (i.e., season-long grazing) that exists in the PRV (Harner and Geluso 2012). The Platte River Caddisfly occupies warm-water slough wetlands with intermittent hydroperiods (Whiles et al. 1999, Harner and Whited 2011, Vivian et al. 2013). Though detailed estimates do not exist, the Platte River Caddisfly's small body size compared to other limnephilids and relatively short adult life stage (~ 3 weeks) suggests that it is unlikely to disperse great distances (Alexander and Whiles 2000, Vivian et al. 2013). Data suggests that caddisfly species disperse under 700 m (0.43 mi) from water on average, with flights of over 1,500 m (0.93 mi) occurring in a small but significant percentage of individuals from a subset of taxa (10%), and dispersals over 5.0 km (3.1 mi) being exceedingly rare (Kovats et al. 1996).

Interestingly, Bumblebees exhibit similar dispersal capabilities with median queen dispersals ranging from 1,265 m (0.79 mi) to 1,820 m (1.13 mi) depending on species and dispersals of over 5.0 km (3.1 mi) being relatively rare (Lepais et al. 2010). Resident flighted insects can likely be treated as a guild for conservation planning purposes given the similarity in dispersal capabilities across species (Lechner et al. 2017). It is likely that concentrations of prairie and wetland-dependent flighted insect species will remain genetically integrated if they are <2 km (1.2 mi) from each other, depending on landscape configuration, but groupings separated by >5.0 km (3.1 mi) may not (Ricketts 2001, Keyghobadi et al. 2006, Caven et al. 2017b). Genetic integration between metapopulations of flighted insects likely varies across species when appropriate habitats are separated by distances ranging from 2 to 5 km. Maintaining population connectivity may be even more challenging regarding small-bodied terrestrial vertebrate species in the PRV.

As a taxa, Keinath et al. (2017) suggests that herpetofauna are particularly sensitive to habitat fragmentation. Research indicates that Red-bellied Snakes (*Storeria occipitomaculata*) and close relatives (e.g., DeKay's Brownsnake – *Storeria dekayi*) tend to disperse less than 250 m (820 ft) during their active season, with longer dispersals reaching near 500 m (1,640 ft) (Blanchard 1937, Lang 1969, Freedman and Catling 1979). Similarly, Boreal Chorus Frogs

(*Pseudacris maculata*) generally disperse less than 250 m (820 ft) with longer movements of up to nearly 700 m (2,297 ft) from breeding sites occasionally observed (Spencer 1964, Kramer 1973). Some priority herpetofauna species are even more restricted in their movements. Northern Prairie Skinks (*Plestiodon septentrionalis*) and analogs rarely disperse over 200 m (656 ft) (Fitch 1954, Bazeau et al. 2018) and the Smooth Greensnakes (*Opheodrys vernalis*) and relatives (e.g., Rough Greensnake – *Opheodrys aestivus*) rarely disperse beyond 100 m (328 ft) during their active periods (Blanchard 1937, Lang 1969, Freedman & Catling 1979). Fire mortality has also been recorded for Smooth Greensnakes regionally, indicating the need to be careful when managing isolated populations (Caven et al. 2017a).

Across taxa, small-bodied terrestrial vertebrates are similarly limited in their dispersal abilities. For instance, rodents like the Plains Pocket Mouse (*Perognathus flavescens perniger*) and analogs (Long-tailed Pocket Mouse – *Chaetodipus formosus*, Little Pocket Mouse – *Perognathus longimembris*) generally disperse between 200 and 900 m (656 and 2,953 ft) (French et al. 1968, Clark et al. 2007). Similarly, the vast majority (>97%) of Meadow Jumping Mouse movements were < 300 m (984 ft) with straight line dispersals rarely exceeding 1 km (0.62 mi) over a one-year period (Wright 2012, Wright and Frey 2015, USFWS 2020).

In summary, to maintain connectivity for the majority of small-bodied terrestrial vertebrates, habitat patches would need to be within ≤500 m (1,640 ft) of each other, with more resilient species maintaining connectivity across ~1 km (0.62 mi) of inappropriate reproductive habitat (i.e., matrix) and the most sensitive requiring appropriate habitats within ≤250 m (820 ft). To effectively conserve populations within this dispersal guild it will be essential to engage with private landowners in the PRV to preserve corridors and steppingstones of appropriate and underrepresented habitats (i.e., prairie and wetlands, etc.) between larger tracts (Ricketts 2001,

Baum et al. 2004, Stewart et al. 2019). Congruently, it will be crucial to preserve sufficiently expansive areas of prairie, wetland, and braided-river habitat to maintain viable metapopulations of small-bodied terrestrial vertebrates where significant connectivity cannot readily be established (Hager 1998, Keinath et al. 2017). Finally, the "resistance" of the landscape surrounding habitat patches (i.e., matrix) is also important to connectivity, and efforts should be made to prevent the expansion of the least permeable matrices (e.g., woodlands, human development, etc.) for key species (e.g., Ricketts 2001, Baum et al. 2004, Caven et al. 2017b, Stewart et al. 2019).

*Scale of Conservation*

A substantial body of literature demonstrates that larger and more connected habitats support a higher diversity, richness, and density of species than smaller patches with equivalent characteristics (MacArthur and Wilson 1967, Yates et al. 1997, Hager 1998, Helzer and Jelinski 1999). Larger habitats tend to be more resilient to disturbances, support a higher number of reproductive individuals, contain more interior and a lower proportion of edge habitat, be less prone to local extirpation and more prone to colonization considering individual species, and support greater resource heterogeneity (MacArthur and Wilson 1967, Hager 1998, Helzer and Jelinski 1999). For these and related reasons, a number of species demonstrate patterns of "area sensitivity" where the probability of occurrence or density of individual species increases with habitat patch size (Herkert 1994, Hager 1998, Helzer and Jelinski 1999, Johnson 2001). This phenomenon has been well documented in a number of taxa but is particularly well described for avifauna (Herkert 1994, Helzer and Jelinski 1999).

Area sensitivity has been documented in a number of grassland birds present in the PRV including the Dickcissel, Grasshopper Sparrow, Western Meadowlark, Eastern Meadowlark, and Savanna Sparrow, with the Bobolink, Henslow's Sparrow, Upland Sandpiper, and Greater Prairie Chicken being among the most "area sensitive" (Herkert 1994, Helzer and Jelinski 1999, Winter and Faaborg 1999). Herkert (1994) estimated that Henslow's Sparrow's probability of occurrence reaches 50% of its maximum value in grasslands of $\geq$55 ha (136 ac) and recommended this metric as an indicator of habitat area requirements. Heckert (1994) similarly valued Bobolink area requirements at $\geq$50 ha (124 ac) and demonstrated that the probability of occurrence continued to increase with patch size (~70% at 1,000 ha (2,470 ac)). Winter and Faaborg (1999) found that Upland Sandpipers only occurred in prairie fragments $\geq$78 ha (193 ac) and Greater Prairie-Chickens in prairies $\geq$130 ha (321 ac). Helzer and Jelinski (1999) similarly found that grasslands of $\geq$50 ha (124 ac) provided sufficient habitat for most grassland breeding birds, but that probabilities of occurrence increased with the ratio of interior area to perimeter length (i.e., patch shape moderates the effects of size and maximizing interior area increases grassland bird species richness). Area sensitivity had been documented in a number of other taxa as well. Despite their comparatively small body size, Regal Fritillaries require a similar amount of space as grassland breeding birds to maintain metapopulations, with most significant concentrations occurring in prairies $\geq$70 ha (173 ac) in size (Kelly and Debinski 1998, Mason 2001, Shepherd and Debinski 2005, Caven et al. 2017b). Mason (2001) found that patch size explained 60% of the variation in Regal Fritillary abundance. Relatedly, Zercher et al. (2002) suggests that Regal Fritillaries require patches of prairie over 104 ha (>257 ac) in Pennsylvania, USA. Research also indicates that a number of herpetofauna species exhibit area-sensitivity (Hager 1998, Keinath et al. 2017, Markle et al. 2018).

The Crane Trust (1998) suggested that to meet the habitat needs of Whooping Cranes, Sandhill Cranes, and other migratory birds, habitat complexes of $\geq$1,069 ha (2,640 acres) including $\geq$3.2 km (2 mi) of $\geq$305 m (1,000 ft) wide channels and $\geq$972 ha (2,400 acres) of lowland grasslands and wet meadows, should be protected within each of the 11 bridge segments (i.e., reaches) between Chapman and Overton, Nebraska (i.e., CPRV). The PRMJS (1990) and Lutey (2002) similarly suggested that habitat complexes of between 1,012 ha (2,500 acres) and 1,417 ha (3,500 acres) would effectively meet species conservation objectives. The objectives of PRRIP are to protect habitat complexes including at least 259 ha (640 acres) of lowland grassland and wet meadow, which is the result of dividing the overall goal of 7,000 new acres of "wet meadow" (*sensu lato*) by 11 bridge segments (USFWS and USBR 2006). However, research indicates that complexes of this size may be insufficient to meet the needs of some species of conservation concern. Whooping Cranes are highly sensitive to human disturbances (Johns et al. 1997, Baasch et al. 2019). For instance, Pearse et al (2021) indicates that Whooping Cranes avoid areas within 5 km (3 mi) of wind turbines. Similarly, Whooping Cranes avoid powerlines, paved roads, human structures, and tall visual disturbances to varying degrees, with effects generally ranging from 0.4 to 1.3 km (0.25 to 0.81 mi) (Brown et al. 1987, Norling et al. 1992, Johns et al. 1997, Pearse et al. 2017b, Baasch et al. 2019c, Pearse et al. 2021, Caven et al. *In Press*). Simple area-based equations ($\pi r^2$, $L^2$) using these avoidance distances suggests that habitat patches likely need to be >530 ha (1,310 ac) (depending on shape) to effectively buffer Whooping Cranes from most edge disturbances. Therefore, it is important to protected large tracts of habitat where Whooping Cranes and other disturbance sensitive species can rest and refuel (Johns et al. 1997, Baasch et al. 2019).

Caven et al. (2019b) found that the proportion of meadow and/or prairie landcover within 800 m (2,625 ft) of the main channel of the Platte River was a top predictor of the trend in Sandhill Crane relative abundance and suggested that Sandhill Cranes could serve as an effective umbrella species for wet meadow, lowland tallgrass prairie, and braided river species of concern within the region. These habitats are the most limited in distribution within the PRV and without intervention on the part of conservation organizations, would be in decline (Sidle et al. 1989, Krapu et al. 2014, Caven et al. 2019b). Caven et al. (2019b) found that reaches of the Platte River that contained on average >12% of Sandhill Cranes annually, or had a significant positive trend in relative abundance, exceeded 20% and averaged >30% prairie-meadow cover within 800 m (2,625 ft) of the main channel ($\bar{x}$ = 31.4%, $sd$ = 11.0, range = 20.7–49.6%). Restoring and protecting >30% meadow-prairie landcover within 800 m (2,625 ft) of the main channel would equate to protecting >575 ha (1420 ac) within a 12 km (7.5 mi) reach of river (mean segment length in the CPRV per Caven et al. 2019b). Prioritizing a zone of land adjacent to the main channel of the Platte River has the potential to create the most connected and largest expanse of herbaceous habitat while also potentially mitigating the impacts of flood pulses on human communities near the river because wet meadows and lowland grasslands have a greater capacity to absorb flood pulses than developed landscapes or woodlands (Hey and Philippi 1995, Caven et al. 2019b).

We generally agree that it will be necessary to restore ≥1,010 ha (~2,500 acres) of meadow-prairie (i.e., lowland tallgrass prairie, wet meadow, and/or shallow marsh, etc.) habitat within each ~12 km (7.5 mi) reach of the PRV to meet species and ecosystem conservation objectives (See PRMJS 1990, Crane Trust 1998, Lutey 2002). Our assessment of available area sensitivity, disturbance avoidance, and dispersal distance data from regional species of concern suggests that at least 575 ha (1,420 acres) of contiguous habitat should be maintained within each

reach (See Johns et al. 1997, Helzer and Jelinski 1999, Caven 2019b, Baasch et al. 2019).

Additional meadow-prairie areas within each reach should be ≥80 ha (~200 acres) and within ≤2

km (1.2 mi) of larger contiguous habitats or each other (Helzer and Jelinski 1999, Winter and

Faaborg 1999, Keyhobadi et al. 2006, Caven et al. 2017b). Smaller areas may be worth

protecting under a limited number of circumstances. For instance, they may fall between larger

meadow-prairie habitats and therefore serve as a steppingstone or movement corridor for

dispersal-limited species or the habitat could be of exceptional quality in some way (e.g.,

remnant, support a high density of species of concern, etc.) (Kramer 1973, Baum et al. 2004,

Wright and Frey 2015, Stewart et al. 2019). Future research should assess the existing degree of

functional connectivity in the PRV for multiple species guilds considering both conservation and

privately owned lands and identify priority areas for protection and restoration (Vogt et al. 2009).


*Habitat Management*

   *Fire and Woody Encroachment* - In Nebraska, the planting of Eastern Redcedar

(hereafter cedar) has been government policy for >100 years (Gardner 2009, Twidwell et al.

2016). In 2001 for example, >1.8 million cedar trees were distributed for planting in the Great

Plains (Ganguli et al. 2008) including Nebraska. Cedars are frequently planted as windbreaks to

provide shelter around buildings, croplands, and livestock (Ganguli et al. 2008). Although cedar

is native to Nebraska, it is invasive, meaning it is actively spreading into formerly unoccupied

habitats and altering the ecosystem. Fire suppression in the Great Plains following European

settlement abetted cedar expansion (Engle et al. 2008, Stambaugh et al. 2008). Cedar spread from

windbreaks and anthropogenic afforestation attempts has been documented for decades (e.g.,

Graf 1965). Rapid increases in cedar abundance following initial invasion changes grassland species composition and structure, as well as soil properties and hydrology (Wilcox and Thurow 2006, McKinley et al. 2008, Mellor et al. 2013). Invasion by cedar leads to the loss or reduction of forage for livestock, increased wildfire risk and a reduction of grassland biodiversity (Briggs et al. 2002, Horncastle et al. 2005, Twidwell et al. 2013). Research indicates that other woody species are also increasingly invading into herbaceous habitats in the central Great Plains and along the Platte River (Briggs et al. 2002, 2005; Lett and Knapp 2005; Caven and Wiese 2022). Caven and Wiese (2022) demonstrated that Siberian Elm and Roughleaf Dogwood (*Cornus drummondii*) have increased markedly on Mormon Island over the last 40 years (1980-2020).

Management to control cedar and other shrub invasions is often insufficient to keep up with new incursions, in Nebraska, the Great Plains, and most grassland biomes globally (Symstad and Leis 2017, Fogarty et al. 2020). This suggests that current control strategies are insufficient. Current strategies to control cedar invasion often focus on a brush management paradigm where tree removal is prioritized over proactive and preventative practices (Symstad and Leis 2017). This strategy may have slowed invasion in some priority areas (Fogarty et al. 2020), and on smaller sites with limited invasion, but overall, this approach is unlikely to be successful at scale, and is expensive in terms of time and money (Symstad and Leis 2017, Fogarty et al. 2020). Proactive prevention is a more robust strategy where possible, and where invasions have progressed, fire is a more successful long-term control strategy that can scale from fields to landscapes (Buehring et al. 1971, Knapp et al. 2009, Bielski et al. 2021).

The expense of mechanical removal limits treatments to small-scales, at a time when the entire Great Plains is threatened by afforestation (Twidwell et al. 2013, Symstad and Leis 2017, Fogarty et al. 2020). Cedar invasion rates often outpace mechanical control efforts, and time and money expended on mechanical control reduce dollars available to protect more intact habitats. In Nebraska, brush management has not kept pace with woody plant encroachment in Biologically Unique Landscapes (Twidwell et al. 2013, Fogarty et al. 2020). From 2004 to 2013, the Natural Resource Conservation Service allocated ~US $8 million towards mechanical tree removal in Nebraska (Simonsen et al. 2015), but woody cover increased in Nebraska over this time period (Fogarty et al. 2020). This suggests a need to implement more diverse strategies with realistic outcome potential and prioritize control locations and the maintenance of uninvaded habitats (Simonsen et al. 2015, Fogarty et al. 2020). In comparison to brush management practices, fire targets all stages of the cedar invasion process, from seeds to mature trees (Bielski et al. 2021). However, data indicates that controlled burns more effectively kill young trees, including cedars (Knapp et al. 2009). For instance, Buehring et al. (1971) found desiccation rates of >50% regarding 3-6 ft cedars following spring burns in pastures containing >2,000 lbs./acre of herbaceous understory but the kill rate was generally >90% for trees <3 ft tall. However, research indicates that to effectively manage broadleaf shrub and tree invasions it may require even shorter fire return intervals than needed to control cedars (Briggs et al. 2002, 2005; Lett and Knapp 2005).

Grasses can re-establish dominance rapidly following fires, even under high intensity conditions (Bielski et al. 2021). For example, in the Loess Canyon of Nebraska, a year following fire, total herbaceous biomass in burned stands was comparable to grasslands sites, having increased from $5 \pm 3$ g m$-2$ (when cedar dominated) to $142 \pm 42$ g m$-2$ (+2,785 $\pm$ 812% with cedars removed by fire; Bielski et al. 2021). Herbaceous dominance in juniper stands continued to persist 15-years after initial treatment, reaching a maximum of $337 \pm 42$ g m$-2$ eight years post-fire (Bielski et al. 2021). The Loess Canyons provides the best example of fire use to stabilize a grassland landscape being lost to cedar invasion (Fogarty et al. 2020). Conservation investments support landowner-led prescribed burn associations in the Loess Canyons, and in practically every Nebraska landscape (Twidwell et al. 2013). Prescribed burn associations in these contexts consist primarily of landowner coalitions, where they work together to implement prescribed fire to reduce cedar invasion (Twidwell et al. 2013).

Incipient invasion by cedar can be controlled by low (or high) intensity fires; cutting is often not possible at this stage because young trees are within the grass canopy and are difficult to find (Fryer and Luensmann 2012, Briggs et al. 2002, Ratajczak et al. 2014). Even mature cedars can be controlled by higher intensity fires, and by using "cut and stack" methods that provide dry ladder fuels into the canopy of mature juniper stands (Crockford et al. 2017, Bielski et al. 2021). Established cedar stands may create enormous seed banks that tend to germinate in the bare ground left by the removal of tree canopies, therefore, several subsequent fires may be needed to control re-establishment via seed banks (Fryer and Luensmann 2012, Ratajczak et al. 2014).

The frequency with which fire is applied to the landscape, the management contexts under which it is applied, and its seasonality are important determinants of its effectiveness in limiting woody encroachment. Ratajczak et al. (2014) suggests that grasslands can be effectively maintained with burn intervals of <3 years, that shrublands tend to predominate under fire return intervals of 3 to 8 years, and that fire frequencies longer than this tended to be associated with woodland land cover. Fryer and Luensmann (2012) similarly suggests that Central Tallgrass Prairie can be maintained by minimum fire return intervals of 3 to 5 years. However, the burn frequency threshold necessary to maintain a prairie landscape largely devoid of shrubs can vary depending on soil features, land management regime, and region (Briggs et al. 2002, Ratajczak et al. 2014).

Briggs et al. (2002) demonstrated that controlled burns killed about 32% of cedars within pastures grazed during the previous growing season but >90% in ungrazed pastures. Relatedly, research indicates that growing season fires may more effectively control woody encroachment than the spring controlled-burns typically implemented by conservation organizations, range managers, and burn associations regionally (Bragg 1998, Knapp et al. 2009). Interestingly, research indicates that natural lightning strike fires in the central and northern Great Plains most frequently occur in the mid to late summer, particularly July and August (Bragg 1982, Knapp et al. 2009). Conservation organizations in the CPRV should work to sustain a fire return interval of at least ≤5 years to maintain herbaceous communities for the benefit of grassland and wetland bird species and integrate summer burns into rotations where possible, particularly where shrub encroachment is a persistent problem. Once a system has shrub encroachment issues, it often requires mechanical and chemical control efforts along with more frequent fire (annual fire interval) to reestablish a grass-dominated ecosystem (Briggs et al. 2005). Burn plans should generally include fire refugia (i.e., unburned areas) for species of concern that could suffer immediate negative impacts from controlled burning (e.g., reproductive losses) to ensure the persistence of dispersal limited species, particularly in isolated habitats (Swengel et al. 2011; Caven et al. 2017a, 2017b; Schultz and Caven 2021).

*Channel Maintenance* – Given the river's inability to maintain vegetation free braided channels, especially in low water years, it is now necessary to remove vegetation mechanically on a regular basis to sustain ecological function (Williams 1978; Currier 1982, 1984; Currier et al. 1985; Pfeiffer and Currier 2005). Mechanical removal of vegetation improves channel widths for Whooping Cranes, Sandhill Cranes, and other waterbirds that prefer open braided river habitats (e.g., Piping Plovers, Least Terns, Baird's Sandpipers, American Avocets; Davis 2003, Pfeiffer and Currier 2005, Farnsworth et al. 2018). Mechanical channel maintenance also improves water conveyance by increasing channel area, reducing the amount of water used by woody and invasive vegetation, and mobilizing sediment that drives sandbar creation and maintains the braided planform (Nagel and Dart 1980, Kinzel et al. 2009, PVWMA 2013, Farnsworth et al. 2018).

Audubon volunteers on Rowe Sanctuary conducted the first channel clearing efforts in the mid 1970's (B. Taddicken pers. comm.; Anderson 2000). These efforts focused on clearing vegetation from a few small islands and sandbars. Initial efforts using hand tools and small power tools were modest but effective at a small scale (B. Taddicken pers. comm.; Anderson 2000). In the mid-1980's, the Crane Trust began the first large-scale clearing efforts using heavy machinery (Currier 1984). The Crane Trust purchased a four-wheel drive tractor and began disking vegetated islands. The Trust soon purchased a Kershaw Klearway to shred larger woody vegetation previous to disking which removed a significant portion of the vegetation load that the disk would have to drive over and maneuver through (Pfeiffer and Currier 2005). This step allowed the disk to penetrate the soil and root systems more efficiently on each pass (B. Taddicken pers. comm.). This process proved to be more efficient at breaking apart the sediment and roots while not clogging the implement with vegetation as frequently (K. Schroeder pers. comm.). These two pieces of heavy equipment working in tandem (i.e., a shredder and a tractor pulling a disk) marked the beginning of large-scale river clearing and management efforts in the CPRV and NPRV (K. Schroeder pers. comm.; Currier 1984, Pfeiffer and Currier 2005).

In the early 1990's the Crane Trust, USFWS, and Audubon collaborated to begin a larger effort using heavy equipment to clear vegetated islands and accreting banks on conservation-managed properties (Currier and Lingle 1993, Pfeiffer and Currier 2005). The Crane Trust later purchased a 1997 Caterpillar Challenger 55 rubber-tracked tractor to replace the older four-wheel drive tractor, which was much more efficient working inside the river channels (Pfeiffer and Currier 2005). As the river channel on both Crane Trust and Audubon properties began to open up, and adjacent untreated areas became more vegetated, treated areas began to attract ever-increasing numbers of waterfowl and Sandhill Cranes (Faanes and LeValley 1993, Krapu et al. 2014). This prompted waterfowl hunters and adjacent landowners of cleared properties to request clearing on their lands (K. Schroeder pers. comm.; Pfeiffer and Currier 2005) . In the late 1990's the number of requests for clearing started increasing as the benefits of this work was realized by landowners throughout the PRV. Demand began to outstrip the capacity of conservation organizations and contractors were hired to fulfill the needs of private landowners (K. Schroeder pers. comm.).

Most of the clearing and channel maintenance work was concentrated from Kearney to about three miles east of the Grand Island (K. Schroeder pers. comm.). By the early 2000's, during a drought period, as many as 50 miles of river channel were disked from bank to bank annually (B. Taddicken pers. comm.; Pfeiffer and Currier 2005). The USFWS Partners for Wildlife Program, the Nebraska Game and Parks Commission, and the Crane Trust [via grants received] funded the majority of this work (K. Schroeder pers. comm.). Caven et al. (2019a) indicates that conservation organizations collectively spend >$300,000 USD in "normal" years and >$1,000,000 USD [adjust to 2017] in "low water" years (i.e., droughts) on channel maintenance with much of it dedicated toward river disking. Collaborative works continue and allow conservation organizations the ability to quickly scale up channel management efforts to address poor riverine conditions, especially during dry periods (B. Krohn pers. comm., B. Taddicken pers. comm.).

An emergent problem is Common Reed (*Phragmites australis*) which has been increasingly invading the channel during dry growing seasons. Disking alone cannot be used to control this plant as it will spread via chopped rhizomes (Rapp et al. 2012, Juneau and Tarasoff 2013). Therefore, it is important to treat Common Reed with herbicide (Glyphosate or Imazapyr) previous to seed viability or disking to ensure maximum effectiveness of control efforts (Rapp et al. 2012, PVWMA 2013). Control efforts can also include flooding young plants, which reduces their establishment rate (Galatowitsch et al. 2016). In all cases effectively controlling Common Reed at a landscape scale in the long-term requires a mixed-methods approach employing some form of herbicide treatment and mechanical removal of above and/or below ground biomass (PVWMA 2013, Juneau and Tarasoff 2013, Hazelton et al. 2014). The Platte Valley Weed Management Area and the West Central Weed Management Area (collectively WMAs) have garnered funding from a diversity of sources including the Nebraska Environmental Trust Fund, PRRIP, Nebraska Department Agriculture, Natural Resources Districts (NRDs) including the Central Platte and Tri-Basin NRDs, as well as conservation organizations to address Common Reed infestations over the last two decades. Efforts have focused east of Kingsley Dam on the North and South Platte Rivers and throughout the CPRV to Columbus, Nebraska (~315 river miles; PVWMA 2013). This project costed $3.54 million from 2007 to 2013, or roughly 0.5 million annually, and similarly to channel disking required more effort in dry years, which provide Common Reed an opportunity to colonize drying channel beds (Galatowitsch et al. 2016). Sustaining funding for this effort should be a collective goal of conservation organizations especially considering uncertainty in the long-term future of the PRRIP (USDOI 2019) and climate change scenarios that predict lower river flows during the Common Reed growing season (Acharya et al. 2012, Fassnacht et al. 2018).

Heavily vegetated islands and accretion land with trees larger than 3 inches diameter (~8 cm) require a bulldozer, crawler loader, or excavator to remove trees, brush and roots. These are then stacked in high piles for later burning to facilitate a chimney effect to allow for more complete burning. Burning is often completed during the winter months to limit the risk of unintended spread (B. Krohn pers. comm.). Once large trees are removed the smaller brush is mulched and a rubber-tracked tractor with ≥36-inch rubber tracks (~91 cm) and 3-point mounted Rome disk are used on islands and sandbars to break up the remaining root structure and allow for the mobilization of sand (Pfeiffer and Currier 2005, Kinzel et al. 2009). The 3-point mounted Rome disk works best because it can be fully lifted from contact with the ground, allowing the machine to extricate itself in very soft areas. Standard disks have a set of wheels that remain on the ground, which become a problem when in deep, fine sand and water (B. Krohn pers. comm.).

Larger in-channel islands where the vegetation is removed are often attractive to Least Terns, Piping Plovers, and occasionally Snowy Plovers (*Charadrius nivosus*) (Currier and Lingle 1993, Ostrom et al. 2020). Repeated annual disking may be necessary on a newly cleared site for the first 2-3 years to foster natural sandbar erosion (B. Krohn pers. comm., B. Taddicken pers. comm). To kill small trees and brush completely each treatment may include multiple disking passes to break down the soil and root structure, which also allows the roots to be exposed to weather elements, enabling the material to dry out and die off. After this initial work it is possible to maintain a site with disking once every ~3 years (B. Krohn pers. comm., B. Taddicken pers. comm). The goal is to maintain the channel bed and islands in an early

81

succussion state that would result from recurrent scouring historically, so when high flows do occur the sand is mobilized and facilitates natural hydrogeomorphic processes (Kinzel et al. 2006, 2009; Farnsworth et al. 2018). Sites with little woody encroachment can be disked using the Rome disk and tractor without additional mulching or preparation. Accretion land, large and elevated islands, and bank edges should be cleared of trees to maintain an open channel width of ≥250 m (820 ft) with additional open visibility on the channel banks (Kinzel et al. 2005, Baasch et al. 2019b). The accretion should be disked to bare sand at least three disk widths back from the river's edge in order to facilitate the widening of the river channel through bank erosion as high flow opportunities arise. These unobstructed views meet the habitat suitability requirements for both Whooping and Sandhill Cranes and prevent establishment of woody vegetation (Baasch et al. 2019a, 2019b).

Clearing work typically begins in mid to late July after the primary nesting season for migratory birds has passed and the bulk of the vegetative growing season has been completed. This prevents regrowth later in the same season and allows sand to remain unbound and free to be redistributed throughout the winter and spring. The end date for clearing is mainly subject to the formation of ice (K. Schroeder pers. comm., B. Taddicken pers comm.). Operating heavy equipment in the river channel becomes more treacherous and difficult after ice forms heavily on the river.

Key Equipment

- Bulldozer, crawler loader, and excavator (large tree removal)
- Heavy duty mowers and/or mulching machines (e.g., Kershaw Klearway)
- Large-tired or rubber-tracked tractor (Caterpillar Challenger, John Deere RT 310, ≥36-inch-wide tracks preferred)

- Large 3-point Rome disks with 36" blades (~91 cm)

- Smaller 3-point field disks in some cases

Islands and banks often have a sharp drop off into the channel making it difficult to drive a machine onto or off them (B. Krohn pers. comm., B. Taddicken pers. comm.). The disk can be run over the bank to create a helpful access ramp. Travelling in the river with a machine can be difficult due to loose sand, deep channels, and holes. Areas of loose "quicksand" can quickly bury a machine, even in very shallow water. It is usually less hazardous to drive upstream because the sandbars move upwards like stairs in this direction, whereas traveling downstream the machine is more likely to drop off into a deeper channel or hole (B. Krohn pers. comm., B. Taddicken pers. Comm). Normally the bottom of the river can be seen from the machine to determine depth. When it cannot be seen flat water is generally shallower than rippling water and the operator must enter slowly to determine depth. Often it is necessary to drive around deeper channels until a shallow area is found for safe crossing. The tracked vehicles have much better mobility in the river than wheeled implements. Using heavy machinery in a very wet environment like the river makes it likely one will eventually get stuck even with care. It is best for safety reasons to have two machines and operators in one area at all times. In case of emergencies, it is best to have one tractor available to pull the other one out when stuck. Very heavy cables capable of handling heavy machinery are required for pulling, as chains are not usually strong enough. Other hazards include objects unseen in tall vegetation. Objects often encountered include woody debris, abandoned hunting blinds made from steel, concrete, or wood, and large holes or sharp bank cuts. Our goal is to continue disking efforts annually focusing on problem as well as key conservation areas in the NPRV and CPRV. The LPRV is less in need of mechanical intervention as a result of the additional sediment loads and flows it receives from the Loup River system.

*Habitat Restoration*

*Meadow and Prairie Restoration* – Over the last three decades, ecological restoration projects in the PRV have played an important role in conservation efforts that aim to maintain biodiversity, promote native vegetation and expand and connect critical habitat (Krapu et al. 2014, Caven et al. 2019b, Caven and Wiese 2022). Restoration projects using high diversity planting techniques in the PRV have developed native vegetation that more closely resembles remnant wet meadows when compared to low diversity grass planting techniques and tree clearing alone (Pfeiffer 1999). Restoration sites that develop diverse plant communities have the ability to support a wider diversity of insects and other wildlife (Pfeiffer 1999, Albrecht et al. 2007, Rowe and Holland 2013, Harmon-Threatt and Hendrix 2015, Lamke 2019, Meissen et al. 2020) and restored prairie surrounding remnant sites can protect native plant communities by providing a buffer from non-native species invasion (Rowe 2013, Caven and Wiese 2022). In the coming decades, prairie and wet meadow restoration will be a critical component of long-term conservation planning with the goals of ecological functionality and resilience in the PRV in mind. Successful restoration work over the past three decades gives us valuable information for future planning, but we must understand potential threats to biodiversity in the PRV to maximize the positive impacts and resilience of restoration efforts moving forward (Suding 2011).

Nebraska Restoration History: Some of the first ecological restoration work in Nebraska began in the 1980s through the work of Bill and Jan Whitney and the founding of Prairie Plains Resource Institute (PPRI). Inspired by prairie restoration efforts in Midwest states like Illinois

84

and Wisconsin, Bill Whitney visited key sites in this region to learn about ecological restoration techniques and prairie management. He brought these concepts back to Nebraska where he studied remnant sites, worked to compile a list of native flora in our region and began harvesting seed locally (Whitney 1997a). Whitney started experimenting with small prairie plantings near the town of Aurora, NE, along Lincoln Creek in the early 1980s. Though these restoration parcels were small, most plantings included 70+ species, with an abundance of forbs – a very different approach from low-diversity grass plantings that were more common at the time (Whitney 1997a, Pfeiffer 1999). There was an opportunity for PPRI to carve a niche for prairie restoration work in Nebraska and these early efforts proved valuable, as techniques were developed for high diversity, local ecotype plantings which led to larger-scale efforts in the PRV in the 1990s (Whitney 1997a, Pfeiffer 1999).

In 1991, PPRI began work through a cooperative agreement to restore wet meadows along the CPRV from cropland (Whitney 1997b, Pfeiffer 1999, Steinauer et al. 2003). This agreement began on Crane Trust land in 1991 with funding from the U.S. Fish and Wildlife Service and grew to include The Nature Conservancy on land near Wood River by 1994 (Whitney 1997b, Pfeiffer 1999). Between 1991 and 1997, PPRI planted approximately ~448 acres to restore prairie and wet meadow habitats along the CPRV (Whitney 1997b, Pfeiffer 1999). Plantings occurred at 11 different locations and included a total of 19 unique projects involving restorations from fields previously row cropped with corn, milo, or soybeans and one gravel pit reclamation site (Whitney 1997b). These early restoration projects allowed PPRI to scale-up restoration efforts which led to the development of better seed harvesting technologies (Whitney 1997b). These early restoration sites also helped Whitney as well as other land managers and researchers gather valuable information regarding ecological restorations as well as the composition, structure and management of prairies and wet meadows in the CPRV (Whitney 1997b, Pfeiffer 1999).

PPRI's high diversity, local ecotype restoration methods set the stage for other conservation agencies in Nebraska to adopt these practices. The Nature Conservancy and the Crane Trust continue to establish high diversity, local ecotype prairie and wet meadow restorations in the CPRV (Steinauer et al. 2003). Since the late 1990s, PPRI has grown considerably in its capacity to restore prairies and wetlands in central and eastern Nebraska. Currently, PPRI has the ability to restore over 1,000 acres per year, offering a contract service to provide high diversity, local ecotype seed mixes and broadcast seeding on site. From its start in the 1980s until today, PPRI has restored >13,500 acres throughout Nebraska. Over 4,900 of those acres have been within the PRV of central and eastern Nebraska (PPRI unpublished data). This work has taken place in partnership with a number of agencies, NGOs and individuals, including the Natural Resources Conservation Service (NRCS; through the Wetland Reserve Easements program), The Nature Conservancy, Crane Trust, U.S. Fish and Wildlife Service, Audubon, PRRIP, Ducks Unlimited, Army Corps of Engineers, Central Platte NRD, Papio-Missouri NRD, Nebraska National Guard – Camp Ashland and a number of private landowners. The Nature Conservancy, Audubon Nebraska, the Crane Trust, and PRRIP have also independently undertaken restorations within the PRV that in addition to PPRI's efforts have resulted in estimated increases of nearly ~35% wet meadow and lowland prairie landcover within <6 km  of the Platte River since the early 1980s (Pfeiffer 1999, Krapu et al., 2014; Caven et al., 2019b, Caven and Wiese 2022)

High Diversity and Local Ecotype: High diversity restoration is defined as a site in which >75 plant species are seeded (Steinauer et al. 2003). High diversity prairie seed mixes set the stage for development of diverse and resilient native plant communities that support a rich diversity of insects, pollinators and other wildlife (Pfeiffer 1999, Albrecht et al. 2007, Rowe and Holland 2013, Harmon-Threatt and Hendrix 2015, Lamke 2019, Meissen et al. 2020). Local ecotype seed is defined as seed collected from native plants that are growing in close proximity to a restoration site. Many restorationists prefer sourcing local ecotype seed for projects because the resulting plant communities will likely contain genetics similar to plants growing on the site prior to settlement (Steinauer et al. 2003). There are some varying opinions about what is considered local ecotype seed. Some restorationists suggest that seed should be harvested within 100 miles north or south and 200 miles east or west of a restoration site, while others might suggest that seed should be harvested within 25 miles of a restoration site (Steinauer et al. 2003). Recent work by Larson et al. (2021) used a model-based framework weighing seed availability against the risks of novel invasive species introduction and suggested that seed sourced from within 272 km (~170 mi) could be considered "local ecotype." Additionally, there have been more recent discussions about what local ecotype seed sourcing should look like with a changing climate (Galliart et al. 2019). Generally, the restoration work discussed in this section uses seed collected within approximately a 100-mile radius of restoration sites in central and eastern Nebraska.

Restorations using species-rich seed mixes that develop diverse plant communities may be better suited to withstand stochastic events such as drought and flooding. Diverse plant communities are predicted to be resilient, having decreased variability in ecosystem processes as some species compensate for others in response to environmental fluctuations, according to the insurance hypothesis (Yachi and Loreau 1999, Carter and Blair 2012). Responses to perturbation differ from species to species, for example, a season-long drought may decrease the ability of some species to contribute to ecosystem processes, while increased contributions may be observed in other species during the same period (Yachi and Loreau 1999). Annual and biennial plants tend to have the ability to respond quickly after drought conditions and are associated with disturbance (McIntyre et al. 1995, Carter and Blair 2012). Including native annual and biennial species in species-rich seed mixes may enhance recovery and resilience at restoration sites after short-term drought (Carter and Blair 2012). This may be of particular importance in the coming decades, as mid-continental regions are predicted to experience increased drought risk due to climate change (Meehl et al. 2007, Carter and Blair 2012). Annual species such as Deervetch (*Lotus purshianus*), Foxtail Dalea (*Dalea leporina*), Marsh Elder (*Iva annua*), Prairie Sunflower (*Helianthus petiolaris*), Woolly Plantain (*Plantago patagonica*), Daisy Fleabane (*Erigeron strigosus*), Partridge Pea (*Chamaecrista fasciculata*), Plains Coreopsis (*Coreopsis tinctoria*), Beggar-ticks (*Bidens* spp.) and some Smartweeds (*Polygonum* spp.) as well as biennials and short-lived perennials such as Common Evening Primrose (*Oenothera villosa*), Fourpoint Primrose (*Oenothera rhombipetala*), Black-eyed Susan (*Rudbeckia hirta*), Canada Wild-rye (*Elymus canadensis*), and Virginia Wild-rye (*Elymus virginicus*) are good candidates for restoration seed mixes in our region.

There is considerable evidence that more diverse seed mixes enhance grassland restoration success through increased species richness, improved native plant cover, and related reductions in exotic species invasion (Carter and Blair 2012, Nemec et al. 2013, Barr et al. 2017). When comparing species-rich mixes and seeding rates, Carter and Blair (2012), Nemec et al. (2013) and Barr et al. (2017) found that increasing the diversity of a seed mix is often more important than increasing the seeding rate (density) when restoring grasslands. In the CPRV near Wood River, NE, Nemec et al. (2013) found that restoration plots establishing from a species-rich seed mix showed increased invasion resistance to unseeded exotic-invasive species such as Smooth Brome (*Bromus inermis*) and Bull Thistle (*Cirsium vulgare*), but a higher seeding density did not appear to have the same benefits. Knowing that management of invasive species is often costly, high diversity seed mixes should also be considered at restoration sites for their potential to reduce exotic-invasive species control expenditures. Though high diversity seed mixes can be costly up front, they may provide a more successful, efficient, and cost-effective restoration approach in the long run (Nemec et al. 2013, Barr et al. 2017).

One of the biggest factors driving project costs and ecological outcomes in grassland restoration is seed mix design (Larson et al. 2011, Barr et al. 2017, Meissen et al. 2020). Limited funding within conservation programs can inhibit the use of species-rich mixes, which are typically more expensive. High initial costs also promote the use of mixes with high grass-to-forb seed ratios for restoration projects, as grass seed is generally less expensive than forb seed to harvest in bulk (Meissen et al. 2020). However, Dickson and Busby (2009) demonstrated the ecological advantages of decreasing grass seeding density in tallgrass prairie restoration projects. Planting a mix with high grass seed density led to swift increases in dominant grass abundance, resulting in poor forb species establishment and low forb species richness (Dickson and Busby 2009). Mixes where dominant grasses were included at a low density allowed for greater forb establishment and higher forb species richness (Dickson and Busby 2009). It is also important that seed mixes are designed with multifunctionality in mind, simultaneously providing ecosystem services such as, pollinator resources, erosion control, and resistance to weeds, rather than focusing on a single conservation objective (Meissen et al. 2020). A "diversity mix" (with 71 species and a balanced grass-to-forb seeding ratio) provided the widest range of ecosystem services when compared to an "economy mix" (21 species and higher grass-to-forb seed ratio) and a "pollinator mix" (38 species and a higher forb-to-grass seed ratio) according to findings by Meissen et al. (2020). Though the "pollinator mix" would adequately provide pollinator resources, it would be unable to provide good weed resistance and erosion control (Meissen et al. 2020). The "economy mix" would provide good weed resistance and erosion control but would not be able to provide adequate pollinator resources, however the "diversity mix" adequately provided all three ecosystem services (Meissen et al. 2020). Prairie restorations can achieve multifunctionality and be more cost-effective with well-designed seed mixes that prioritize species richness, site-customization, and maintain carefully balanced grass-to-forb seeding ratios (Dickson and Busby 2009, Drobney et al. 2020, Meissen et al. 2020).

Pollinators can benefit from restoration efforts, as there is evidence that restored habitats support increases in pollinator abundance and diversity on the landscape (Fiedler et al. 2011, Williams 2011, Tonietto and Larkin 2018, Lamke 2019). Restorations support similar species of native bees to remnant sites depending on site condition but community composition (i.e., species relative abundance) generally varies based on the functional characteristics of the restored site (Lamke 2019, Larose et al. 2020). Research demonstrates that restorations with diverse floral resources support diverse native bee and pollinator communities (Harmon-Threatt and Hendrix 2015, Lane et al. 2020). Relatedly, research indicates that effective invasive species control can promote pollinator communities (Fiedler et al. 2011). Studies also demonstrate that high diversity pollinator communities help sustain diverse plant communities better than low diversity pollinator communities (Fontaine et al. 2005). The pollination services to native forbs that are provided by diverse assemblages of pollinators can help promote the success of grassland restorations (Fontaine et al. 2005, Slagle and Hendrix 2009, Harmon-Threatt and Hendrix 2015). Pollinators utilizing restoration sites play an important role in the long-term maintenance of plant species richness and community composition (Fontaine et al. 2005, Harmon-Threatt and Hendrix 2015). Thus, monitoring of native bees and other pollinators at restoration sites should be implemented along with other protocols assessing restoration success when possible.

Other insect guilds also benefit from diverse native plant communities resulting from restoration efforts (Albrecht et al. 2007, Rowe and Holland 2013). When comparing leafhopper (Hemiptera: Cicadellidae) communities in prairie restorations with high plant species richness to those with low plant species richness, Rowe and Holland (2013) found that higher plant richness resulted in significant increases in leafhopper diversity and richness and that species-rich restorations appear to offer comparable leafhopper habitat to remnant sites. These findings indicate that animal food webs may be better supported by high diversity restorations (Rowe and Holland 2013). Albrecht et al. (2007) demonstrated that insect species diversity and the abundance and diversity of their trophic interactions increased significantly where plant species diversity was higher. More diverse community interactions involving parasitoid and predator insects (natural enemies of bees and wasps) occurred within restored meadows with greater plant species richness than in intensively managed agricultural meadows with lower plant species richness (Albrecht et al. 2007). This also supports the idea that the structure, function and stability of insect communities and their associated food webs can be improved by diverse restorations.

One of the benefits of local ecotype restoration work, is that the resulting plant communities likely have similar genetics to plants growing in the region historically (Steinauer et al. 2003, Bucharova et al. 2016). When examining the overall fitness consequences of translocating plant populations across Minnesota, Rushing et al. (2021) found that populations sourced from locations farther to the north tended to flower earlier and exhibited higher fitness than populations that were sourced from more southern locations. Based on these findings, the latitude where seed is sourced from may be an important consideration for restoration work (Rushing et al. 2021). Sourcing seed mixes for restoration projects from appropriate latitudes may be beneficial to native pollinators and developing plant communities by reducing the risk of phenological mismatch (Bucharova et al. 2017). Spring ephemerals are of particular concern, as phenological mismatch can limit their reproductive success and affect plant-pollinator interactions (Kudo and Ida 2013).

Restoration Methods: The high diversity, local ecotype restoration methods described here have been developed by and are implemented by PPRI in central and eastern Nebraska. Similar methods have been used by other organizations and agencies, such as The Nature Conservancy and Crane Trust along the PRV (Note: uncited content in the following paragraphs corresponds to unpublished data from PPRI and personal communications from S. Bailey).

The majority of species included in a PPRI ecological restoration mix are harvested by hand. This includes nearly all forb species, along with sedges, rushes and minor grass species. Hand harvesting takes place from the end of May until the end of October each year, as various species mature and produce seed throughout different times in the growing season. Seed is harvested from various locations in central and eastern Nebraska including, remnant prairies/wetlands, local ecotype restored prairies/wetlands, and roadside ditches (predominantly county roadsides) where wild plant populations remain. It is important to avoid overharvesting from remnant and restored sites, thus a general rule of thumb is to harvest 50% or less of the seed available in these areas. When feasible, seed from a particular species is harvested from many different locations (within an approx. 100-mile radius) with the hope of increasing genetic diversity within seed mixes. Once seed is hand-harvested in the field, the seed/plant material is then spread out on tarps on the open floor of an outbuilding for drying. Proper drying of seed is necessary to avoid issues caused by mold. After drying, all of the hand harvested seed is processed through a Hammermill to break up the plant material, allowing the seed to fall out of chaff or capsules. This takes place in November after the harvest season is complete. After processing, individual lots of seed are labeled and stored in barrels and buckets until it is time to create seed mixes. PPRI does not clean the seed (i.e., remove lingering chaff, bracts, and capsules) used in their restoration projects, as broadcast seeding can easily be done with the extra chaff included in the mix.

Warm season grass species (i.e. *Andropogon gerardii*, *Sorghastrum nutans*, *Panicum virgatum*, *Schizachyrium scoparium*, *Elymus canadensis* and occasionally *Spartina pectinata*, *Sporobolus asper*, *Bouteloua* spp. and *Calamovilfa longifolia*) are needed in greater bulk quantities and are harvested by combine in late September and early October. Combine harvesting is also handy for creating a "granola mix" of both major grasses and forb species that are ready for harvest at the same time. Forb seed that is also brought in through the combine may include, *Silphium* spp., *Helianthus* spp., *Monarda fistulosa*, *Desmodium* spp., *Desmanthus illinoensis*, *Solidago* spp., *Astragalus canadensis*, *Cirsium altissimum*, *Eupatorium altissimum*, *Bickellia eupatorioides*, *Oenothera villosa*, *Lotus purshianus*, *Vernonia* spp., *Verbena* spp., *Salvia azurea* and *Symphyotrichum* spp. Combine harvest locations typically include previously restored (local ecotype) as well as remnant prairie and meadow sites with very limited invasive-exotic plant cover. PPRI uses older Gleaner combines for bulk harvest (i.e., 1983 Gleaner L3 and a 1974 Gleaner K). Combine and seed harvested mixes are integrated to meet specific project objectives.

In the 1990s, during early CPRV high diversity restoration efforts, PPRI harvested seed from between 150 -170 species each year (Whitney 1997a). Today, PPRI harvests between 225-250 species that get incorporated into seed mixes that are tailored to specific soil types and hydrological regimes. These seed mixes are designated as: upland prairie, sand prairie, eastern tallgrass prairie, mesic prairie, ephemeral wetland and emergent wetland. Mixes contain around 50+ species at the low end and 150+ species at the high end and are typically blended or sometimes customized based on particular restoration site attributes. Often, multiple mixes are broadcast onto a restoration site which can increase the number of species used on a particular project to over 200. GIS mapping of a restoration site prior to seeding allows for targeted application of seed mixes to appropriate microsites. Mapping helps determine soil types and their locations on site and LiDAR data reveals subtle changes in topography across a site in order to gain a better understanding of the hydrological characteristics present. Once these restoration site attributes are determined, site-specific mixes are prepared in appropriate quantities for the mapped areas. Recommendations vary by a factor of ≥10 concerning the necessary seeding rate for prairie and meadow restorations ranging from ~5 to ~50 lbs. pure live seed per acre depending on region and seed mixture composition (Glaves 2009, Rowe et al. 2010). However, as research demonstrates, seed diversity can often be more important than seed volume to restoration outcomes (Dickson and Busby 2009, Carter and Blair 2012, Nemec et al. 2013, Barr et al. 2017). Given a diverse seed mix it is likely acceptable to reseed meadows and prairies with seed volumes closer to the lower end of the recommendation spectrum. PPRI actually estimates their volume in gallons and uses about 10 – 23 gallons of hammer-milled but otherwise "uncleaned" seed per acre depending on project needs.

Site preparation ahead of seeding can vary considerably by type of restoration project and site history. This can include restoring historic topography with heavy machinery (e.g., bulldozer), mechanical seedbed preparation (e.g., disks, harrows), altering crop rotations in the growing season before planting (e.g., soybeans for nitrogen fixing), and occasionally spraying dominant exotic-invasive species with herbicide (Rowe 2010, Deák et al. 2015, Shaw et al. 2020). Research indicates that restoring natural topographical variation to formerly land-leveled agricultural lands previous to seeding improves long-term restoration outcomes (Deák et al. 2015). Planting work generally takes place from December through April or early May regionally (Steinauer et al. 2003, Rowe 2010, Larson et al. 2011). Seed can be spread through a number of methods including broadcast seeding, drill seeding, or hydroseeding, and they can all be highly effective depending on the restoration contexts such as slope, season, and site preparation and condition (Rowe 2010, Larson et al. 2011, Shaw et al. 2020). In Nebraska, dormant-season broadcast seeding is the dominant restoration approach, which allows seeds to go through a moist-cold stratification process that generally enhances germination (Steinauer et al. 2003). Seed is often broadcast directly into light snow which allows for easy tracking and may maximize moist-cold stratification effects (Steinauer et al. 2003). PPRI uses an EZEE-Flow drop spreader followed by a spring-tooth (i.e., drag) harrow pulled with an ATV to broadcast seed prairie-meadow restorations (S. Bailey pers. comm., Steinauer et al. 2003).

Based on findings from Lamke (2019) and long-term observations of PPRI's high diversity restorations, improvements need to be made to increase abundance and species richness of early blooming forbs within restoration sites. When Lamke (2019) compared remnant plots to high diversity restoration plots, the remnant plots supported a greater abundance and richness of early blooming forbs. Though high diversity restoration plots supported high abundance and richness of flowering forbs in the mid-season and late -season and high bee richness in the mid-season and late-season, they did not support bees as consistently across all seasons like the remnant plots did (Lamke 2019). Observations of PPRI's restorations over the years have revealed a fairly predictable subset of predominantly early-maturing plant species that do not establish well from seed. Some examples include, *Astragalus crassicarpus*, *Viola* spp., *Lithospermum incisum*, *Anemone* spp., *Nothocalias cuspidata*, *Packera plattensis*, *Echinacea angustifolia*, *Tradescantia* spp. *Hesperostipa* spp. *Pediomelum esculentum* and some *Carex* spp. We find there to be a lack of reliable and abundant seed sources for some of these species, which leads to underrepresentation and sometimes absence from seed mixes. This is one highly plausible explanation for poor establishment or absence of certain species at restoration sites. However, in our experience, other species may be fairly well represented in certain seed mixes, but may not germinate well on site. Frischie and Rowe (2012) found that timing of seed sowing can play a significant role in establishment of a particular subset of early-maturing species. Early-maturing species that were sown in the summer established sooner than those sown in the dormant season and after 4 years, diversity in summer sown plots was higher than in dormant season sown plots (Frischie and Rowe 2012). Though dormant season sowing works well for many species, this summer sowing method should be considered for some early-maturing species and put to the test in our region. Another potential method for establishing early-maturing species, is through growing out seedling plugs that get planted into restoration sites as they develop. This method is discussed in the following section.

Plug Plantings: Whether it is early blooming forbs and other species that don't establish well from seeding, rarer species with limited seed sources or species that meet certain habitat conservation objectives, greenhouse grown seedling plugs offer a way to introduce these species of interest to prairie and wetland restoration sites to improve plant species diversity and habitat quality (Wallin et al. 2009). Over the last decade, PPRI has successfully grown plugs for over 100 native plant species and the Crane Trust has also grown a subset of these species in their greenhouse. Violets (*Viola* spp.), some Sedges (*Carex* spp.), and Lobelias (*Lobelia* spp.) represent taxa that grow well in the greenhouse but are often underrepresented in broadcast seeded restorations (A. Caven pers. comm.). Bonesets (*Eupatorium* spp.), Beardtongues (*Penstemon* spp.), Beebalms (*Monarda* spp.), and Milkweeds (*Asclepias* spp.) represent taxa that grow well in the greenhouse and can be effectively established through plugs or broadcast seeding (J. Wiese pers. comm.). However, plug planting provides additional control over where particular floral resources are ultimately sited and can increase the chances of establishment for particular species at degraded sites (Wallin et al. 2009). Plug planting appears most effective in the spring (~mid-May) or early fall (~mid-late September; S. Bailey pers. comm.). Plug planting is easier when soil moisture is high which likely also increases the probability that plants effectively establish (J. Wiese pers. comm.). Moving forward, more research and monitoring efforts are needed to assess the effectiveness of planting plugs into restoration sites as well as in degraded remnant sites. There is very little research that addresses questions related to this in our region.

In recent years there has been a growing need for restoration work that is tailored to benefit insect pollinator species, especially those listed as Tier-1 at-risk species in Nebraska (Schneider et al. 2018). An example of this is the growing concern over declining Regal Fritillary populations (Swengel and Swengel 2016) and the need to connect and expand existing habitat by enhancing degraded prairie and meadow remnant sites and restoring adjacent lands. These prairie specialist insects rely on violet species as a larval food source including *Viola pedatifida* (Prairie Violet) in upland prairies and *Viola missouriensis* (Missouri Violet) as well as *Viola sororia* (Common Violet) in lowland prairie and wet meadow sites (Caven et al. 2017). However, these species are often absent from restorations, limiting the Regal Fritillary's ability to successfully colonize new restorations (Caven et al. 2017).

Since building a greenhouse facility in 2010, PPRI has worked toward providing *V. pedatifida* plugs for Regal Fritillary habitat restoration projects and is now working to provide *V. missouriensis* and *V. sororia* as well. In recent years, PPRI has experienced a growing demand with partner agencies and organizations for these local ecotype violet plugs. The Crane Trust has also been growing and installing *Viola* spp. for enhancement and restoration work on conservation lands in the CPRV. It is highly likely that this demand will continue to grow and there will be need for expansion of greenhouse operations and more people involved in growing violet plugs. However, more research and monitoring efforts will also be needed to establish best practices for growing and planting violets regionally. Larger-scale monitoring of current Regal Fritillary populations and *Viola* spp. populations in the CPRV are needed to help determine where violet plug planting efforts are best spent. Research will then be needed to assess survivorship of *Viola* spp. plugs being planted at various PRV restoration and enhancement sites. The Crane Trust has been monitoring Regal Fritillary abundance, violet abundance, and violet plug establishment on their lands in the CPRV and these efforts should be expanded throughout the PRV to determine if violet restorations are influencing long-term Regal Fritillary abundance or site use (Caven et al. 2017).

Initial data taken to assess survivorship among *Viola pedatifida* plugs planted in groupings into a degraded upland prairie site in eastern Nebraska are showing some promising results. In September 2020, *V. pedatifida* plugs grown out by PPRI were installed into a degraded remnant prairie at Pioneers Park. Groupings of 10 plugs were installed within a few feet of each other around marked locations. When the site was re-visited in May 2021 and the number of live violets were tallied, two of the planting blocks were found to have >60% *V. pedatifida* survivorship (63% survivorship in the northwest planting block and 67% survivorship in the southwest block; D. Wedin pers. comm.). *V. pedatifida* plug survivorship fared much worse in the third (southeast) planting block, with 16% survivorship. (D. Wedin pers. comm.). It was noted that the condition of the surrounding plant community in this southeast planting block was much poorer than in the northwest and southwest blocks. The local land manager also noted a history of invasive plants and woody encroachment that were treated and cleared within the southeast block (S. Bailey pers. comm.). Considering that approximately 750 violets were planted in these groupings, the results for the >60% survivorship planting blocks are quite promising. It is highly plausible that a number of these *V. pedatifida* plugs that survived from fall 2020 until May 2021 may even set seed within this first year. Though this is preliminary data, it may also be useful in understanding how site conditions and history may impact the success of *Viola* spp. that are plugged into degraded remnants and restoration sites. More data taken from other sites could help inform restorationists about the best locations for successful *Viola* spp. plug planting efforts, especially in the CPRV. The Crane Trust has also monitored *V. sororia* plantings and consistently documented post-planting persistence in subsequent growing seasons (J. Wiese pers. comm.).

It is also important to note that growing native plant plugs and planting them into restoration sites serves as a useful educational tool that introduces conservation and ecological restoration work in Nebraska to new audiences. Volunteer efforts to plant plugs into restoration sites has proved successful and has raised peoples' awareness about local conservation efforts and how restoration work plays a critical role. An example of this is taking place in the Prairie

Corridor on Haines Branch near Lincoln, NE. The City of Lincoln and PPRI have worked with

Nebraska Master Naturalist volunteers to install *Viola pedatifida* plugs into restoration sites in

the Prairie Corridor to improve Regal Fritillary habitat over the last few years (S. Bailey pers.

comm.). School partnerships with local conservation organizations have also proved successful

in introducing young audiences to conservation and restoration work in Nebraska. Two local

high school classes are involved in hands-on restoration efforts on PPRI preserves through

growing native plant plugs in their school greenhouses. Students practice identifying native

plants and learn about prairie ecology, local restoration work, and how to grow native plants in a

greenhouse setting. They grow their own plugs which they bring to local restoration sites for

planting.

Post-restoration Management: The management applied after restoring prairies is highly

important to project outcomes (Steinauer et al. 2003, Helzer 2009, Meissen et al. 2020). Burning

can generally be introduced as soon as there is enough fuel to initiate one as burning adds

phosphorus and other nutrients to the system that stimulate growth of above and below ground

biomass as well as seed production (Steinauer et al. 2003, Helzer 2009). However, burning can

occasionally lead to the desiccation of the seedbed during dry conditions (Steinauer et al. 2003).

Mowing can have the opposite effect as it can create cover for sprouting seedlings and help

retain moisture while reducing competition from early successional ruderal species (Steinauer et

al. 2003, Rowe 2010, Meissen et al. 2020). The season and climatic conditions when burning or

mowing occur can influence restoration community composition in subsequent years (Steinauer

et al. 2003, Helzer 2009, Meissen et al. 2020). Though mowing and burning can both be useful

tools early in the restoration process it is important to wait to intensively graze until after perennial warm season grasses have established robust root systems, which generally requires 3–5 years at minimum (Steinauer et al. 2003, Rowe 2010). However, regarding restorations with high forb to grass ratios it may require even more time for restorations to develop resilience to season-long grazing (Crane Trust unpublished data).

Restored systems that had been heavily grazed over a 30-year period had reduced warm season grass cover and increased bare ground cover as well as reduced soil nutrient and organic matter accumulation relative to less intensively grazed restorations and remnant sites regardless of management (Fuhlendorf et al. 2002). These findings suggest that restored prairies may never be as resilient to intensive season-long grazing as remnant systems. While mowing or haying are singular disturbances, season-long cattle grazing provides a more chronic disturbance that can result in decreased vigor of native perennial graminoids which provide an important buffer against exotic-invasive species invasion in relatively new restorations (Fuhlendorf et al. 2002, Steinauer et al. 2003, Meissen et al. 2020). Grazing too hard and early in the successional process can result in a loss of natural grassland structure and ultimately increased exotic species cover (Steinauer et al. 2003, Crane Trust unpublished data). Another important consideration in prairie and meadow restoration management is the control of woody and exotic-invasive species colonization, which can be exacerbated by premature season-long grazing and may require repeat, targeted herbicide applications to control (Steinauer et al. 2003, Rowe 2010, Archer et al. 2017).

Goals: Our long-term goal is to use restoration to improve habitat connectivity and availability for a diversity of dispersal-limited and area-sensitive species (Herkert 1994, Winter and Faaborg 1999, Vogt et al. 2009, Lechner et al. 2017). To truly succeed in this effort, we need to engage private landowners in the PRV. Relatedly, it is a priority to identify degraded grasslands and restore missing components through overseeding and plug planting (Wallin et al. 2009). We also hope to scale up restoration monitoring efforts across the PRV to further refine best restoration practices regionally (Steinauer et al. 2003, Török 2021). Engaging the public in restoration and monitoring efforts can help us build support for and ramp up regional conservation work. Seed collection is an effort that can generally benefit from robust volunteer support. Estimating the importance of diverse grassland restorations for carbon sequestration regionally presents another emerging opportunity (Hungate et al. 2017).

*Warm-water Slough Restoration* – Slough wetlands provide important habitat for several threatened and endangered species including Whooping Cranes, Plains Topminnows, Platte River Caddisflies, and Cardinal Flowers (Harner and Whited 2011, Vivian et al. 2013, Zambory et al. 2017, Caven and Wiese 2022, Caven et al. *In Press*; Appendix 1). These habitats are also critical to migrating and wintering waterfowl, such as American wigeon, as well as hundreds of other native species, and provide many recreational opportunities (Goldowitz and Whiles 1999, Conly 2001, Whiles and Goldowitz 2001, Ducks Unlimited 2011; Appendix 1). Slough wetlands further benefit the community by mitigating water shortages, through recharging groundwater aquifers, and providing flood control (Chen 2007, Brinley Buckley et al. 2021). Many of these habitats were lost via altered hydrology and land use conversion by humans (Currier 1982, Sidle et al. 1989, Henszey et al. 2004). Since the 1990s, there were concerted efforts to restore sloughs by the U.S. Fish and Wildlife Service, Nebraska Game and Parks Commission, Crane Trust, Ducks Unlimited, Audubon's Rowe Sanctuary, The Nature Conservancy, Platte River Basin Environments, Natural Resources Conservation Service, and private landowners (See Meyer and Whiles 2008, Meyer et al. 2010). Slough restoration techniques have continued to evolve, and hundreds of miles of slough have been restored throughout the Platte and North Platte River

Valleys. Despite the investment of time and resources, few studies have systematically evaluated slough habitat post-restoration, and those that have only investigated a small subset on conservation-owned and managed lands (Meyer and Whiles 2008, Meyer et al. 2010).

Continued warm-water slough restoration is a key conservation objective for the PRV. However, recurrent assessment years after restoration is needed to evaluate the long-term ecological benefits of slough restoration, the impacts of differing restoration techniques and management, and their cost effectiveness. Specifically, we need to take stock of what we have done, evaluate the success of past efforts, and the describe gaps in spatial coverage of this important habitat type. Ultimately, we need to develop regionally specific warm-water slough restoration goals following inventory and condition assessment efforts (e.g., restore >2,000 acres in the LPRV). Additionally, we need to protect the functionality of existing remnant and reconstructed sloughs by promoting grassland buffers around them (>100 m width), supporting no-till agriculture, and managing woody encroachment in the PRV (See Appendix 2).

*Land Protection and Restoration Programs*

Numerous conservation programs exist in the PRV that restore and/or protect habitat, and are provided by federal agencies, other government agencies, and non-governmental organizations (NGOs). One such option is a conservation easement, which is a way to preserve property that has high habitat values while keeping the property in its natural and undeveloped state. The landowner still maintains ownership of the property with the property being protected for a term of years or in perpetuity. Conservation easements are an instrument that is a legal document between a willing landowner and a conservation organization. Each organization has its own values and goals as well as rules and requirements in an easement, so properties considered for conservation easements typically align with a specific organization's objectives. Nonfederal agencies who extend these programs in the PRV are the Crane Trust, The Nature Conservancy, Ducks Unlimited, the Nebraska Land Trust, Platte River Basin Environments, the Platte River Recovery Implementation Program, Audubon Nebraska, and some Natural Resources Districts. Therefore, several different conservation easement options are available for a property to align with an organization's/agency's and landowner's ideals.

Although each easement is different, several features are common to conservation easements offered by the various nonfederal organizations (Cheever and McLaughlin 2015). An entire tract does not have to be entered into an easement program as long as the identified land encompasses the conservation values and, if developed, the portion left out would not adversely affect conservation values of the easement tract. Depending upon the landowner's tax situation, donation of a conservation easement also may reduce estate, income, and property taxes but the entire property should be donated to receive full tax benefits. Working lands, such as active ranching and farming operations, can continue to function normally under a conservation easement. The willing landowner keeps the right to use property for economic gain or recreation and the right to sell or deed the property to another. However, the conservation easement is attached to the deed and remains active through that transfer to ensure protection in perpetuity or the full length of the agreement (Cheever and McLaughlin 2015). Also, by the discretion of the landowner, an easement can remain private, but it can also be made available for public access. Developing an easement document acceptable to both the conservation organization and the willing landowner is important to growing strong partnerships and protecting vital habitat.

In the PRV, working lands conservation easements provided by nonfederal organizations are generally valued between 15% and 30% of the site's total value but can exceed this level under special circumstances (Tom Peterson, Ducks Unlimited, personal communication, January 28, 2021; Tim Smith, Crane Trust, pers. comm., April 5, 2021). Because of the high cost to NGOs, easements are often partially or fully donated. The donated easement value can be tax deductible, but to receive a federal tax deduction, the easement must strictly follow Internal Revenue Service (IRS) rules and requirements (e.g., Internal Revenue Code § 170(h)). One such rule is the easement must be in perpetuity (Internal Revenue Code § 170(h)(2)(C)), so NGOs generally require permanent easements. IRS requirements need not be followed if the landowner does not plan to deduct his/her donation or if the easement is fully paid (i.e., not donated).

In addition to nonfederal agency easements, federally-held and/or -funded easements are also available. Three easement options are available through United States Department of Agriculture (USDA): the Wetland Reserve Easement (WRE), Emergency Watershed Protection - Floodplain Easement (EWP-FPE), and Agricultural Land Easement (ALE). Through WRE, a landowner is compensated for placing a 30-year or perpetual conservation easement held by USDA on a property containing wetland and associated upland habitats (USDA 2020). USDA restores the site, providing 75 or 100% cost-share, depending on the length of the easement. The landowner cannot crop the site and can only manage per USDA approval and guidelines, so WRE is not generally a good option for landowners wanting to manage or graze however they see fit. WRE is much more controlled by the easement holder, but also compensates the landowner more than other easement options along the Platte River, except EWP-FPE. Due to the WRE ranking process, sites with little to no hydrologic modification have a low chance of being enrolled in WRE.

EWP-FPE is a perpetual easement option that is only available for a limited time after a U.S. presidential declaration of disaster (USDA 2016). For land to be eligible during the limited application window, it must have been damaged by a flood the previous year or twice in the last ten years, or would be adversely impacted by a dam breach (USDA 2016). Habitat restoration is often limited to establishing native plants and/or removing existing buildings. EWP-FPE is similar to WRE in terms of its compensation, restoration payments, and management requirements, including all of the pros and cons thereof. Because EWP-FPE is so seldom available, it can only be used in the PRV during very limited timeframes.

ALE is used to preserve farmland from development. A permanent easement held by an eligible entity (e.g., local government, NGO) is placed on the site, usually the entire tract, and the landowner receives a one-time payment, 50 – 75% of which is paid by USDA and the remainder must be paid by the eligible entity and/or donated by the landowner (USDA 2020). No restoration costs are paid by USDA. The easement deed must contain minimum terms by USDA but the eligible entity can include additional terms, such as provisions for habitat restoration on the property. If a portion of the easement value is donated, the easement must follow IRS rules for the landowner to receive a tax deduction. Because ALE was created to protect farmland from development, some PRV sites might not have sufficient development pressure to receive funding.

The United States Fish and Wildlife Service (USFWS) also has a permanent easement option, under which the habitat is restored at no cost to the landowner (USFWS 2001, USFWS 2011). Cropping is prohibited on USFWS easements, but landowners can generally graze and manage the sites as they choose. However, the PRV is outside priority easement areas for USFWS, except limited areas along the CPRV and by North Platte National Wildlife Refuge (USFWS 2001). In addition, outside funds are needed to deliver USFWS easements, which have been difficult to attain for numerous years prior to the writing of this document, although that could change in the future.

Fee title acquisition of a willing seller's property is another tool to protect ecosystems in the Platte River watershed. This process involves a conservation agency purchasing a property that meets its conservation goals. Purchase price can be determined by fair market value or appraised value. Depending upon the purchasing agency/organization, it can remain the holder or the agency/organization can place a conservation easement on the property then transfer it to a partnering conservation agency or private landowner. This approach to protecting lands has been successful but can also require several conservation partners to contribute funding from various sources.

Shorter-term programs are also available to protect and restore habitat along the Platte River. Most of these programs are administered by USDA and range from one-year contracts to long-term easements. For landowners interested in cost-share for restoration with no annual payment, the Environmental Quality Incentives Program (EQIP) is an option, although the land must be used to produce an agricultural commodity at the time of enrollment in EQIP (USDA 2018a). This program provides cost-share for specific conservation practices (e.g., native plant seeding, wetland restoration) with one- to five-year contracts. The Conservation Stewardship Program (CSP) provides landowners with an annual payment for completing farming conservation practices on their entire operation, but does not pay directly for the practice itself (USDA 2018b). Unlike other USDA programs, CSP is for the whole suite of conservation practices (e.g., cover crops, wildlife-friendly fences) used across an entire farming operation rather than a specific area of the operation, so is not widely used for habitat restoration and has limited utility in the PRV. Through the Conservation Reserve Program (CRP), landowners enroll in 10- or 15-year contracts or occasionally 30-year contracts, during which the land is usually planted to native grasses and forbs, the land cannot be cropped, and the landowner must follow USDA guidelines for management (USDA 2021). Most CRP options are only available on cropped sites, with the exception of CRP Grasslands for use on range and pastureland. In addition, Regional Conservation Partnership Program grants are available that give conservation organizations more flexibility within programs (e.g., modifying eligible land types, tweaking requirements) and the opportunity to target funds to a specific region, such as the PRV (USDA 2017).

Each conservation program option has its pros and cons. USDA programs are available in the entire PRV and funding is generally better than other conservation programs. Also, Regional Conservation Partnership Program grants help provide some flexibility in USDA programs. However, USDA programs have some drawbacks. Most programs are only available on land that produces an agricultural commodity, with the exceptions being WRE and EWP-FPE, and only landowners who make less than $900,000 annually are eligible, other than for EWP-FPE (USDA 2016, 2017, 2018a, 2018b, 2020, 2021). Also, demand is usually greater than funding, so only a portion of projects can be enrolled based on application ranking. Furthermore, USDA programs except EWP-FPE are authorized by U.S. Farm Bills and are therefore subject to change or termination by Congress whenever a new Farm Bill is passed (e.g., Stubbs 2014, 2019). In addition, funds allocated to each program change over time (e.g., Stubbs 2014, 2019). So, programs available at the time of this document may be modified or renamed in future Farm Bills. EWP-FPE is instead authorized by numerous laws such as Public Law 81-516, Section 216 (USDA 2016), and also is subject to modification or termination by Congress.

Numerous agencies and organizations also provide cost-share for habitat projects, such as USFWS (USFWS 2017), Nebraska Game and Parks Commission, Natural Resource Districts, Ducks Unlimited (Ducks Unlimited 2019), Pheasants Forever, the Crane Trust, Audubon Nebraska, and The Nature Conservancy (K. Schroeder pers. comm.). Each agency has its own requirements but generally will provide wetland restoration, river channel clearing, tree removal, slough restorations, high diversity native seeding, and/or nonnative plant species removal, among other activities. Landowners sign an agreement for a term of years, which outlines the restoration and enhancement activities on the project and cost-share. Restoration and management activities associated with projects are negotiated between the landowner and the agency/conservation organizations involved with the project, making them a flexible option. Cost-share from different agencies/organizations is often combined on projects. Because each agency has its own priorities, particular projects may only fit with certain agencies. For example, USFWS cost-share is available on any land use type, but the vast majority occur in their focus areas that, which along the Platter River only includes the CPRV and portions of the NPRV (USFWS 2017), while Ducks Unlimited cost-share is available throughout the PRV, but projects must benefit wetland habitat (Ducks Unlimited 2019). Additional management options are also available through conservation partners. Pheasants Forever, through their prescribed burn associations, provides tools for completing prescribed burns (https://nebraskapf.com/prescribed-burn-associations-pba/). Some Nebraska Natural Resources Districts provide prescribed fire training and/or will help complete prescribed burns. Ducks Unlimited can disk wetlands to control undesirable plants and the Crane Trust will help landowners clear unwanted trees near the main channel of the Platte River.

Short-term easements, restoration programs, and cost-share programs all have their place in managing and restoring habitat in the PRV. However, it is important to note that some programs only provide benefits for a limited amount of time, so their benefits last only as long as the restoration or contract. Morefield et al. (2016) found that almost 30% of expiring CRP in the Midwest from 2010 to 2013 was converted back to annual row crops—with areas of Nebraska having particularly high conversion rates—while only 3% remained under conservation protection. That being said, short-term programs have their utility. These programs can sometimes be used in combination with long-term easements and fee title acquisitions when the long-term program does not directly pay for restoration. For example, a landowner can receive EQIP cost-share for habitat restoration on a site protected by an ALE (USDA 2020). Another reason for using short-term programs is simply because a landowner may not be interested in a permanent option.

It is also important to note that easement protection coverage is not always complete and may not preserve lands in conditions comparable to public lands (Rissman et al. 2007, Quintas-Soriano et al. 2021). Additionally, the rules associated with many restoration and easement-related programs can be confusing to landowners (Lute et al. 2018). However, conservation easements are one of the fastest growing forms of land protection, preserving >50 million acres (>20 million ha) in the US from development (McLaughlin 2013, Dayer et al. 2016). Conservation easements have come under fire regarding their legal framework and the public can at times demonstrate significant misunderstandings regarding their implications (McLaughlin 2013, Lute et al. 2018). This has been concerning to conservation agencies as easements are an important tool that has been a great benefit in protecting habitat. Conservation easements have a long history of successful application in the U.S., first being used to protect land along the Blue

Ridge Parkway in North Carolina and Virginia in the 1930s (Cheever and McLaughlin 2015).

Research highlights that landowners entering into easements regularly do so as much for the

environmental and cultural services they provide as for the funding incentives (Lute et al. 2018,

Aoyama and Huntsinger 2019). Moreover, both landowners and conservationist often highlight

the importance of developing relationships to the success of easement programs (Lute et al.

2018, Aoyama and Huntsinger 2019). This highlights the need for VESPR working group

members to not only find the best conservation programs to support working lands in the Platte

River but to develop close relationships with our neighbors.

**Social Context**

Although this paper has focused mostly on an ecological vision for the Platte River to this

point, human communities are also part of the system and are essential to any successful

conservation effort. The Platte River watershed is a social-ecological system that is complex and

dependent upon feedbacks between social and ecological processes. It is critical, therefore, to

review the social and political factors that interact with, shape, and are shaped by shifting

ecological dynamics (Dunham et al. 2018). A great deal of resources have been directed toward

increasing our understanding of and restoring the many vital ecological functions of the Platte

River watershed through research and management efforts, but less has been done to investigate

the perceptions, needs, or opinions of the human communities within the watershed that impact

and are impacted by those ecological processes (Dunham et al. 2018). In order to achieve a

higher level of success in the implementation of conservation efforts within this riverscape, we

recognize the need to engage with the human communities of the Platte River Basin.

In the Methods section, we referenced landscape design as an interdisciplinary conservation planning process that incorporates components of landscape ecology and social dimensions (Nassauer and Opdam 2008, Bartuszevige et al. 2016). The data driven practice classifies important ecological events or mechanisms as processes that create landscape patterns, and the human influence on those processes as drivers. For example, bridge building (driver) may result in changes to streamflow and sediment transport (ecological process). Here, the goal-based approach to landscape design is important to review because drivers are addressed in the context of meeting quantitative ecological goals in the face of societal desires, which can be measured in many cases (i.e. cost to community associated with replacing bridges) but are also felt or experienced (i.e. historical significance of certain bridges, desire to reconstruct damaged bridges to same design standards as previous).

This is where the use of various social sciences can be critical in understanding motivations and desires for different management strategies and engaging the community to address problems that impact people as well as the plants and animals that call the riverscape home. Social science can help us understand the broader community's underlying perspective on natural resource-related phenomena. Using the driver above (i.e., bridges) as an example, social scientists can help us determine whether community members understand that bridge designs which do not consider social-ecological resilience can negatively impact ecological function downstream (e.g., channel capacity) while causing undesired impacts to human communities upstream (e.g., property flooding). Social science can also help us determine how to engage people in crafting solutions that are mutually beneficial to both the ecosystem and embedded human communities.

Below are a few examples of how social science will be applied to building a more holistic understanding of the drivers of landscape processes along the Platte River and the contexts within which they interact. The potential benefit of social science application to conservation efforts in the Platte River Basin include understanding the historical context of human development of the riverscape, understanding where human needs and goals match or are in conflict with ecological needs, and understanding the values and opinions of various human groups within the watershed. Social science is a foundational aspect of our vision and will help us consider the various benefits and impacts of conservation work on the human community. It will also help us test assumptions about what people think, do, and feel; and also help shape future social science work to answer new questions. Through the use of social science disciplines, we believe novel and actionable pathways toward a socio-ecologically sound Platte River will result from new synergies rooted in linking a better understanding ecological function with societal benefit.

*Application of social science in landscape design*

Beyond the urban areas at the headwaters and the river's mouth, the Platte River basin is defined by rural, private, agricultural, and grazing lands. The development of agriculture in the region has been important to support a growing population but has also been a significant driver of many of the landscape, river channel, and water use legacies influencing the ecological processes referenced above. For example, thousands of agricultural diversion dams have been built in the basin, significantly adjusting hydrologic flow paths, trapping sediment, and altering surface and groundwater interactions (Winter et al. 1998, Simons and Associates 2000, Caven et al. 2019a). Determining their location and then prioritizing dams for modification to release sediment, or removal in the case that they may now be non-functional, will require the development of trust and cooperation between conservation professionals, regulatory authorities, and private landowners, with a clear understanding of the benefits and costs to each party.

Total population across the basin has increased in every county over the last 50 years, although in the rural counties, the rate of growth was generally below the national average (NASS 2017). Between 2000 and 2010, rural counties saw slight population decreases (especially in the PRV), while urban centers grew substantially –we expect the 2020 census data to confirm the continuation of this trend. As development pressures shift, various stakeholder groups in the PRV will need to collectively determine what landscape features they want to protect and what strategies they will use to adapt to change while still preserving ecological and community resilience.

The North and South Platte River subbasins include mostly private rangelands, where grazing and crops such as alfalfa and hay dominate. However, the corn belt has been expanding west with new drought tolerant crop varieties, more efficient equipment, and farm bill programs that provide incentives to put marginal land into monoculture production (Higgins et al. 2002, Cooper et al. 2014, Wang et al. 2017, Wright et al. 2017). Corn and soybeans dominate the central Platte River through the heart of Nebraska, which has seen a dramatic consolidation of both crop types and agricultural operations over the past 50+ years (Figures 4 and 5). This has also been accompanied by an increase in fertilizer use consistent with a shift to monocropping (Figure 6). Essentially, these trends suggest a movement away from the "family farm" as historically conceptualized and toward industrial agriculture focused on producing multi-use agricultural commodities (e.g., corn ethanol, corn silage, etc.; Higgins et al. 2002, McNew and Griffith 2005, Wang et al. 2017). Interestingly, Wright et al. (2017) found that grassland losses were concentrated around ethanol refineries indicating that even as "food" prices fluctuate the corn crop's value for ethanol provides additional economic stability. This assumption is supported by research from McNew and Griffith (2005) which indicates ethanol plants boost corn prices within a nearly 70 mi radius. Wang et al. (2017) suggests that larger industrial agricultural producers and those that rent land appear to exhibit more sensitivity to fluctuations in policy, prices, and technological shifts. Ultimately, this indicates we may be dealing with fewer landowners with more clearly defined economic objectives than during earlier conservation efforts in the PRV.

As highlighted in this plan, the continued loss of grassland and wetland habitats to agricultural production will have wide-ranging negative impacts on native fauna and flora populations, which tend to be closely linked to habitat availability (Winter and Faaborg 1999, Rosenberg et al. 2016, Markle et al. 2018). Higgins et al. (2002) suggests that financially supporting ranching operations through stewardship programs or conservation easements may offer the best approach to preserving intact grasslands and embedded wetlands in privately owned areas of the Great Plains. Additionally, agricultural lands can provide significant value to some wildlife populations (e.g., cranes, grassland birds), especially when best conservation practices such as "no-till" farming are utilized (Basore et al. 1986, Krapu et al. 2014). Agricultural lands are generally superior to suburban or industrial development from a wildlife conservation perspective (e.g., Krapu et al. 2014, Pearse et al. 2015, Baasch et al. 2019c). Therefore, stewardship programs that support agricultural livelihoods in suburbanizing landscapes could also be highly valuable to our landscape conservation efforts. Considering both social and ecological processes will be valuable in determining where inroads toward improving riverscape resilience can be made.

Social science can reveal the personal motivations of individuals influencing landscape change, restoration, or protection, and the institutional factors that might encourage or prevent someone from doing so. The complexity involved in landowner decision-making to enter into conservation easements or re-enroll in the Conservation Reserve Program, for example, have been documented in previous studies (e.g., place attachment, financial implications, trust in conservation programs, land management concerns, resource availability, and family legacy; Barnes et al. 2020, Farmer et al. 2011). Because grassland conservation is key to building broader ecosystem health, it is imperative that conservation proponents listen to the range of concerns and desires felt by landowners who may be interested in protecting their land from future development (Barnes et al 2020). As conservation practitioners engage more local communities and other stakeholder groups, collaborative opportunities to improve landscape-level health and social well-being may be uncovered.

As demand for groundwater resources continues to grow, associated decreases in groundwater levels throughout the PRV result in the hydrological detachment of sub-irrigated wetlands and have been shown to have implications for the quality of local groundwater supplies (Currier 1994, Gurdak et al. 2009). Here, combining a spatial understanding of changes in water supplies with water quality-related outreach efforts to communities on the importance of maintaining river streamflows, groundwater supplies, and the filtration benefits of wetlands, may help define a more desirable socio-ecological condition. Within Nebraska alone, groundwater withdrawals for irrigation (which account for 93% of the state's groundwater use) quadrupled from 1955 to 2005 (NNRC 1995, 1998, Hoffman and Zellmer 2012). This trend is most likely due to the widespread adoption of center-pivot irrigation technology (Hiller et al. 2009).

Policy is also a driver influencing the governance of ecological processes across the region from every level of government, as well as a myriad of conservation, agricultural, and community-based NGOs operating in the basin. Federal and state compliance with the federal Endangered Species Act (ESA) precipitated the establishment of PRRIP, which spurred a number of actions at different governance levels to restore some streamflow and improve critical habitat for endangered species in the PRV, with varying levels of success. For example, in order to comply with the PRRIP, the State of Nebraska developed more hydrologically integrated water use policies and stakeholder-based planning actions in the PRV with the goal of decreasing depletions to streamflow (NeDNR et al. 2019). On the other hand, PRRIP has not yet been able to address the North Platte Choke Point which limits our ability to manipulate flows to manage critical Whooping Crane habitat in the CPRV (Stella 2020).

In Nebraska, the unicameral state legislature created one of the most unique local-level natural resource management approaches found in the United States, Natural Resource Districts (NRDs), governed by local districts based roughly on sub-watershed boundaries. NRDs were founded in 1972 to better solve flood control, soil erosion, irrigation run-off, and groundwater quality issues by consolidating irrigation districts, local flood control authorities, soil and water conservation districts, and other special use districts under one roof at the subwatershed scale (Jenkins and Hyer 2009, NARD 2020). Elected, non-partisan boards of directors govern the districts individually, with some district funding coming from local property taxes. This NRD system was designed to decouple the local demands from state demands, giving more power and autonomy to local natural resource governance (Jenkins and Hyer 2009). However, in more recent research, there is evidence that NRD boards can be dominated by agricultural interests which are not representative of all stakeholders within the districts (Hiller et al. 2009; Hoffman et al. 2015).

Although our description here of socio-political dynamics of the Platte River basin is coarse, it underscores the complexity of the region, both spatially and temporally, and reminds us that the ecological dynamics of the basin cannot be decoupled from the human drivers behind landscape change, nor human needs for water. Historical legacies of agricultural development, as well as economic and demographic change, are layered upon the landscape in lasting land conversion and hydrologic alteration. In addition, political systems set into place for the preservation, conservation, and restoration efforts are nested, overlapping, and sometimes in conflict. To create a socio-ecologically sound vision for the Platte River, these large-scale dynamics will need to be understood; as well as the perceptions and desires of individual landowners and other stakeholders in the Platte River watershed.

*Inclusion of community values through social science*

All communities within the Platte River watershed are connected by their need for clean and reliable supplies of water. Carrying out our long-term vision for the Platte River is dependent on our ability to understand the motivations behind drivers of landscape change, and the various human needs for and connections to water in this riverscape (Bogart et al. 2009, Dunham et al. 2017). Decisions and behaviors are rooted in the fundamental values held by humans living and working within the watershed (Dunham et al. 2017). In order to connect the goals that conservation practitioners have for the Platte's riverine ecosystems with the social and economic values of the humans living within the riverscape, we need to integrate social and ecological research, planning, and management already being done (Dunham et al. 2018, Nassauer and

Opdam 2008). As we work toward our vision, unanswered questions will be identified and additional research will be stimulated by what we learn along the way.

Just as the environmental concerns held by those interested in the ecological function of the watershed vary across the landscape, it is assumed that public perceptions of those concerns and methods used to address them vary as well. To more effectively focus future conservation work within the riverscape, it will be important to have a social and spatial understanding of where community support for those efforts already exists and where it needs to be fostered (Villamagna et al. 2017). An effective management plan will require the inclusion of a communication strategy that is intended to build a better understanding of the cultural, environmental, economic, and policy-related pressures experienced by stakeholders within the watershed and how those factors vary from one location to another within the riverscape (Bogart et al. 2009, Villamagna et al. 2017).

Historically, the social implications of environmental conservation efforts have often been decoupled, either due to constrained directives, negligent planning, naivety in regard to cultural norms, or outright disregard for marginalized communities. Bringing a social science research component into the Platte riverscape will assist conservation practitioners in identifying where discrepancies exist in how the benefits from ecosystem services and conservation efforts are distributed (Villamagna et al. 2017). If we can identify where communities are located that have seen few obvious benefits from the services provided by the Platte River and associated ecosystems, or where detrimental impacts from the river or past conservation efforts have been felt, conservation managers will be able to more critically assess where overlaps between ecosystem restoration needs and community needs exist (Villamagna et al. 2017).

The first step in integrating the human dimensions component into a long-term vision for the Platte River watershed will require an effort to collect social science data from individuals and communities across the riverscape. In order to most appropriately prioritize, place, and design upcoming conservation efforts (including communications, policy, and on-the-ground habitat work) the level of agreement or mis-match between the desired conditions held by conservation scientists will be considered in relation to those held by communities within the riverscape. To this end, a social science-based project is now being funded and developed that will make an initial effort at better framing a spatial and social understanding of how our future conservation work will provide the most value to the Platte riverscape (Villamagna et al. 2017).

## CONCLUSIONS

This long-term vision document focuses on conservation priorities in the mainstem Platte River including the Central Platte River Valley (CPRV) and the Lower Platte River Valley (LPRV). However, we ultimately plan to expand this work throughout the Platte River watershed including the headwaters states of Wyoming and Colorado. It provides relatively specific objectives for conservation delivery and research over the coming years. This vision should provide a basis for developing smaller, more specific, and targeted projects to address significant conservation issues. Portions of this vision document should be valid for decades while other components may only be applicable for a number of years. Ultimately, this plan represents a path forward and not an end in and of itself.

The Platte River is an amazing ecosystem not just for what it continues to support biologically but for the number of threats it continues to endure. It displays the characteristics of a biodiversity hotspot and exemplifies the challenges faced by threatened ecosystems.

Nonetheless, it continues to persist as a riverine ecosystem of continental importance for migratory birds, fish, and other taxa. Success on the Platte River is a litmus test for conservation in the Great Plains and beyond across highly transformed landscapes with intensive developmental and agricultural pressures. If we can succeed on the Platte River, we can do great things for conservation throughout the prairie province. However, if we fail on the Platte River and it functionally "dies" like so many of the rivers to its south and west, it signals poor things to come for biodiversity conservation at a much larger scale.

The Platte has high biological value (diversity, endemism, rare species) and more financial and institutional support than the majority of other Great Plains rivers, but faces most of the major threats impacting riverine ecosystems in modern agricultural landscapes including extensive water appropriation, massive structural augmentation, invasive species, warmer and drier conditions associated with climate change, nutrient and pesticide pollution, and more. Nonetheless, the Platte River looks objectively better in most respects than it did 45 years ago when conservation efforts began in earnest regionally. The extent of target habitats (e.g., wet meadow, braided river, etc.) and river flows have generally increased as a result of cooperative conservation efforts. However, the Platte River remains very conservation-dependent and habitat quality is highly variable throughout its length. Additionally, the list of species in decline throughout the Great Plains has continued to increase. Continuing to restore ecological connectivity, functionality, and resilience within the Platte River Valley can safeguard the ecosystem's role as a refugium for a diversity of taxa for many generations to come. However, this must be done in a way that also meets the needs of human communities so that conservation efforts are sustainable.

Through the landscape design process we identified a number of approaches that research indicates will improve our chances of successfully preserving biodiversity in the Platte River Valley. First, conservation efforts that are ecosystem- rather than species-centric may improve long-term outcomes. Secondly, if conservation efforts focus on promoting ecological functionality as compared to meeting minimum suitability thresholds for target species, improvements in ecosystem condition may be more resilient to future stressors. Restoring hydro-geomorphologic processes and improving habitat connectivity are essential to advancing ecosystem function. Finally, successful conservation efforts will need to consider the needs of the human community and actively engage partners whose interests align with conservation objectives. Improving community engagement will be key to long-term conservation success.

## ACKNOWLEDGEMENTS

The findings and conclusions in this article are those of the authors and do not necessarily represent the views of the U.S. Fish and Wildlife Service. We would like to thank Matt Rabbe, Amy Jones, John Denton, Kenny Dinan, Mark Burbach, Douglas R. Hallum, Andrew Pierson, and Bethany Ostrom for workshop participation. We would also like to thank Keith Koupal and Eleanor Nugent for providing technical feedback and content for sections of this document. Additionally, we would like to thank Emma M. Brinley Buckley for GIS support. We thank Audubon Nebraska, the Crane Trust, the Nebraska Game and Parks Commission, The Nature Conservancy, Ducks Unlimited, Prairie Plains Resource Institute, the U.S. Fish and Wildlife Service, the Center for Resilience in Agricultural Working Landscapes at the University of Nebraska-Lincoln, and the Playa Lakes Joint Venture for their support for this planning effort in terms of person-hours and direct financial support as well as providing housing, meeting spaces, and meals. Faculty at the W.A. Franke College of Forestry & Conservation at the University of Montana and staff from the International Crane Foundation also participated in meetings and workshops. A big thank you to Paul Royster, Coordinator of Scholarly Communications for the University of Nebraska-Lincoln, for his support turning this manuscript into a Zea E-Book. We also want to provide a special thank you to Carrie Roberts for supplying a technical review of this work and Catherine Cargill for providing an editorial review. Thank you to Alyx Vogel for creating the cover photo with content from the Crane Trust, Nebraskaland Magazine, Nebraska Game and Parks Commission, Nebraska Master Naturalists, the United States Fish and Wildlife Service, Kirk Steffensen, Jonathan Nikkila, Neil Dankert, Jayne O'Connell, Melvin Nenneman, Keith Geluso, and Sharla Meester. Finally, we want to thank all of you who love the Platte River as well as the Great Plains and advocate for their conservation. Keep up the good work.

# LITERATURE CITED

Acharya, A., T. C. Piechota, and G. Tootle. 2012. Quantitative assessment of climate change impacts on the hydrology of the North Platte River watershed, Wyoming. Journal of Hydrologic Engineering 17(10):1071-1083.

Adams, M. J., D. A. Miller, E. Muths, P. S. Corn, E. H. C. Grant, L. L. Bailey, G. M. Fellers, R. N. Fisher, W. J. Sadinski, H. Waddle, and S. C. Walls. 2013. Trends in amphibian occupancy in the United States. PloS one 8(5):e64347.

Aiken, J. D. 1998. Balancing endangered species protection and irrigation water rights: the Platte River cooperative agreement. Great Plains Natural Resources Journal 3:119-158.

Albrecht, M., P. Duelli, B. Schmid, C. B. Müller. 2007. Interaction Diversity within Quantified Insect Food Webs in Restored and Adjacent Intensively Managed Meadows. Journal of Animal Ecology 76:1015-1025.

Alexander, J. S., D. M. Schultze, and R. B. Zelt. 2013. Emergent sandbar dynamics in the lower Platte River in eastern Nebraska—methods and results of pilot study, 2011. U.S. Geological Survey Scientific Investigations Report 2013-55031, 42 pp.

Alexander, J. S., M. Bomberger Brown, and J. G. Jorgensen. 2018. Reproductive ecology of interior least tern and piping plover in relation to Platte River hydrology and sandbar dynamics: Letter to the Editor. Ecology and Evolution 8(11):5674-5679.

Alexander, J. S., B. McElroy, S. Huzurbazar, C. Elliott, and M. L. Murr. 2020. Deposition potential and flow- response dynamics of emergent sandbars in a braided river. Water Resources Research 56(1):e2018WR024107.

Alexander, K. D., and M. R. Whiles. 2000. New species of *Ironoquia* (Trichoptera:

Limnephilidae) from an intermittent slough of the central Platte River, Nebraska. Entomological News 111(1):1-7.

Allen, C. R., H. E. Birge, D. G. Angeler, C. A. Arnold, B. C. Chaffin, and D. A. DeCaro, A. S. Garmestani, and L. Gunderson. 2018. Quantifying uncertainty and trade-offs in resilience assessments. Ecology and Society 23(1):3.

Allen, R. P. 1952. The Whooping Crane. Research Report No. 3 of the National Audubon Society. National Audubon Society, New York, NY, USA.

Anderson, D. M., and M. W. Rodney. 2006. Characterization of hydrologic conditions to support Platte River species recovery efforts. Journal of the American Water Resources Association 42(5):1391-1403.

Anderson, J. M. 2000. Wildlife Sanctuaries and the Audubon Society. In Wildlife Sanctuaries and the Audubon Society. University of Texas Press, Austin, TX, USA, 285 pp.

Archer, S. R., E. M. Andersen, K. I. Predick, S. Schwinning, R. J. Steidl, and S. R. Woods. 2017. Woody plant encroachment: causes and consequences. Pages 25-84 *in* D. D. Briske, editor, Rangeland Systems: Processes, Management and Challenges. Springer Publishing, New York, NY, USA.

Aronson, J. G., and S. L. Ellis. 1979. Monitoring, maintenance, rehabilitation and enhancement of critical Whooping Crane habitat, Platte River, Nebraska. Environmental Research and Technology, Incorporated, Fort Collins, Colorado, USA.

Austin, J. E., A. L. Richert. 2001. A comprehensive review of observational and site evaluation data of migrant whooping cranes in the United States, 1943-1999. US Geological Survey, Reston, VA, USA.

Austin, J., and A. Richert. 2005. Patterns of habitat use by whooping cranes during migration:

summary from 1977-1999 site evaluation data. Proceedings of the North American Crane Workshop 9:79-104.

Baasch, D. M., P. D. Farrell, J. M. Farnsworth, and C. B. Smith. 2017. Nest- site selection by Interior Least Terns and Piping Plovers at managed, off- channel sites along the Central Platte River in Nebraska, USA. Journal of Field Ornithology 88(3):236-249.

Baasch, D. M., P. D. Farrell, S. Howlin, A. T. Pearse, J. M. Farnsworth, and C.B. Smith. 2019a. Whooping crane use of riverine stopover sites. PLoS ONE 14(1):e0209612.

Baasch, D. M., P. D. Farrell, A. J. Caven, K. C. King, J. M. Farnsworth, and C. B. Smith. 2019b. Sandhill Crane use of riverine roost sites along the central Platte River in Nebraska, USA. Monographs of the Western North American Naturalist 11(1):1-13.

Baasch, D. M., P. D. Farrell, A. T. Pearse, D. A. Brandt, A. J. Caven, M. J. Harner, G. D. Wright and K. L. Metzger. 2019c. Diurnal habitat selection of migrating Whooping Crane in the Great Plains. Avian Conservation and Ecology 14(1):6.

Babbitt, C. H., M. Burbach, and L. Pennisi. 2015. A mixed-methods approach to assessing success in transitioning water management institutions: a case study of the Platte River Basin, Nebraska. Ecology and Society 20(1):54.

Baker, B. W., E. P. Hill. 2003. Beaver (*Castor canadensis*). Pages 288-310 *in* G. A. Feldhamer, and B. C. Thompson, editors. John Hopkins University Press, Baltimore, MD, USA.

Ballinger, R. E., and K. S. Watts. 1995. Path to extinction: impact of vegetational change on lizard populations on Arapaho Prairie in the Nebraska Sandhills. American Midland Naturalist 134(2):413-417.

Bartuszevige, A. M., K. Taylor, A. Daniels, and M. F. Carter. 2016. Landscape design: integrating ecological, social, and economic considerations into conservation planning. Wildlife Society Bulletin 40(3):411-422.

Barr S., J. L. Jonas, M. W. Paschke. 2017. Optimizing Seed Mixture Diversity and Seeding Rates for Grassland Restoration. Restoration Ecology 25(3):396-404.

Basore, N. S., L. B. Best, and J. B. Wooley Jr.1986. Bird nesting in Iowa no-tillage and tilled cropland. The Journal of wildlife management 50:19-28.

Baum, K. A., K. J. Haynes, F. P. Dillemuth, and J. T. Cronin. 2004. The matrix enhances the effectiveness of corridors and stepping stones. Ecology 85(10):2671-2676.

Bawa, R., and P. Dwivedi. 2019. Impact of land cover on groundwater quality in the Upper Floridan Aquifer in Florida, United States. Environmental pollution 252:1828-1840.

Bielski, C. H., R. Scholtz, V. M. Donovan, C. R. Allen, and D. Twidwell. 2021. Overcoming an "irreversible" threshold: A 15-year fire experiment. Journal of environmental management 291:112550.

Birge, H. E., C. R. Allen, K. R. Craig, A. S. Garmestani, J. A. Hamm, and C. Babbitt. 2014. Social-ecological resilience and law in the Platte River Basin. Idaho Law Review 51:229.

Blanchard, F. N. 1937. Data on the natural history of the red-bellied snake, *Storeria occipito-maculata* (Storer), in northern Michigan. Copeia 1937(3):151-162.

Blanchong, J. A., M. D. Samuel, and G. Mack. 2006. Multi-species patterns of avian cholera mortality in Nebraska's Rainwater Basin. Journal of Wildlife Diseases 42(1):81-91.

Blum, D. A., J. D. Carr, R. K. Davis, and D. T. Pederson. 1993. Atrazine in a Stream- Aquifer System: Transport of Atrazine and Its Environmental Impact Near Ashland, Nebraska. Groundwater Monitoring & Remediation 13(2):125-133.

Bogart, R. E., J. N. Duberstein, and D. F. Slobe. 2009. Strategic communications and its critical role in bird habitat conservation: understanding the social-ecological landscape. Proceedings of the International Partners in Flight Conference: Tundra to Tropics 4:441-452.

Boyd, K. M. 1995. Sand removal at a diversion dam. Pages 1951-1955 *in* J. J. Cassidy, editor, Proceedings of the International Conference on Hydropower: Waterpower '95, 25-28 July, San Francisco, California, USA. American Society of Civil Engineers, New York, NY, USA.

Bragg, T. B. 1982. Seasonal variations in fuel and fuel consumption by fires in a bluestem prairie. Ecology 63(1):7-11.

Bragg, T. B. 1998. Fire in the Nebraska Sandhills prairie. Pages 179-194 *in* Fire in ecosystem management: shifting the paradigm from suppression to prescription. Tall Timbers Fire Ecology Conference Proceedings, No. 20.

Brakebill, J. W. and J. M. Gronberg. 2017. County-Level Estimates of Nitrogen and Phosphorus from Commercial Fertilizer for the Conterminous United States, 1987-2012: U.S. Geological Survey data release, https://doi.org/10.5066/F7H41PKX.

Brazeau, D. J., and S. J. Hecnar. 2018. Summer movements of the common five-lined skink (*Plestiodon fasciatus*). Herpetological Conservation and Biology 13(3):743-752.

Briggs, J. M., G. A. Hoch, and L. C. Johnson. 2002. Assessing the rate, mechanisms, and consequences of the conversion of tallgrass prairie to Juniperus virginiana forest. Ecosystems 5(6):578-586.

Briggs, J. M., A. K. Knapp, J. M. Blair, J. L. Heisler, G. A. Hoch, M. S. Lett, and J. K. McCarron. 2005. An ecosystem in transition: causes and consequences of the conversion of mesic grassland to shrubland. BioScience 55(3):243-254.

Brinley Buckley, E. M. 2016. Applications of time-lapse imagery for monitoring and illustrating ecological dynamics in a water-stressed system. Thesis. University of Nebraska-Lincoln, Lincoln, NE, USA, 228 pp.

Brinley Buckley, E. M., A. J. Caven, J. D. Wiese, and M. J. Harner. 2021a. Assessing the hydroregime of an archetypal riverine wet meadow in the central Great Plains using time-lapse imagery. Ecosphere 12(11):e03829.

Brinley Buckley, E. M., B. L. Gottesman, A. J. Caven, M. J. Harner, and B. C. Pijanowski. 2021b. Assessing ecological and environmental influences on Boreal chorus frog (*Pseudacris maculata*) spring calling phenology using multimodal passive monitoring technologies. Ecological Indicators 121:107171.

Brown, W. M., R. C. Drewien, and E. G. Bizeau. 1987. Mortality of cranes and waterfowl from power line collisions in the San Luis Valley, Colorado. Pages 128–136 *in* J. C. Lewis, editor. Proceedings of the 1985 Crane Workshop. Platte River Whooping Crane Habitat Maintenance Trust, Grand Island, Nebraska, USA.

Brown, M. B., and P. A. Johnsgard. 2013. Birds of the Central Platte River Valley and Adjacent Counties. Zea Books, University of Nebraska-Lincoln, Lincoln, NE, USA.

Bucharova, A., S. Michalski, J. M. Hermann, K. Heveling, W. Durka, N. Hölzel, J. Kollmann, O. Bossdorf. 2017. Genetic differentiation and regional adaptation among seed origins used for grassland restoration: lessons from a multispecies transplant experiment. Journal of Applied Ecology 54(1):127-136.

Burbrink, F. T., C. A. Phillips, and E. J. Heske. 1998. A riparian zone in southern Illinois as a potential dispersal corridor for reptiles and amphibians. Biological conservation 86(2):107-115.

Buehring, N., P. W. Santelmann, H. M. Elwell. 1971. Responses of eastern red cedar to control procedures. Journal of Range Management 24(5):378-382.

Catlin, D. H., S. L. Zeigler, M. B. Brown, L. R. Dinan, J. D. Fraser, K. L. Hunt, and J. G. Jorgensen. 2016. Metapopulation viability of an endangered shorebird depends on dispersal and human-created habitats: Piping Plovers (*Charadrius melodus*) and prairie rivers. Movement Ecology 4(1):6.

Carignan, V., and M. A. Villard. 2002. Selecting indicator species to monitor ecological integrity: a review. Environmental monitoring and assessment 78(1):45-61.

Carter, D. L., and J. M. Blair. 2012. High Richness and Dense Seeding Enhance Grassland Restoration Establishment but have Little Effect on Drought Response. Ecological Applications 22(4):1308-1319.

Carwardine, J., C. J. Klein, A. K. Wilson, R. L. Pressey, and H. P. Possingham. 2009. Hitting the target and missing the point: target- based conservation planning in context. Conservation Letters 2(1):4-11.

Castelle, A. J., A. W. Johnson, and C. Conolly. 1994. Wetland and stream buffer size requirements—a review. Journal of environmental quality 23(5):878-882.

Carroll, C., D. J. Rohlf, Y. W. Li, B. Hartl, M. K. Phillips, and R. F. Noss. 2015. Connectivity conservation and endangered species recovery: A study in the challenges of defining conservation- reliant species. Conservation Letters 8(2):132-138.

Caven, A. J., J. Salter, and K. Geluso. 2017a. *Opheodrys vernalis* (*Liochlorophis vernalis*)

(Smooth Greensnake). Fire mortality and phenology. Herpetological Review 48(4):864-865.

Caven, A. J., K. C. King, J. D. Wiese, E. M. Brinley Buckley. 2017b. A descriptive analysis of Regal Fritillary (*Speyeria idalia*) habitat utilizing biological monitoring data along the Big Bend of the Platte River, NE. Journal of Insect Conservation 21(2):183-205.

Caven, A. J., E. M. Brinley Buckley, J. D. Wiese, B. Taddicken, B. Krohn, T. J. Smith, and A. Pierson. 2019a. Appeal for a Comprehensive Assessment of the Potential Ecological Impacts of the Proposed Platte-Republican Diversion Project. Great Plains Research 29(2):123-135.

Caven, A. J., E. M. Brinley Buckley, K. C. King, J. D. Wiese, D. M. Baasch, G. D. Wright, M. J. Harner, A. T. Pearse, M. Rabbe, D. M. Varner, B. Krohn, N. Arcilla, K. D. Schroeder, K. F. Dinan. 2019b. Temporospatial shifts in Sandhill Crane staging in the Central Platte River Valley in response to climatic variation and habitat change. Monographs of the Western North American Naturalist 11(1):33-76.

Caven, A. J., J. Malzahn, T. Franti, and E. M. Brinley Buckley, editors. 2019c. Proceedings of the Thirteenth Platte River Basin Ecosystem Symposium, 5-6 June 2018, Wood River, NE, USA. Nebraska Water Center, University of Nebraska-Lincoln, Lincoln, NE, USA.

Caven, A. J., J. M. Malzahn, K. D. Koupal, E. M. Brinley Buckley, J. D. Wiese, R. Rasmussen, and C. Steenson. 2019d. Adult Whooping Crane (*Grus americana*) consumption of juvenile channel catfish (*Ictalurus punctatus*) during the avian spring migration in the Central Platte River Valley, Nebraska, USA. Monographs of the Western North American Naturalist 11(1):14-23.

Caven, A. J., M. Rabbe, J. Malzahn, and A. E. Lacy. 2020b. Trends in the occurrence of large

Whooping crane groups during migration in the Great Plains, USA. Heliyon 6:e03549.

Caven, A. J., D. M. Varner, J. and J. Drahota. 2020a. Sandhill Crane abundance in Nebraska during spring migration: making sense of multiple data points. Transactions of the Nebraska Academy of Sciences and Affiliated Societies 40:6-18.

Caven, A .J., K. D. Koupal, D. M. Baasch, E. M. Brinley Buckley, J. Malzahn, M. L. Forsberg, and M. Lundgren. 2021. Whooping Crane (*Grus americana*) family consumes a diversity of aquatic vertebrates during fall migration stopover at the Platte River, Nebraska. Western North American Naturalist 81(4):592–607.

Caven, A. J., A. T. Pearse, D. A. Brandt, M. J. Harner, G. D. Wright, D. M. Baasch, E. M. Brinley Buckley, K. L. Metzger, M. R. Rabbe, and A. E. Lacy. *In Press*. Whooping Crane stay length in relation to stopover site characteristics. Proceedings of the North American Crane Workshop 15.

Caven, A. J., and J. D. Wiese. 2022. Reinventory of the Vascular Plants of Mormon Island Crane Meadows after Forty Years of Restoration, Invasion, and Climate Change. Heliyon 8: e09640.

Chen, A. H., D. L. Rus, and C. P. Stanton. 1999. Trends in channel gradation in Nebraska streams, 1913-95. US Department of the Interior, US Geological Survey, Water Resources Investigations Report 99-4103.

Chen, X. 2007. Hydrologic connections of a stream–aquifer-vegetation zone in south-central Platte River valley, Nebraska. Journal of Hydrology 333(2-4):554-568.

Clark, M. E., B. J. Danielson, M. V. Santelmann, J. I. Nassauer, D. White, and K. F. Lindsay. 2007. Impacts on Mammal Communities: A Spatially Explicit Model. Pages 115-146 *in* J. I. Nassauer, M. V. Santelmann, and D. Scavia, editors, From the Corn Belt to the Gulf:

Societal and Environmental Implications of Alternative Agricultural Futures. Resources for the Future, Washington, D.C., USA.

Conly, F. Malcolm, and G. Van der Kamp. 2001. Monitoring the hydrology of Canadian prairie wetlands to detect the effects of climate change and land use changes. Environmental Monitoring and Assessment 67(1):195-215.

Cooper, M., C. Gho, R. Leafgren, T. Tang, and C. Messina. 2014. Breeding drought-tolerant maize hybrids for the US corn-belt: discovery to product. Journal of Experimental Botany 65(21):6191-6204.

Crockford, J. F., J. R. Weir, C. E. Blocksome, M. L. Russell, and D. L. Twidwell. 2017. Cut and stuff practices for enhanced cedar control with prescribed fire. Oklahoma Cooperative Extension Service, Oklahoma State University, Stillwater, OK, USA, Report No. NREM-2902, 2 pp.

Currier, P. J. 1982. The floodplain vegetation of the Platte River: phytosociology, forest development, and seedling establishment. Dissertation. Iowa State University, Ames, Iowa, 332 pp.

Currier, P. J. 1984. Response of Prairie White-fringed Orchid to fire and grazing recovery. Restoration and Management Notes 2:28.

Currier, P. J., and L. M. Eisel. 1984. The impact of flow level on Sandhill Crane and Whooping Crane roosting habitat on the Platte River, Nebraska. Whooping Crane Habitat Maintenance Trust, Grand Island, NE, USA.

Currier, P.J. 1989. Plant species composition and groundwater levels in a Platte River wet meadow. Proceedings of the North American Prairie Conference 11:19-24.

Currier, P .J. 1994. Restoration of functioning wet meadows on the Platte River— experimenting with reseeding, constructed wetlands, and hydrology. Final report submitted to the U.S. Fish and Wildlife Service (Project No. 14-16-0006-90-917), Grand Island, NE, USA.

Currier, P. J., G. R. Lingle, and J. G. VanDerwalker. 1985. Migratory bird habitat on the Platte and North Platte Rivers in Nebraska. Platte River Whooping Crane Critical Habitat Maintenance Trust, Grand Island, Nebraska, USA, 177 pp.

Currier, P. J. 1997. Woody vegetation expansion and continuing declines in open channel habitat on the Platte River in Nebraska. Proceedings of the North American Crane Workshop 7:141-152.

Currier, P. J., and C. A. Davis. 2000. The Platte as a prairie river: a response to Johnson and Boettcher. Great Plains Research 10:69-84.

Currier, P. J. and R. J. Henszey. 1996. Platte River wet meadows: a primer on their flora, fauna, hydrology, management, and restoration. Platte River Whooping Crane Maintenance Trust, Grand Island, Nebraska, USA, 25 pp.

Currier, P. J., and G. R. Lingle. 1993. Habitat restoration and management for Least Terns and Piping Plovers by the Platte River Trust. Page 92 *in* K. F. Higgins and M. R. Brashler, editors, Proceedings, the Missouri River and its Tributaries: Piping Plover and Least Tern Symposium/Workshop. South Dakota State University, Brookings, SD, USA.

Currier, P. J. and G. R. Lingle. 1996. Wild Rose wetland restoration project. Final Report submitted to the U.S. Fish and Wildlife Service (Project No. 14-48-0006-92-925), Grand Island, Nebraska, USA, 10 pp.

Cushman, S. A., and K. McGarigal. 2008. Landscape metrics, scales of resolution. Pages 33-51 *in* K. von Gadow, T. Pukkala, editors, Designing Green Landscapes, Designing green landscapes. Springer, Dordrecht, Netherlands.

Davis, C. A. 2003. Habitat use and migration patterns of Sandhill Cranes along the Platte River, 1998-2001. Great Plains Research 13:199-216.

Davis, C. 2005a. Breeding and migrant bird use of a riparian woodland along the Platte River in central Nebraska. North American Bird Bander 30:109–114.

Davis, C. 2005b. Breeding bird communities in riparian forests along the Central Platte River, Nebraska. Great Plains Research 15:199–211.

Deák, B., O. Valkó, P. Török, A. Kelemen, T. Miglécz, S. Szabó, Gergely Szabóc, and B. Tóthmérész. 2015. Micro-topographic heterogeneity increases plant diversity in old stages of restored grasslands. Basic and Applied Ecology 16(4):291-299.

Dickson, T. L., W. H. Busby. 2009. Forb Species Establishment Increases with Decreased Grass Seeding Density and with Increased Forb Seeding Density in a Northeast Kansas, U.S.A, Experimental Prairie Restoration. Restoration Ecology 17(5):597-605.

Dinan, K. F. 1992. Application of the Stream Network Temperature Model (SNTEMP) to the central Platte River, Nebraska. M. S. Thesis. Colorado State University, Fort Collins, CO, USA, 87 pp.

Drobney, P., D. L. Larson, J. L. Larson, K. Viste-Sparkman. 2020. Toward Improving Pollinator Habitat: Reconstructing Prairies with High Forb Diversity. Natural Areas Journal 40(3):252-261.

Ducks Unlimited. 2011. The Platte River initiative: Flowing past the challenges of a changing river. Fiscal Year 2011 Progress Report, Ducks Unlimited, Great Plains Regional Office, Bismarck, ND, USA.

Dunham, J. B., P. L. Angermeier, S. D. Crausbay, A. E. Cravens, H. Gosnell, J. McEvoy, M. A. Moritz, N. Raheem, and T. Sanford. 2018. Rivers are social-ecological systems: Time to integrate human dimensions into riverscape ecology and management. Wiley Interdisciplinary Reviews: Water 5(4):e1291.

Echeverria, J. D. 2000. No success like failure: The Platte River collaborative watershed planning process. William & Mary Environmental Law and Policy Review 25:559-604.

Eisel, L., and D. Aiken. 1997. Platte River Basin Study, Report to the Western Water Policy Review Advisory Committee. University of Nebraska– Lincoln Faculty Publications: Agricultural Economics, No. 25.

Eisenhauer, J. G. 2003. Regression through the origin. Teaching statistics 5(3):76-80.

Emmons, P. J. 1996. Water Quality in a Wet Meadow, Platte River Valley, Central Nebraska. US Department of the Interior, US Geological Survey Fact Sheet FS-097-96, 4 pp.

Engle, D. M., B. R. Coppedge, S. D. Fuhlendorf. 2008. From the dust bowl to the green glacier: human activity and environmental change in Great Plains grasslands. Pages 253-271 *in* Western North American Juniperus Communities. Springer, New York, NY, USA.

Eschner, T. R., R. F. Hadley, and K. D. Crowley. 1981. Hydrologic and morphologic changes in channels of the Platte River basin: a historical perspective. US Geological Survey Open-File Report 81–1125.

Eschner, T. R., R. F. Hadley, and K. D. Crowley. 1983. Hydrologic and geomorphic studies of the Platte River Basin. U.S. Geological Survey Professional Paper 1277-A, United States Government Printing Office, Washington, DC, USA, 297 pp.

Executive Director of the Platte River Recovery Implementation Program (PRRIP). 2021. North Platte Chokepoint Alternatives. Headwaters Corporation, Kearney, NE, USA, 11 pp.

Faanes, C. A. 1983. Aspects of the Nesting Ecology of Least Terns and Piping Plovers in Central Nebraska. The Prairie Naturalist 15(4):145-154.

Faanes, C. A., and D. B. Bowman. 1992. Relationship of channel maintenance flows to Whooping Crane use of the Platte River. Proceedings of the North American Crane Workshop 6:111-116.

Faanes, C. A., G. R. Lingle, and D. H. Johnson. 1992. Characteristics of Whooping Crane roost sites in the Platte River. Proceedings of the North American Crane Workshop 6:90-94.

Faanes, C. A., M. J. LeValley. 1993. Is the distribution of Sandhill Cranes of the Platte River changing? Great Plains Research 3:297–304.

Farmer, A. H., B. S. Cade, J. W. Terrell, J. H. Henriksen, and J. T. Runge. 2005. Evaluation of models and data for assessing whooping crane habitat in the central Platte River, Nebraska. U.S. Geological Survey, Scientific Investigations Report 2005-5123, 64 pp.

Farmer, J. R., D. Knapp, V. J. Meretsky, C. Chancellor, and B. C. Fischer. 2011. Motivations influencing the adoption of conservation easements. Conservation Biology 25(4):827-834.

Farnsworth, J., C. B. Smith, and D. Baasch. 2011. Adaptive Management Implementation Plan – Version 2.0. Executive Director's Office, Platte River Recovery Implementation Program, Kearney, NE, USA, 96 pp.

Farnsworth, J. M., D. M. Baasch, C. B. Smith, and K. L. Werbylo. 2017. Reproductive ecology of interior least tern and piping plover in relation to Platte River hydrology and sandbar dynamics. Ecology and evolution 7(10):3579-3589.

Farnsworth, J. M., D. M. Baasch, P. D. Farrell, C. B. Smith, and K. L. Werbylo. 2018. Investigating whooping crane habitat in relation to hydrology, channel morphology and a water-centric management strategy on the central Platte River, Nebraska. Heliyon 4(10): e00851.

Farrell, P., D. Baasch, J. Farnsworth, and C. Smith. 2018. Interior Least Tern and Piping Plover nest and brood survival at managed, off-channel sites along the central Platte River, Nebraska, USA 2001-2015. Avian Conservation and Ecology 13(1):1-10.

Fassnacht, S. R., N. B. Venable, D. McGrath, and G. G. Patterson. 2018. Sub- Seasonal Snowpack Trends in the Rocky Mountain National Park Area, Colorado, USA. Water 10 (5):562.

Ferguson, R. B. 2015. Groundwater quality and nitrogen use efficiency in Nebraska's Central Platte River Valley. Journal of environmental quality 44(2):449-459.

Ferguson, R. I. 1984. The threshold between meandering and braiding. Pages 749-763 *in* K. V. H. Smith, editor, Channels and channel control structures. Springer, Berlin, Heidelberg, Germany.

Ferguson, E. L., D. S. Gilmer, D. H. Johnson, N. Lyman, and D. S. Benning. 1979. Experimental surveys of Sandhill Cranes in Nebraska. Pages 41–52 *in* J. C. Lewis, editor, Proceedings 1978 Crane Workshop, Rockport, Texas, December 6–8, 1978. National Audubon Society and Colorado State University, Boulder, CO, USA.

Ferster, B., and K. Vulinec. 2010. Population size and conservation of the last eastern remnants of the regal fritillary, *Speyeria idalia* (Drury)[Lepidoptera, Nymphalidae]; implications for temperate grassland restoration. Journal of Insect Conservation 14(1):31-42.

Fiedler A. K., D. A. Landis, and M. Arduser. 2011. Rapid Shift in Pollinator Communities Following Invasive Species Removal. Restoration Ecology 20:593-602.

Fitch, H. S. 1954. Life history and ecology of the five-lined skink, *Eumeces fasciatus*. Univ. of Kansas Publ. Mus. Nat. Hist. 8:213-274.

Fogarty, D. T., C. P. Roberts, D. R. Uden, V. M. Donovan, C. R. Allen, D. E. Naugle, M. O.

Jones, B. W. Allred, D. Twidwell. 2020. Woody plant encroachment and the
    sustainability of priority conservation areas. Sustainability 12(20):8321.

Folk, M. J., and T. C. Tacha. 1990. Sandhill Crane roost site characteristics in the North Platte
    River Valley. Journal of Wildlife Management 54:480–486.

Fontaine, C., I. Dajoz, J. Meriguet, M. Loreau. 2005. Functional Diversity of Plant–Pollinator
    Interaction Webs Enhances the Persistence of Plant Communities. PLoS Biology 4(1):e1
    <https://doi.org/10.1371/journal.pbio.0040001>

Frey, J. K., and J. L. Malaney. 2009. Decline of the meadow jumping mouse (*Zapus hudsonius
    luteus*) in two mountain ranges in New Mexico. The Southwestern Naturalist 54(1):31-
    44.

Freedman, W., and P. M. Catling. 1979. Movement of sympatric species of snakes at
    Amherstburg, Ontario. Canadian Field-Naturalist 93(4):399-404.

Freeman, D. M. 2008. Negotiating for endangered and threatened species habitat in the Platte
    River Basin. Pages 59-67 *in* M. Doyle, C. A. Drew, editors, Large-scale ecosystem
    restoration: five case studies from the United States. Island Press, Washington, DC, USA.

French, N. R., T. Y. Tagami, and P. Hayden. 1968. Dispersal in a population of desert rodents.
    Journal of Mammalogy 49(2):272-280.

Frischie, S. L., H. I. Rowe. 2012. Replicating Life Cycle of Early-Maturing Species in the
    Timing of Restoration Seeding Improves Establishment and Community Diversity.
    Restoration Ecology 20:188-193.

Frith, C. R. 1974. The ecology of the Platte River as related to Sandhill Cranes and other
    waterfowl in south central Nebraska. Thesis. Kearney State College, Kearney, NE, USA,
    111 pp.

Fryer, J. L., and P. S. Luensmann. 2012. Fire regimes of the conterminous United States. *In* Fire

    Effects Information System (FEIS). U.S. Department of Agriculture, U.S. Forest Service,

    Rocky Mountain Research Station, Fire Sciences Laboratory, Missoula, MT, USA

    [Online].

Fuhlendorf, S. D., H. Zhang, T. R. Tunnell, D. M. Engle, and A. F. Cross. 2002. Effects of

    grazing on restoration of southern mixed prairie soils. Restoration Ecology 10(2):401-

    407.

Galatowitsch, S. M., D. L. Larson, and J. L. Larson. 2016. Factors affecting post-control

    reinvasion by seed of an invasive species, *Phragmites australis,* in the central Platte

    River, Nebraska. Biological Invasions 18(9):2505-2516.

Ganguli, A. C., D. M. Engle, P. M. Mayer, S. D. Fuhlendorf. 2008. When are native

    species inappropriate for conservation plantings? Rangelands 30(6):27–32.

Gardner, R. 2009. Constructing a technological forest: Nature, culture, and tree- planting in the

    Nebraska Sand Hills. Environmental History 14(2):275–297.

Geluso, K., and M. J. Harner. 2013. Reexamination of herpetofauna on Mormon Island, Hall

    County, Nebraska, with notes on natural history. Transactions of the Nebraska Academy

    of Sciences 33:7-20.

Glaves, B. P. 2009. Seed rate study for restoration ecology: What weight of seed should be

    planted for the best results? Dissertation. Northern Illinois University, DeKalb, IL, USA.

Goldowitz, B. 1996. Summer fish kills on the central Platte River: a summary of events, 1974-

    1995. Platte River Whooping Crane Maintenance Trust, Grand Island, NE, USA, 18 pp.

Goldowitz, B.S. and Whiles, M.R., 1999. Investigations of Fish, Amphibians and Aquatic

    Invertebrate Species Within the Middle Platte River System. Final Report, Platte

Watershed Program Cooperative Agreement X99708101. U.S. EPA region VII, Kansas City, Missouri, USA.

Gosselin, D. C., J. Headrick, R. Tremblay, X. H. Chen, X. and S. Summerside. 1997. Domestic well water quality in rural Nebraska: Focus on nitrate- nitrogen, pesticides, and coliform bacteria. Groundwater Monitoring & Remediation 17(2):77-87.

Graf, D. I., R. Q. Landers, and R. W. Poulter. 1965. Distribution patterns of eastern red-cedar *Juniperus virginiana* L. in Henry County, Iowa. Proceedings of the Iowa Academy of Science 72(1):98-105.

Gurdak, J. J., P. B. McMahon, K. Dennehy, and S. L. Qi. 2009. Water Quality in the High Plains Aquifer, Colorado, Kansas, Nebraska, New Mexico, Oklahoma, South Dakota, Texas, and Wyoming, 1999-2004. U.S. Geological Survey, Circular 1337.

Harmon-Threatt, A. N., and S. D. Hendrix. 2015. Prairie Restorations and Bees: The Potential Ability of Seed Mixes to Foster Native Bee Communities. Basic and Applied Ecology 16(1):64-72

Harner, M. J., and D. C. Whited. 2011. Modeling inundation of sloughs to determine changes in suitable habitat for the Platte River Caddisfly (*Ironoquia plattensis*). Final Report submitted to the U.S. Fish and Wildlife Service, Grand Island, Nebraska, USA.

Harner, M. J. and K. Geluso. 2012. Effects of cattle grazing on the Platte River caddisfly (*Ironoquia plattensis*) in central Nebraska. Freshwater Science 31:389-394.

Harner, M. J., G. D. Wright, and K. Geluso. 2015. Overwintering Sandhill Cranes (*Grus canadensis*) in Nebraska, USA. The Wilson Journal of Ornithology 127(3):457-466.

Hart, R. H. 2001. Where the buffalo roamed—or did they? Great Plains Research 11:83-102.

Haukos, D. A., L. A. Johnson, L. M. Smith, and S. T. McMurry. 2016. Effectiveness of

vegetation buffers surrounding playa wetlands at contaminant and sediment amelioration.

Journal of environmental management 181:552-562.

Hazelton, E. L., T. J. Mozdzer, D. M. Burdick, K. M. Kettenring, and D. F. Whigham. 2014.

*Phragmites australis* management in the United States: 40 years of methods and

outcomes. AoB plants 6: plu001 https://doi.org/10.1093/aobpla/plu001

He, S., P. Li, J. Wu, V. Elumalai, and N. Adimalla. 2020. Groundwater quality under land

use/land cover changes: a temporal study from 2005 to 2015 in Xi'an, northwest China.

Human and Ecological Risk Assessment: An International Journal 26(10):2771-2797.

Jenkins, H. M., and R. B. Hyer. 2009. A history of Nebraska's natural resources districts.

Nebraska Department of Natural Resources, Lincoln, NE, USA, 24 pp.

He, S., P. Li, P., J. Wu, V. Elumalai, and N. Adimalla. 2020. Groundwater quality under land

use/land cover changes: a temporal study from 2005 to 2015 in Xi'an, northwest China.

Human and Ecological Risk Assessment: An International Journal 26(10):2771-2797.

Helzer, C. 2009. The ecology and management of prairies in the central United States, Bur Oak

Book. University of Iowa Press, Iowa City, IA, USA.

Helzer, C. J., and D. E. Jelinski. 1999. The relative importance of patch area and perimeter–area

ratio to grassland breeding birds. Ecological applications 9(4):1448-1458.

Henszey, R. J. and T. A. Wesche. 1993. Hydrologic components influencing the condition of wet

meadows along the Central Platte River, Nebraska. Nebraska Game and Parks

Commission, Lincoln, Nebraska, USA, 112 pp.

Henszey, R. J., K. Pfeiffer, and J. R. Keough. 2004. Linking surface- and ground-water levels to riparian grassland species along the Platte River in central Nebraska, USA. Wetlands 24:665-687.

Herkert, J. R. 1994. The effects of habitat fragmentation on midwestern grassland bird communities. Ecological applications 4(3):461-471.

Hey, D. L., and N. S. Philippi. 1995. Flood reduction through wetland restoration: the Upper Mississippi River Basin as a case history. Restoration Ecology 3(1):4-17.

Higgins, K. F., D. E. Naugle, and K. J. Forman. 2002. A case study of changing land use practices in the northern Great Plains, USA: an uncertain future for waterbird conservation. Waterbirds 25:42-50.

Hiller, T. L., L. A. Powell, T. D. McCoy, and J. J. Lusk. 2009. Long-term agricultural land-use trends in Nebraska, 1866—2007. Great Plains Research 19:225-237.

Hintz, W. D., and J. E. Garvey. 2012. Considering a species-loss domino-effect before endangered species legislation and protected area implementation. Biodiversity and Conservation 21(8):2017-2027.

Hoagstrom, C. W., J. E. Brooks, and S. R. Davenport. 2018. A large-scale conservation perspective considering endemic fishes of the North American plains. Biological Conservation 144(1):21-34.

Hobbs, R. J., S. Arico, J. Aronson, J. S. Baron, P. Bridgewater, V. A. Cramer, P. R. Epstein, J. J. Ewel, C. A. Klink, A. E. Lugo, D. Norton. 2006. Novel ecosystems: theoretical and management aspects of the new ecological world order. Global ecology and biogeography (1):1-7.

Hoffman, C. and S. Zellmer. 2012. Assessing institutional ability to support adaptive, integrated water resources management. Nebraska Law Review 91:805-865.

Horn, J. D., R. M. Joeckel, and C. R. Fielding. 2012. Progressive abandonment and planform changes of the central Platte River in Nebraska, central USA, over historical timeframes. Geomorphology 139:372-383.

Horncastle, V. J., E. C. Hellgren, P. M. Mayer, A. C. Ganguli, D. M. Engle, and D. M. Leslie. 2005. Implications of invasion by Juniperus virginiana on small mammals in the southern Great Plains. Journal of Mammalogy 86(6):1144-1155.

Hungate, B. A., E. B. Barbier, A. W. Ando, S. P. Marks, P. B. Reich, N. Van Gestel, D. Tilman, J. M. H. Knops, D. U. Hooper, B. J. Butterfield, and B. J. Cardinale. 2017. The economic value of grassland species for carbon storage. Science Advances 3(4):e1601880.

Jenniges, J. J. and R. G. Plettner. 2008. Least tern nesting at human created habitats in central Nebraska. Waterbirds: The International Journal of Waterbird Biology 31(2):274-282.

Johns, B. W., E. J. Woodsworth, and E. A. Driver. 1997. Habitat use by migrant Whooping Cranes in Saskatchewan. Proceedings of the North American Crane Workshop 7:123-131.

Johnsgard, P.A. 1983. Cranes of the World. Indiana University Press, Bloomington, Indiana, USA.

Galliart, M., N. Bello, M. Knapp, J. Poland, P. St. Amand, S. Baer, B. Maricle, A. B. Smith, and L. Johnson. 2019. Local adaptation, genetic divergence, and experimental selection in a foundation grass across the US Great Plains' climate gradient. Global Change Biology 25(3):850-868.

Johnson, D. H. 2001. Habitat fragmentation effects on birds in grasslands and wetlands: a critique of our knowledge. Great Plains Research 11:211-231.

Johnson, O. J., and K. Geluso. 2017. Distributional and reproductive records of bats from south-central Nebraska. Museum of Texas Tech University Occasional Papers 347:1-16.

Johnson, W. C. 1994. Woodland Expansion in the Platte River, Nebraska: Patterns and Causes. Ecological Monographs 64(1):45-84.

Johnson, W. C. 1996. Monitoring of tree reproduction and survival in the Platte River 1994-95. Final Report, Nebraska Public Power District Columbus, NE, USA, and the Central Nebraska Public Power, and Irrigation District. Holdrege, NE, USA.

Johnson, W. C. 1997. Equilibrium response of riparian vegetation to flow regulation in the Platte River, Nebraska. Regulated Rivers: Research & Management: An International Journal Devoted to River Research and Management 13(5):403-415.

Johnston, C. A. 1991. Sediment and nutrient retention by freshwater wetlands: effects on surface water quality. Critical Reviews in Environmental Science and Technology 21(5-6):491-565.

Jorgensen, J. G., S. J. Brenner, L. R. Greenwalt, and M. P. Vrtiska. 2021. Decline of novel ecosystems used by endangered species: the case of piping plovers, least terns, and aggregate mines. Ecosphere 12(4):e03474.

Joshi, J., P. Stoll, H. P. Rusterholz, B. Schmid, C. Dolt, and B. Baur. 2006. Small-scale experimental habitat fragmentation reduces colonization rates in species-rich grasslands. Oecologia 148(1):144-152.

Juneau, K. J., and C. S. Tarasoff. 2013. The seasonality of survival and subsequent growth of common reed (*Phragmites australis*) rhizome fragments. Invasive Plant Science and Management 6(1):79-86.

Junk, W. J., P. B. Bayley, and R. E. Sparks. 1989. The flood pulse concept in river-floodplain systems. Canadian special publication of fisheries and aquatic sciences 106(1):110-127.

Junk, W. J., and K. M. Wantzen. 2004. The flood pulse concept: new aspects, approaches and applications-an update. Pages 117-149 *in* the Second International Symposium on the Management of Large Rivers for Fisheries. Food and Agriculture Organization and Mekong River Commission, FAO Regional Office for Asia and the Pacific, Bangkok, Thailand.

Kantrud, H. A., G. L. Krapu, and G. A. Swanson. 1989. Prairie basin wetlands of the Dakotas: a community profile. U.S. Fish and Wildlife Service, Biological Report 85, Washington, DC, USA.

Karlinger, M. R., R. C. Mengis, J. E. Kircher, and T. Eschner. 1981. Application of theoretical equations to estimate the discharge needed to maintain channel width in a reach of the Platte River near Lexington, Nebraska. US Geological Survey Open File Report 81-697.

Kaul, R. B., D. Sutherland, and S. Rolfsmeier. 2006. The flora of Nebraska. School of Natural Resources, University of Nebraska–Lincoln, Lincoln, NE, USA.

Keinath, D. A., D. F. Doak, K. E. Hodges, L. R. Prugh, W. Fagan, C. H. Sekercioglu, S. H. M. Buchart, M. Kauffman. 2017. A global analysis of traits predicting species sensitivity to habitat fragmentation. Global Ecology and Biogeography 26(1):115-127.

Keyghobadi, N., K. P. Unger, J. D. Weintraub, and D. M. Fonseca. 2006. Remnant populations of the regal fritillary (*Speyeria idalia*) in Pennsylvania: local genetic structure in a high gene flow species. Conservation Genetics 7(2):309.

Kim, D. H. 2005. First Nebraska nest record for Henslow's Sparrow. The Prairie Naturalist 37:171-173.

Kinbacher, K. E. 2012. Indians and Empires: Cultural Change among the Omaha and Pawnee, from Contact to 1808. Great Plains Quarterly 32(3):207-221.

Kinzel, P. J., J. M. Nelson, and R. S. Parker. 2005. Assessing Sandhill Crane roosting habitat along the Platte River, Nebraska. Fact Sheet 2005-3029. U.S. Geological Survey, Denver, CO, USA.

Kinzel, P. J., J. M. Nelson, and A. K. Heckman. 2006. Channel morphology and bed-sediment characteristics before and after riparian vegetation clearing in the Cottonwood Ranch, Platte River, Nebraska, water years 2001–2004. Scientific Investigations Report 2005–5285. U.S. Geological Survey, Reston, VA, USA.

Kinzel, P. J. 2009. Channel morphology and bed sediment characteristics before and after habitat enhancement activities in the Uridil Property, Platte River, Nebraska, water years 2005–2008. Open-File Report 2009-1147. U.S. Geological Survey, Reston, VA, USA.

Kinzel, P., and J. Runge. 2010. Summary of bed-sediment measurements along the Platte River, Nebraska, 1931–2009. US Geological Survey Fact Sheet 2010-3087, 4 pp.

Kirsch, E. M., and G. R. Lingle. 1993. Habitat use and nesting success of Least Terns along the Platte River, Nebraska. Pages 73-74 *in* Higgins and M.R. Brashler, editors, Proceedings of the Missouri River and its Tributaries: Piping Plover and Least Tern Symposium 1992. South Dakota State University, Brookings, SD, USA.

Kirsch, E. M. 1996. Habitat selection and productivity of Least Terns on the lower Platte River, Nebraska. Wildlife Monographs 132:3-48.

Kircher, J. T. 1983. Interpretation of sediment data for the South Platte River in Colorado and Nebraska, and the North Platte and Platte Rivers in Nebraska. U.S. Geological Survey, Reston, VA, USA, Professional Paper 1277-D.

Klug, P. E., J. Fill, and K. A. With. 2011. Spatial ecology of eastern yellow-bellied racer

(*Coluber constrictor flaviventris*) and Great Plains rat snake (*Pantherophis emoryi*) in a contiguous tallgrass-prairie landscape. Herpetologica 67(4):428-439.

Knapp, E. E., B. L. Estes, C. N. Skinner. 2009. Ecological effects of prescribed fire season: a literature review and synthesis for managers. U.S. Department of Agriculture, U.S. Forest Service, Pacific Southwest Research Station, Albany, CA, USA. Gen. Tech. Rep. PSW-GTR-224, 80 pp.

Kondolf, G. M., Y. Gao, G. W. Annandale, G. L. Morris, E. Jiang, J. Zhang, Y. Cao, P. Carling, K. Fu, Q. Guo, and R. Hotchkiss. 2014. Sustainable sediment management in reservoirs and regulated rivers: Experiences from five continents. Earth's Future 2(5):256-280.

Kovats, Z., J. J. H. Ciborowski, and L. Corkum. 1996. Inland dispersal of adult aquatic insects. Freshwater biology 36(2):265-276.

Kramer, D. C. 1973. Movements of western chorus frogs *Pseudacris triseriata triseriata* tagged with Co 60. Journal of Herpetology 7:231–235.

Krapu, G. L., K. J. Reinecke, and C. R. Frith. 1982. Sandhill Cranes and the Platte River. Pages 542–552 *in* K. Sabol, editor, Transactions of the 47th North American Wildlife and Natural Resources Conference. Wildlife Management Institute, Washington, DC, USA.

Krapu, G. L., D. A. Brandt, K. L. Jones, and D. H. Johnson. 2011. Geographic distribution of the mid- continent population of sandhill cranes and related management applications: Wildlife Monographs 175(1):1-38.

Krapu, G. L., D. A. Brandt, P. J. Kinzel, and A. T. Pearse. 2014. Spring migration ecology of the mid- continent sandhill crane population with an emphasis on use of the Central Platte River Valley, Nebraska. Wildlife Monographs 189(1):1-41.

Kudo, G. and T. Y. Ida. 2013. Early Onset of Spring Increases the Phenological Mismatch Between Plants and Pollinators. Ecology 94 (10):2311-2320.

Lamke, K. 2019. A Descriptive Study of Wild Bees (Hymenoptera: Apoidea: Apiformes) and Angiosperms in a Tallgrass Prairie Corridor of Southeastern Nebraska. Thesis. University of Nebraska at Lincoln, Lincoln, NE, USA, 130 pp.

Lane, I. G., C. R. Herron- Sweet, Z. M. Portman, and D. P. Cariveau. 2020. Floral resource diversity drives bee community diversity in prairie restorations along an agricultural landscape gradient. Journal of Applied Ecology 57(10):2010-2018.

Lang, J. W. 1969. Hibernation and movements of *Storeria occipitomaculata* in northern Minnesota. Journal of Herpetology 3(3-4):196-197.

Larson, D. L., J. B. Bright, P. Drobney, J. L. Larson, N. Palaia, P. A. Rabie, S. Vacek, and D. Wells. 2011. Effects of Planting Method and Seed Mix Richness on the Early Stages of Tallgrass Prairie Restoration. Biological Conservation 144(12):3127-3139.

Larson, J. L., D. L. Larson, and R. C. Venette. 2021. Balancing the need for seed against invasive species risks in prairie habitat restorations. PloS one 16(4):e0248583.

LaRue, M. A., and C. K. Nielsen. 2008. Modelling potential dispersal corridors for cougars in midwestern North America using least-cost path methods. Ecological modelling 212(3-4):372-381.

Lechner, A. M., D. Sprod, O. Carter, and E. C. Lefroy. 2017. Characterising landscape connectivity for conservation planning using a dispersal guild approach. Landscape Ecology 32(1):99-113.

Lemke, P, and J. Ren, coordinating lead authors. 2007. Climate Change 2007: The Physical Science Basis. Contributions of Working Group I to the Fourth Assessment Report of the

Intergovernmental Panel on Climate Change. Cambridge University Press, Cambridge, UK.

Lett, M. S., and A. K. Knapp. 2005. Woody plant encroachment and removal in mesic grassland: production and composition responses of herbaceous vegetation. The American Midland Naturalist 153(2):217-231.

Lingle, G. R., and M. A. Hay. 1982. A checklist of the birds of Mormon Island Crane Meadows. Nebraska Bird Review 50:27-36.

Lingle, G. R. 1993. Nest success and flow relationships on the Central Platte River. Pages 69-72 *in* Higgins and M.R. Brashler, editors, Proceedings, the Missouri River and its Tributaries: Piping Plover and Least Tern Symposium 1992, Lincoln, Nebraska, USA.

Lingle, G. R., editor. 2001. Proceedings of the Eleventh Platte River Basin Ecosystem Symposium, 27 February 2001, Kearney, NE, USA. Nebraska Water Center, University of Nebraska-Lincoln, Lincoln, NE, USA.

Lutterschmidt, W. I., V. H. Hutchison. 1997. The critical thermal maximum: data to support the onset of spasms as the definitive end point. Canadian Journal of Zoology 75(10):1553-1560.

MacArthur, R. H., and E. O. Wilson. 1967. The theory of island biogeography. Princeton University Press. Princeton, NJ, USA.

Markle, C. E., G. Chow-Fraser, and P. Chow-Fraser. 2018. Long-term habitat changes in a protected area: implications for herpetofauna habitat management and restoration. PloS one 13(2):e0192134.

Mariappan, S. 2001. Impact of lagoon leakage at confined animal feeding operations in Nebraska on shallow ground water nitrate concentrations and N-isotope variability. Thesis. University of Nebraska-Lincoln, Lincoln, NE, USA.

Mason, K. R. 2001. Comparison of prairie sites and classification of their habitat attributes in relation to abundance of the Regal Fritillary butterfly (*Speyeria idalia*). Minnesota Department of Natural Resources, Saint Paul, MN, USA.

Matthews, W. J., and E. G. Zimmerman. 1990. Potential effects of global warming on native fishes of the southern Great Plains and the Southwest. Fisheries 15(6):26-32.

McElfish Jr, J. M., R. L. Kihslinger, and S. Nichols. 2008. Setting buffer sizes for wetlands. National Wetlands Newsletter 30(2):6-17.

McIntyre, S., S. Lavorel, R. M. Tremont. 1995. Plant Life-History Attributes – Their Relationship to Disturbance Responses in Herbaceous Vegetation. Journal of Ecology 83:31-44.

McKee, J. 2006. Wetland Analysis: Platte River Recovery Implementation Program. Programmatic Environmental Impact Statement – Wetlands Appendix. U.S. Department of the Interior, Bureau of Reclamation, Platte River Office, Mills, Wyoming, USA.

McKinley, D. C., M. D. Norris, J. M. Blair, and L. C. Johnson. 2008. Altered ecosystem processes as a consequence of *Juniperus virginiana* L. encroachment into North American tallgrass prairie. Pages 170-187 *in* Western North American Juniperus Communities. Springer, New York, NY, USA.

McMahon, P. B., D. W. Litke, J. E. Paschal, and K. F. Dennehy. 1994. Groundwater as a source of nutrients and atrazine to streams in the South Platte River Basin. Journal of the American Water Resources Association 30(3):521-530.

McNew, K., and D. Griffith. 2005. Measuring the impact of ethanol plants on local grain prices. Applied Economic Perspectives and Policy 27(2):164-180.

Meissen, J. C., A. J. Glidden, M. E. Sherrard, K. J. Elgersma, and L. L. Jackson. 2020. Seed Mix Design and First Year Management Influence Multifunctionality and Cost-Effectiveness in Prairie Reconstruction. Restoration Ecology 28(4):807-816.

Mellor, N. J., J. Hellerich, R. Drijber, S. J. Morris, M. E. Stromberger, and E. A. Paul. 2013. Changes in ecosystem carbon following afforestation of native sand prairie. Soil Science Society of America Journal 77(5):1613-1624.

Meyer, C. K., and M. R. Whiles. 2008. Macroinvertebrate communities in restored and natural Platte River slough wetlands. Journal of the North American Benthological Society 27:626-639.

Meyer, C. K., M. R. Whiles, and S. G. Baer. 2010. Plant community recovery following restoration in temporally variable riparian wetlands. Restoration Ecology 18:52-64.

Miller, R. S., D. B. Botkin, R. Mendelssohn. 1974. The whooping crane (*Grus americana*) population of North America. Biological Conservation 6(2):106-111.

Monsarrat, S., S. Jarvie, and J. C. Svenning. 2019. Anthropocene refugia: integrating history and predictive modelling to assess the space available for biodiversity in a human-dominated world. Philosophical Transactions of the Royal Society B 374(1788):20190219.

Moser, M. T. 2014. Microbial water quality during the northern migration of Sandhill Cranes (*Grus canadensis*) at the Central Platte River, Nebraska: U.S. Geological Survey Fact Sheet 2014–3094, 4 pp.

Murphy, P. J., T. J. Randle, L. M. Fotherby, and J. A. Daraio. 2004. Platte River channel: history and restoration. U.S. Department of the Interior, Bureau of Reclamation, Technical

    Service Center, Denver, Colorado, USA.

Murphy, P. J., L. M. Fotherby, T. J. Randle, R. Simons. 2006. Platte River Sediment

    Transport and Riparian Vegetation Model. U.S. Department of the Interior, Bureau of

    Reclamation, Technical Service Center, Denver, Colorado, USA.

Mussetter, R. A. 2019. Uncertainty in Sediment Transport Balance Estimates using Sediment

    Load and River Transect Data. Proceedings of SEDHYD 2019: Conferences on

    Sedimentation and Hydrologic Modeling, 24-28 June 2019 in Reno Nevada, USA, 2:1-

    16.

Nagel, H. G., and M. S. Dart. 1980. Platte River evapotranspiration: A historical perspective in

    central Nebraska. Transactions of the Nebraska Academy of Sciences 8:55-76.

Nagel, H. G., and O. A. Kolstad. 1987. Comparison of plant species composition of Mormon

    Island Crane Meadows and Lillian Annette Rowe Sanctuary in central Nebraska.

    Transactions of the Nebraska Academy of Sciences 15:37-48.

Nebraska Association of Resources Districts (NARD). 2020. Nebraska's NRDs: 23 Natural

    Resources Districts Established Along River Basins. Lincoln, NE, USA, 2 pp.

Nassauer, J. I., P. Opdam. 2008. Design in science: extending the landscape ecology

    paradigm. Landscape ecology 23(6):633-644.

National Research Council (NRC). 2005. Endangered and Threatened Species of the Platte River

    National Academy Press, Washington, DC, USA.

Nebraska Department of Natural Resources (NeDNR). 2013. Flood Hazard Mitigation Plan.

    Floodplain and Dam Safety Division, Nebraska Department of Natural Resources, State

    of Nebraska, Lincoln, NE, USA, 140 pp.

https://nema.nebraska.gov/sites/nema.nebraska.gov/files/doc/flood-hazmit-plan.pdf

Nebraska Department of Natural Resources, Central Platte NRD, North Platte NRD, South Platte NRD, Tri-Basin NRD, and Twin Platte NRD (NeDNR et al). 2019. Basin-wide Plan for Joint Integrated Water Resources Management of Overappropriated Portions of the Platte River Basin, Nebraska. Second Increment (2019-2029). <https://dnr.nebraska.gov/sites/dnr.nebraska.gov/files/doc/water-planning/upper-platte/upper-platte-basin-wide-meetings-and-annual-reports/Second-Increment-Basin-Wide-Plan/20190911_UPB%20Plan_2ndInc_Final_wAppendices.pdf>

Nemec, K. T., J. Chan, C. Hoffman, T. L. Spanbauer, J. A. Hamm, C. R. Allen, T. Hefley, D. Pan, and P. Shrestha. 2014. Assessing resilience in stressed watersheds. Ecology and Society 19(1):34.

Nemec K. T., C. Allen, D. Wedin, C. Helzer. 2013. Influence of Richness and Seeding Density on Invasion Resistance in Experimental Tallgrass Prairie Restorations. Ecological Restoration 31:168-185.

Nguyen, Q. M., and M. W, Gilliland. 1988. Effects of no-flow river conditions on the Platte River well field. Journal of the American Water Resources Association 24(1):103-111.

Norling, B. S., S. H. Anderson, and W. A. Hubert. 1992. Roost sites used by Sandhill Crane staging along the Platte River, Nebraska. Great Basin Naturalist 53:253–261.

Noss, R. F., E. T. LaRoe, J. M. Scott. 1995. Endangered ecosystems of the United States: a preliminary assessment of loss and degradation, vol 28. U.S. Department of the Interior, National Biological Service, Washington, D.C., USA.

O'Brien, J. S., and P. J. Currier. 1987. Platte River channel morphology and riparian vegetation changes in the Big Bend Reach and minimum streamflow criteria for channel

maintenance. Platte River Whooping Crane Critical Habitat Maintenance Trust, Grand

Island, NE, USA.

O'Neill, B. J., and J. H. Thorp. 2011. A simple channel complexity metric for analyzing river

ecosystem responses. River systems 19:327-335.

Olson, R. A., E. C. Seim, and J. Muir. 1973. Influences of agricultural practices on water quality

in Nebraska: A survey of streams, groundwater, and precipitation. Journal of the

American Water Resources Association 9(2):301-311.

Opdam, P., R. Pouwels, S. van Rooij, E. Steingröver, and C. C. Vos. 2008. Setting biodiversity

targets in participatory regional planning: introducing ecoprofiles. Ecology and Society

13(1):20.

Ostrom, B. L., A. J. Caven, J. M. Malzahn, and A. Vogel. 2020. Snowy Plover Activity in the

Central Platte River Valley in May 2019. Transactions of the Nebraska Academy of

Sciences 40:24-29.

Palmer, M. A., E. S. Bernhardt, J. D. Allan, P. S. Lake, G. Alexander, S. Brooks, J. Carr, S.

Clayton, C. N. Dahm, J. Follstad Shah, D. L. Galat, S. G. Loss, P. Goodwin, D. D. Hart,

B. Hassett, R. Jenkinson, G. M. Kondolf, P. Lave, J. L. Meyer, T. K. O'Donnell, L.

Pagano, and E. Sudduth. 2005. Standards for ecologically successful river restoration.

Journal of applied ecology 42(2):208-217.

Panella, M. J., and S. P. Wilson. 2018. Delisting Proposal for North American River Otter

(*Lontra canadensis*) in Nebraska. Nebraska Game and Parks Commission, Lincoln, NE,

USA.

Panella, M. 2020. Enhancing and Restoring Monarch Butterfly Habitat in Eastern Nebraska:

Final Programmatic Report. Submitted to the Monarch Butterfly Conservation Fund –
2017, National Fish and Wildlife Foundation, Washington, DC, USA. Nebraska Game
and Parks Commission, Lincoln, NE, USA.

Parsons, M., M. C. Thoms. 2018. From academic to applied: Operationalising resilience in river
systems. Geomorphology 305:242-251.

Pauley, N. M., M. J. Harner, E. M. Brinley Buckley, P. R. Burger, and K. Geluso. 2018. Spatial
analysis of borrow pits along the Platte River in south-central Nebraska, USA, in 1957
and 2016. Transactions of the Nebraska Academy of Sciences 38:36-46.

Pearse, A. T., D. A. Brandt, W. C. Harrell, K. L. Metzger, D. M. Baasch, and T. J. Hefley. 2015.
Whooping Crane stopover site use intensity within the Great Plains. U.S. Geological
Survey Open-File Report 2015-1166, 12 p.

Pearse, A. T., G. L. Krapu, and D. A. Brandt. 2017a. Sandhill Crane roost selection, human
disturbance, and forage resources. Journal of Wildlife Management 81:477–486.

Pearse, A. T., M. J. Harner, D. M. Baasch, G. D. Wright, A. J. Caven, and K. L. Metzger. 2017b.
Evaluation of nocturnal roost and diurnal sites used by Whooping Cranes in the Great
Plains, USA. U.S. Geological Survey Open-File Report 2016–1209, 29 pp.

Pearse, A. T., K. L. Metzger, D. A. Brandt, J. A. Shaffer, M. T. Bidwell, and W. Harrell. 2021.
Migrating whooping cranes avoid wind-energy infrastructure when selecting stopover
habitat. Ecological Applications 31(5):e02324.

Perkin, J. S., K. B. Gido, A. R. Cooper, T. F. Turner, M. J. Osborne, E. R. Johnson, and K. B.
Mayes. 2015. Fragmentation and dewatering transform Great Plains stream fish
communities. Ecological Monographs 85(1):73-92.

Pfeiffer, K. 1999. Evaluation of wet meadow restorations in the Platte River Valley. Pages 202–

206 *in* J.T. Springer, editor, Proceedings of the 16th North American Prairie Conference, Kearney, Nebraska, July 26–29, 1998. University of Nebraska–Kearney, Kearney, NE, USA.

Pfeiffer, K., and P. Currier. 2005. An adaptive approach to channel management on the Platte River. Proceedings North American Crane Workshop 9:151–154.

Piégay, H., G. Grant, F. Nakamura, and N. Trustrum. 2006. Braided river management: from assessment of river behaviour to improved sustainable development. Pages 257-275 *in* G. H. Sambrook Smith, J. L. Best, C. Bristow, and G. E. Petts, editors, Braided Rivers: process, deposits, ecology and management. John Wiley & Sons, Inc., Hoboken, NJ, USA.

Platte River Recovery Implementation Program (PRRIP). 2018. Restoration and management framework for PRRIP habitat complexes. Executive Director's Office of the Platte River Recovery Implementation Program, Kearney, NE, USA, 34 pp.

Platte River Whooping Crane Maintenance Trust, Inc. (Crane Trust). 1998. Habitat management, restoration, and acquisition plan for the Big Bend reach of the Platte River in Central Nebraska. Platte River Whooping Crane Maintenance Trust, Inc., Wood River, NE, USA, 70 pp.

Platte Valley Weed Management Area and West Central Weed Management Area (PVWMA). 2013. Platte Valley and West Central Weed Management Area's Invasive Species Control in the Central Platte River 2008– 2013 Summary. Kearney and North Platte, NE, USA. <http://www.plattevalleywma.org/Documents/08-13summary.pdf >

Poff, N. L. 2018. Beyond the natural flow regime? Broadening the hydro- ecological foundation to meet environmental flows challenges in a non- stationary world. Freshwater Biology 63(8):1011-1021.

Poff, N. L., J. D. Allan, M. B. Bain, J. R. Karr, K. L. Prestegaard, B. D. Richter, R. E. Sparks, and J. C. Stromberg. 1997. The natural flow regime. BioScience 47(11):769-784.

Powers, C. A., C. G. Henry, R. Walkowiak, J. Gross, J. A. George, K. D. Gustafson, R. T. Burns, B. L Woodbury, R. A. Eigenberg, and D. Gangwish. 2010. Vegetated treatment system design and monitoring at two large CAFO beef feedlots in Nebraska. Page 1 *in* International Symposium on Air Quality and Manure Management for Agriculture Conference Proceedings, 13-16 September 2010, Dallas, Texas. American Society of Agricultural and Biological Engineers.

PRMJS Biology Workgroup (PRMJS). 1990. Platte River Management Joint Study. U.S. Department of Interior, Denver, CO, USA, 139 pp.

Rabalais, N. N. 2002. Nitrogen in aquatic ecosystems. AMBIO: a Journal of the Human Environment 31(2):102-112.

Randle, T. J., and M. A. Samad. 2003. Platte River flow and sediment transport between North Platte and Grand Island, Nebraska (1895-1999). U.S. Department of the Interior, Bureau of Reclamation, Technical Service Center, Denver, Colorado, USA.

Rapp, R. E., A. Datta, S. Irmak, T. J. Arkebauer, S. Z. Knezevic. 2012. Integrated management of common reed (*Phragmites australis*) along the Platte River in Nebraska. Weed Technology 26(2):326-333.

Ratajczak, Z., J. B. Nippert, J. M., Briggs, and J. M. Blair. 2014. Fire dynamics distinguish grasslands, shrublands and woodlands as alternative attractors in the Central Great Plains of North America. Journal of Ecology 102(6):1374-1385.

Ratcliffe, B. C., and P. C. Hammond. 2002. Insects and the native vegetation of Nebraska. Transactions of the Nebraska Academy Sciences 28:29–47

R Core Team. 2019. R: A language and environment for statistical computing. R Foundation for Statistical Computing, Vienna, Austria. URL https://www.R-project.org/.

Reeder, K., and J. Clymer. 2015. Iowa's Wildlife Action Plan: Securing a future for fish and wildlife. Iowa Department of Natural Resources, Des Moines, Iowa, USA.

Reinecke, K. J., and G. L. Krapu. 1986. Feeding ecology of Sandhill Cranes during spring migration in Nebraska. Journal of Wildlife Management 50:71–79.

Ricketts, T. H. 2001. The matrix matters: effective isolation in fragmented landscapes. The American Naturalist 158(1):87-99.

Riens, J. R., M. S. Schwarz, F. Mustafa, and W. W. Hoback. 2013. Aquatic macroinvertebrate communities and water quality at buffered and non-buffered wetland sites on federal waterfowl production areas in the Rainwater Basin, Nebraska. Wetlands 33(6):1025-1036.

Ries, L., and D. M. Debinski. 2001. Butterfly responses to habitat edges in the highly fragmented prairies of Central Iowa. Journal of Animal Ecology 70(5):840-852.

Roche, E. A., M. H. Sherfy, M. M. Ring, T. L. Shaffer, M. J. Anteau, and J. H. Stucker. 2016. Demographics and movements of Least Terns and Piping Plovers in the Central Platte River Valley, Nebraska. U.S. Geological Survey Open-File Report 2016-1061, 38 pp.

Roemer, G. W., and R. K. Wayne, R. K. 2003. Conservation in conflict: the tale of two endangered species. Conservation Biology 17(5):1251-1260.

Rohweder, M. R. 2015. Kansas Wildlife Action Plan. Ecological Services Section, Kansas

Department of Wildlife, Parks and Tourism, Pratt, KS, USA, and Kansas Biological

Survey, University of Kansas, Lawrence, KS, USA.

Rolfsmeier, S. B., and G. Steinauer 2010. Terrestrial ecological systems and natural communities

of Nebraska (Version IV). Nebraska Natural Heritage Program, Nebraska Game and

Parks Commission, Lincoln, Nebraska, USA.

Rondeau, R., K. Decker, J. Handwerk, J. Siemers, L. Grunau, and C. Pague. 2011. The state of

Colorado's biodiversity. Colorado Natural Heritage Program, Colorado State

University, Fort Collins, Colorado, USA.

Rosenberg, K. V., J. A. Kennedy, R. Dettmers, R. P. Ford, D. Reynolds, J. D. Alexander, C. J.

Beardmore, P. J. Blancher, R. E. Bogart, G. S. Butcher, A. F. Camfield, A. Couturier, et

al. 2016. Partners in Flight Landbird Conservation Plan: 2016 revision for Canada and

continental United States. Partners in Flight Science Committee.

Rowe, H. I. 2010. Tricks of the trade: techniques and opinions from 38 experts in tallgrass prairie

restoration. Restoration Ecology 18:253-262.

Rowe, H. I. 2013. Prairie Restorations can Protect Remnant Tallgrass Prairie Plant Communities.

The American Midland Naturalist 170(1):26-38.

Rowe, H. I., and J. D. Holland. 2013. High Plant Richness in Prairie Reconstructions Support

Diverse Leafhopper Communities. Restoration Ecology 21:174-180.

Rushing, N. S., S. A. Flint, R. G. Shaw. 2021. Latitude of Seed Source Impacts Flowering

Phenology and Fitness in Translocated Plant Populations. Restoration Ecology

29:e13464.

Sacerdote- Velat, A. B., J. M. Earnhardt, D. Mulkerin, D. Boehm, and G. Glowacki. 2014.

Evaluation of headstarting and release techniques for population augmentation and reintroduction of the smooth green snake. Animal Conservation 17:65-73.

Samson, F. B., F. L. Knopf, and W. R. Ostlie. 2004. Great Plains ecosystems: past, present, and future. Wildlife Society Bulletin 32(1):6-15.

Schaefer, J. F., E. Marsh-Matthews, D. E. Spooner, K. B. Gido, and W. J. Matthews. 2003. Effects of barriers and thermal refugia on local movement of the threatened leopard darter, *Percina pantherina*. Environmental Biology of Fishes 66(4):391-400.

Scharf, W. C., J. Kren, P. A. Johnsgard, and L. R. Brown. 2008. Body weights and species distributions of birds in Nebraska's Central and Western Platte Valley. Papers in Ornithology No. 43, University of Nebraska–Lincoln, Lincoln, NE, USA.

Schneider, R., M. Fritz, J. Jorgensen, S. Schainost, R. Simpson, G. Steinauer, and C. Rothe-Groleau. 2018. Revision of the Tier 1 and 2 Lists of Species of Greatest Conservation Need: A Supplement to the Nebraska Natural Legacy Project State Wildlife Action Plan. The Nebraska Game and Parks Commission, Lincoln, NE, USA.

Schultz, C., and A. J. Caven. 2021. Lined Snake (*Tropidoclonion lineatum*) prescribed fire mortality. Transactions of the Nebraska Academy of Sciences (41):42–45.

Schwartz, M. W. 1999. Choosing the appropriate scale of reserves for conservation. Annual Review of Ecology and Systematics 30(1):83-108.

Schwenk, W. S., and T. M. Donovan. 2011. A multispecies framework for landscape conservation planning. Conservation Biology 25(5):1010-1021.

Selby, G. 2007. Regal Fritillary (*Speyeria idalia* Drury): a technical conservation assessment. USDA Forest Service, Rocky Mountain Region, Lakewood, CO, USA, 53 pp.

Schepker, T. J., E. B. Webb, D. Tillitt, and T. LaGrange. 2020. Neonicotinoid insecticide concentrations in agricultural wetlands and associations with aquatic invertebrate communities. Agriculture, Ecosystems & Environment 287:106678.

Kent Shannon, D., D. E. Clay, and K. A. Sudduth. 2018. An introduction to precision agriculture. Pages 1-12 *in* D. Kent Shannon, D. E. Clay, N. R. Kitchen, editors, Precision Agriculture Basics. American Society of Agronomy, Inc., Crop Science Society of America, Inc., Soil Science Society of America, Inc., Madison, WI, USA, 265 pp.

Shaw, N., R. S. Barak, R. E. Campbell, A. Kirmer, S. Pedrini, K. Dixon, and S. Frischie. 2020. Seed Use in the Field: Delivering Seeds for Restoration Success. Restoration Ecology 28(3):276-285.

Sherfy, M. H., M. M. Ring, J. H. Stucker, M. J. Anteau, T. L. Shaffer, T. L., and M. A. Sovada. 2021. Foraging Movements and Colony Attendance of Least Terns (*Sternula antillarum*) on the Central Platte River, Nebraska, USA. Waterbirds 44(1):38-54.

Silcock, W. R., and J. G. Jorgensen. 2022a. Least Tern (*Sternula antillarum athalassos*). *In* Birds of Nebraska — Online. www.BirdsofNebraska.org

Silcock, W. R., and J. G. Jorgensen. 2022b. Piping Plover (*Charadrius melodus*). *In* Birds of Nebraska — Online. www.BirdsofNebraska.org

Silvia, T. D. 1995. Riparian habitats of the Central Platte as a corridor for dispersal of small mammals in Nebraska. Thesis. University of Nebraska-Lincoln, Lincoln, Nebraska, USA, 80 pp.

Simons & Associates, Inc, 2000. Physical History of the Platte River in Nebraska: Focusing Upon Flow, Sediment Transport, Geomorphology, and Vegetation. Simons & Associates, Inc., Fort Collins, CO, USA.

Simonsen, V., J. Fleischmann, D. Whisenhunt, J. Volesky, and D. Twidwell. 2015. Act Now or Pay Later: Evaluating the Cost of Reactive versus Proactive Eastern Redcedar Management. University of Nebraska—Lincoln, Extension, Institute of Agriculture and Natural Resources, Lincoln, NE, USA, Report No. EC1784, 9 pp.

Slagle, M., and S. D. Hendrix. 2009. Reproduction of *Amorpha canescens* (Fabaceae) and Diversity of its Bee Community in a Fragmented Landscape. Oecologia 161:813-823.

Smith, C. B. 2011. Adaptive management on the central Platte River–science, engineering, and decision analysis to assist in the recovery of four species. Journal of Environmental Management 92(5):1414-1419.

Smith, N. D. 1971. Transverse bars and braiding in the lower Platte River, Nebraska. Geological Society of America Bulletin 82:3407–3420.

Soulé, M. E., and M. A. Sanjayan. 1998. Ecology: conservation targets: do they help? Science 279(27):2060-2061.

South Dakota Department of Game, Fish and Parks (SD GFP). 2014. South Dakota Wildlife Action Plan. Wildlife Division, South Dakota Department of Game, Fish and Parks, Pierre, SD, USA.

South Platte Regional Opportunities Water Group (SPROWG). 2020. Feasibility Study Report. Lower South Platte Water Conservancy District, Sterling, CO, USA, 56 pp.

Spencer, W. A. 1964. The relationship of dispersal and migration to gene flow in the Boreal Chorus Frog. Dissertation. Colorado State University, Fort Collins, Colorado, USA.

Sprunt, A., IV and F. J. Ligas. 1963. Continental Bald Eagle Project: progress report No. III. Proceedings of the National Audubon Society's Convention, Miami, FL, USA, pp. 2-7.

Stambaugh, M. C., R. P. Guyette, E. R. McMurry, J. M. Marschall, and G. Willson. 2008. Six centuries of fire history at Devils Tower National Monument with comments on regionwide temperature influence. Great Plains Research 18:177-187.

Steinauer, G., B. Whiney, K. Adams, M. Bullerman, and C. Helzer. 2003. A Guide to Prairie and Wetland Restoration in Eastern Nebraska. Joint publication of Prairie Plains Resource Institute & Nebraska Game and Parks Commission. Aurora, NE, USA, 84 pp.

Stella, C. (2020, July 10). Conservationists prepare to study Platte River chokepoint. Nebraska Public Media. https://nebraskapublicmedia.org/en/news/news-articles/conservationists-prepare-to-study-platte-river-chokepoint/

Stewart, F. E., S. Darlington, J. P. Volpe, M. McAdie, and J. T. Fisher. 2019. Corridors best facilitate functional connectivity across a protected area network. Scientific reports 9(1):1-9.

Stoffer, D. 2020. astsa: Applied Statistical Time Series Analysis. R package version 1.10. https://CRAN.R-project.org/package=astsa

Strange, E. M., K. D. Fausch, and A. P. Covich. 1999. Sustaining ecosystem services in human-dominated watersheds: biohydrology and ecosystem processes in the South Platte River Basin. Environmental management 24(1):39-54.

Suding, K. N. 2011. Toward an era of restoration in ecology: successes, failures, and opportunities ahead. Annual review of ecology, evolution and systematics 42(1):465-487.

Sumi, T., M. Okano, and Y. Takata. 2004. Reservoir sedimentation management with bypass tunnels in Japan. Pages 1036–1043 *in* Proceedings of 9th International Symposium on River Sedimentation, Yichang, China.

Sumi, T., and T. Hirose. 2009. Accumulation of sediment in reservoirs. Pages 224-252 *in* Y.

Takahasi, editor, Water storage, transport and distribution. Eolss Publishers Co. Ltd., Oxford, United Kingdom.

Sutton, R. 2005. Analysis of Impacts to Riverine Fish Communities in the Central Platte River. Programmatic Environmental Impact Statement – Technical Appendix. U.S. Department of the Interior, Bureau of Reclamation, Platte River Office, Mills, Wyoming, USA.

Swengel, S. R., D. Schlicht, F. Olsen, and A. B. Swengel. 2011. Declines of prairie butterflies in the midwestern USA. Journal of Insect Conservation 15:327–339

Swengel, S. R., and A. B. Swengel. 2016. Status and Trend of Regal Fritillary (*Speyeria idalia*) (Lepidoptera: Nymphalidae) in the 4th of July Butterfly Count Program in 1977–2014. Scientifica 2016:1-10.

Symstad, A. J., and S. A. Leis. 2017. Woody encroachment in northern Great Plains grasslands: perceptions, actions, and needs. Natural Areas Journal 37(1):118-127.

Tibbs, J. E., and D. L. Galat. 1998. The influence of river stage on endangered least terns and their fish prey in the Mississippi River (USA). Regulated Rivers: Research & Management: An International Journal Devoted to River Research and Management 14(3):257-266.

Tiner, R. W. 2016. Wetland indicators: a guide to wetland formation, identification, delineation, classification, and mapping. Crc Press, Boca Raton, FL, USA.

The Flatwater Group, Inc. 2010. Platte River from the Lexington to Odessa bridges sediment augmentation experiment alternatives screening study: summary report. Platte River Recovery Implementation Program, Kearney, NE, USA, 174 pp.

The Flatwater Group, Inc. 2014. Sediment augmentation final pilot study report. Platte River

Recovery Implementation Program, Kearney, NE, USA, 123 pp.

Tonietto, R. K. and D. J. Larkin. 2018. Habitat Restoration Benefits Wild Bees: A Meta-analysis. Journal of Applied Ecology 55:582-590.

Tonitto, C., and S. J. Riha. 2016. Planning and implementing small dam removals: lessons learned from dam removals across the eastern United States. Sustainable Water Resources Management 2(4):489-507.

Török, P., L. A. Brudvig, J. Kollmann, J. N. Price, and B. Tóthmérész. 2021. The present and future of grassland restoration. Restoration Ecology 29:e13378.

Trainor, A. M., T. M. Shenk, and K. R. Wilson. 2012. Spatial, temporal, and biological factors associated with Preble's meadow jumping mouse (*Zapus hudsonius preblei*) home range. Journal of Mammalogy 93(2):429-438.

Turner, S. M. 2021. North Platte Choke Point: North Platte Chokepoint Planning Workgroup Meeting. Platte River Recovery Implementation Program, Kearney, Nebraska, USA, 04-13-2021, 32 pp. https://platteriverprogram.org/system/files/2021-04/NPchokepointWorkgroupPresentation_20210413.pdf

Turner, M. G., R. H. Gardner, and R. V. O'Neill. 2001. Landscape ecology in theory and practice: pattern and process. Springer-Verlag, New York, New York, USA.

Twidwell, D., W. E. Rogers, S. D. Fuhlendorf, C. L. Wonkka, D. M. Engle, J. R. Weir, U. P. Kreuter, and C. A. Taylor Jr. 2013. The rising Great Plains fire campaign: citizens' response to woody plant encroachment. Frontiers in Ecology and the Environment 11(s1):e64-e71.

Twidwell, D., A. S. West, W. B. Hiatt, A. L. Ramirez, J. Taylor Winter, D. M. Engle, S. D.

    Fuhlendorf, and J. D. Carlson. 2016. Plant invasions or fire policy: which has altered fire

    behavior more in tallgrass prairie? Ecosystems 19(2):356-368.

Tye, S. P., K. Geluso, and M. J. Harner. 2017. Early emergence and seasonality of the Red-

    bellied Snake (*Storeria occipitomaculata*) along the Platte River in south-central

    Nebraska, USA. Transactions of the Nebraska Academy of Sciences 37:11-17

U.S. Department of Agriculture. National Agricultural Statistics Service (NASS). 2017. Census

    of Agriculture. Complete data available at www.nass.usda.gov/AgCensus.

U.S. Department of the Interior (USDOI). 2019.  Interior Extends Platte River Recovery

    Implementation Program to Protect Endangered Species. Press Release, U.S. Department

    of the Interior, Washington, DC, USA, 12/30/2019.

U.S. Fish and Wildlife Service (USFWS). 1978. Title 50, Wildlife and Fisheries: Part 17,

    Endangered and Threatened Wildlife and Plants. Determination of Critical Habitat for the

    Whooping Crane Federal Register 43(94):20938-20942.

U.S. Fish and Wildlife Service. 1981. The Platte River Ecology Study: Special Research: Report.

    Northern Prairie Wildlife Research Center, Jamestown, ND, USA.

U.S. Fish and Wildlife Service and U.S. Bureau of Reclamation (USFWS and USBR). 2006.

    Platte River Recovery Implementation Program: Final Environmental Impact Statement.

    U.S. Department of the Interior, Denver, CO, USA.

U.S. Fish and Wildlife Service (USFWS). 2019. Waterfowl population status 2019. U.S.

    Department of the Interior, Washington, D.C., USA.

U.S. Fish and Wildlife Service (USFWS). 2020. Species status assessment report for the New

Mexico meadow jumping mouse (*Zapus hudsonius luteus*), 1st Revision. U.S. Department of the Interior, U.S. Fish and Wildlife Service – Southwest Region, Albuquerque, NM, USA, 160 pp.

U.S. Geological Survey (USGS). 2020. National Water Information System. U.S. Department of Interior, U.S. Geological Survey, Reston, VA, USA. https://waterdata.usgs.gov/nwis

VanDerwalker, J.G. 1982. The Platte River Whooping Crane Critical Habitat Maintenance Trust. Proceedings of the 1981 Crane Workshop, Tavernier, Florida, USA, pp. 4-6.

Vannote, R. L., G. W. Minshall, K. W. Cummins, J. R. Sedell,  and C. E. Cushing. 1980. The river continuum concept. Canadian journal of fisheries and aquatic sciences 37(1):130-137.

Villamagna, A. M., B. Mogollón, and P. L. Angermeier. 2017. Inequity in ecosystem service delivery: socioeconomic gaps in the public-private conservation network. Ecology and Society 22(1):36.

Vivian, L. A., M. Cavallaro, K. Kneeland, E. Lindroth, W. W. Hoback, K. M. Farnsworth-Hoback, R. R. Harms, and J. E. Foster. 2013. Current known range of the Platte River caddisfly, *Ironoquia plattensis*, and genetic variability among populations from three Nebraska Rivers. Journal of Insect Conservation 17(5):885-895.

Vogt, P., J. R. Ferrari, T. R. Lookingbill, R. H. Gardner, K. H. Riitters, and K. Ostapowicz. 2009. Mapping functional connectivity. ecological indicators 9(1):64-71.

Vrtiska, M. P., and S. P. Sullivan. 2009. Abundance and distribution of lesser snow and Ross's geese in the Rainwater Basin and central Platte River Valley of Nebraska. Great Plains Research 19:147-155.

Vymazal, J. 2010. Constructed wetlands for wastewater treatment. Water 2(3):530-549.

Walkinshaw, L. H. 1956. Two visits to the Platte Rivers and their Sandhill Crane migration.

    Nebraska Bird Review 24:18–21.

Wallin, L., B. M. Svensson, and M. Lönn. 2009. Artificial dispersal as a restoration tool in

    meadows: sowing or planting? Restoration Ecology 17(2):270-279.

Wang, M., L. Duan, J. Wang, J. Peng, and B. Zheng. 2020. Determining the width of lake

    riparian buffer zones for improving water quality base on adjustment of land use

    structure. Ecological Engineering 158:106001.

Wang, T., M. Luri, L. Janssen, D. A. Hennessy, H. Feng, M. C. Wimberly, and G. Arora. 2017.

    Determinants of motives for land use decisions at the margins of the Corn Belt.

    Ecological economics 134:227-237.

Ward, J. V., and J. A. Stanford. 1995. Ecological connectivity in alluvial river ecosystems and its

    disruption by flow regulation. Regulated rivers: research & management 11(1):105-119.

Wenger, S. 1999. A review of the scientific literature on riparian buffer width, extent and

    vegetation. Office of Public Service & Outreach, Institute of Ecology, University of

    Georgia, Athens, GA, USA, 59 pp.

Wesche, T. A., O. D. Skinner, and R. J. Henszey. 1994. Platte River wetland hydrology study.

    U.S. Bureau of Reclamation and Wyoming Water Resources Center, University of

    Wyoming, Laramie, Wyoming, 165 pp.

Whiles, M. R., and B. S. Goldowitz. 2001. Hydrologic influences on insect emergence

    production from central Platte River wetlands. Ecological Applications 11(6):1829-1842.

Whiles, M. R., B. S. Goldowitz, and R. E. Charlton. 1999. Life history and production of a semi-

    terrestrial Limnephilid caddisfly in an intermittent Platte River wetland. Journal of the

    North American Benthological Society 18:533-544.

White, J. M., and J. C. Stromberg. 2011. Resilience, restoration, and riparian ecosystems: case study of a dryland, urban river. Restoration Ecology 19(1):101-111.

Whitney, B. 1997. Platte River Country Restoration Part I. Getting Started. Restoration & Management Notes 15(1):6-13.

Whitney, B. 1997. Platte River Country Restoration Part II. At Work on the Plains. Restoration & Management Notes 15(2):126-137.

Whitney, W. S. 1999. Prairie and wetland restoration along the Central Platte River, 1991-1998. Proceedings of the North American Prairie Conference 16:207-215.

Wiese, J. D., A. J. Caven, T. Smith, and B. Krohn. 2019. Heather Henson property vegetation assessment: with notes on plants of ecological and human interest. Platte River Whooping Crane Maintenance Trust, Inc., Wood River, NE, USA, 12 pp.

Wilcox, B. P., and T. L. Thurow. 2006. Emerging issues in rangeland ecohydrology: vegetation change and the water cycle. Rangeland Ecology & Management 59(2):220-224.

Wille, M., and L. G. Barr. 2022. Resurgence of avian influenza virus. Science 376(6592):459-460.

Williams, G. P. 1978. The case of the shrinking channels: the North Platte and Platte Rivers in Nebraska. Geological Survey Circular 781, U.S. Geological Survey, Arlington, VA.

Williams, N. M. 2011. Restoration of Non-target Species: Bee Communities and Pollination Function in Riparian Forests. Restoration Ecology 19:450-459.

Wilsey, C. B., J. Grand, J. Wu, N. Michel, J. Grogan-Brown, and B. Trusty. 2019. North American Grasslands. National Audubon Society, New York, New York, USA.

Winter, T. C., J. W. Harvey, O. L. Franke, and W. M. Alley. 1998. Ground water and surface water: a single resource. U.S. Geological Survey Circular 1139.

Worthington, T. A., A. A. Echelle, J. S. Perkin, R. Mollenhauer, N. Farless, J. J. Dyer, D. Logue, S. K. Brewer. 2018. The emblematic minnows of the North American Great Plains: a synthesis of threats and conservation opportunities. Fish and Fisheries 19(2):271-307.

Wright, C. K., B. Larson, T. J. Lark, and H. K. Gibbs. 2017. Recent grassland losses are concentrated around US ethanol refineries. Environmental Research Letters 12(4):044001.

Wright, C. K., and M. C. Wimberly. 2013. Recent land use change in the Western Corn Belt threatens grasslands and wetlands. Proceedings of the National Academy of Sciences 110(10):4134-4139.

Wright, G. D. 2012. Multiple scale habitat selection by a small mammal habitat specialist (*Zapus hudsonius luteus*) in a managed floodplain landscape. Thesis. New Mexico State University, Las Cruces, NM, USA.

Wright, G. D., and J. K. Frey. 2015. Habitat selection by the endangered New Mexico meadow jumping mouse on an irrigated floodplain. Journal of Fish and Wildlife Management 6(1):112-129.

Yachi, S., and M. Loreau. 1999. Biodiversity and Ecosystem Productivity in a Fluctuating Environment: The Insurance Hypothesis. Proceedings of the National Academy of Sciences USA 96(4):1463-1468.

Yates, M. D., S. C. Loeb, and D. C. Guynn. 1997. The effect of habitat patch size on small mammal populations. Proceedings of the Southeastern Association of Fish and Wildlife Agencies 51:501-510.

Yamamuro, M., T. Komuro, H. Kamiya, T. Kato, H. Hasegawa, and Y. Kameda. 2019. Neonicotinoids disrupt aquatic food webs and decrease fishery yields. Science 366(6465):620-623.

Zambory, C. L., A. P. Bybel, C. L. Pierce, K. J. Roe, and J. M. Weber. 2017. Habitat improvement projects for stream and oxbow fish of greatest conservation need. 2017. Annual Progress Report. U.S. Fish and Wildlife Service, Iowa Department of Natural Resources, and Minnesota Department of Natural Resources, Ames, IA, USA, 41 pp.

Zuerlein, E. J., J. L. Hutchinson, S. Schainost, and R. Lock, R. 2001. Instream Flow Rights for the Platte River— A Major Tributary of the Missouri River. In G. Lingle, editor, Proceedings of the 11th Platte River Basin Ecosystem Symposium, Kearney, NE. University of Nebraska– Lincoln, Lincoln, Nebraska, USA.

## TABLES AND FIGURES

**Figure 1.** Map of the Platte River and major tributaries comprising the North and South Platte Rivers, the Loup River, and the Elkhorn Rivers, including major dams/reservoirs (>30,000 acre-feet capacity) and U.S. Geological Survey gage stations in Nebraska (State line, Roscoe, Overton, Grand Island, Duncan, North Bend, Louisville, from left to right respectively). Data from USACE (2018) National Inventory of Dams, USGS (2019) National Hydrography Dataset, USGS (2019) The National Map, 3D Elevation Program.

*Map credit E.M. Brinley Buckley.*

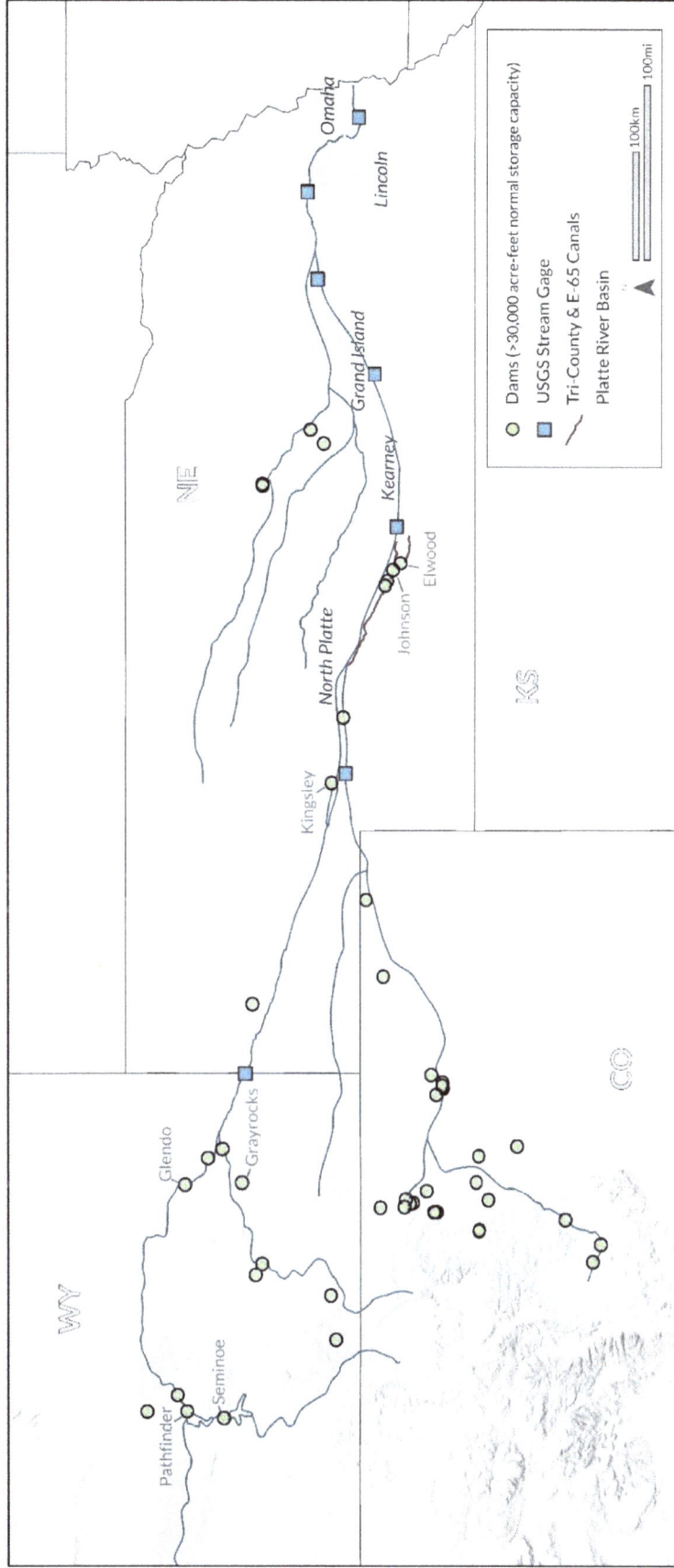

**Figure 2.** Target peak flows (red) and maximum daily discharge (blue) by day of year for the period of record at Overton (a), Grand Island (b), and Duncan (c), Nebraska.

a)

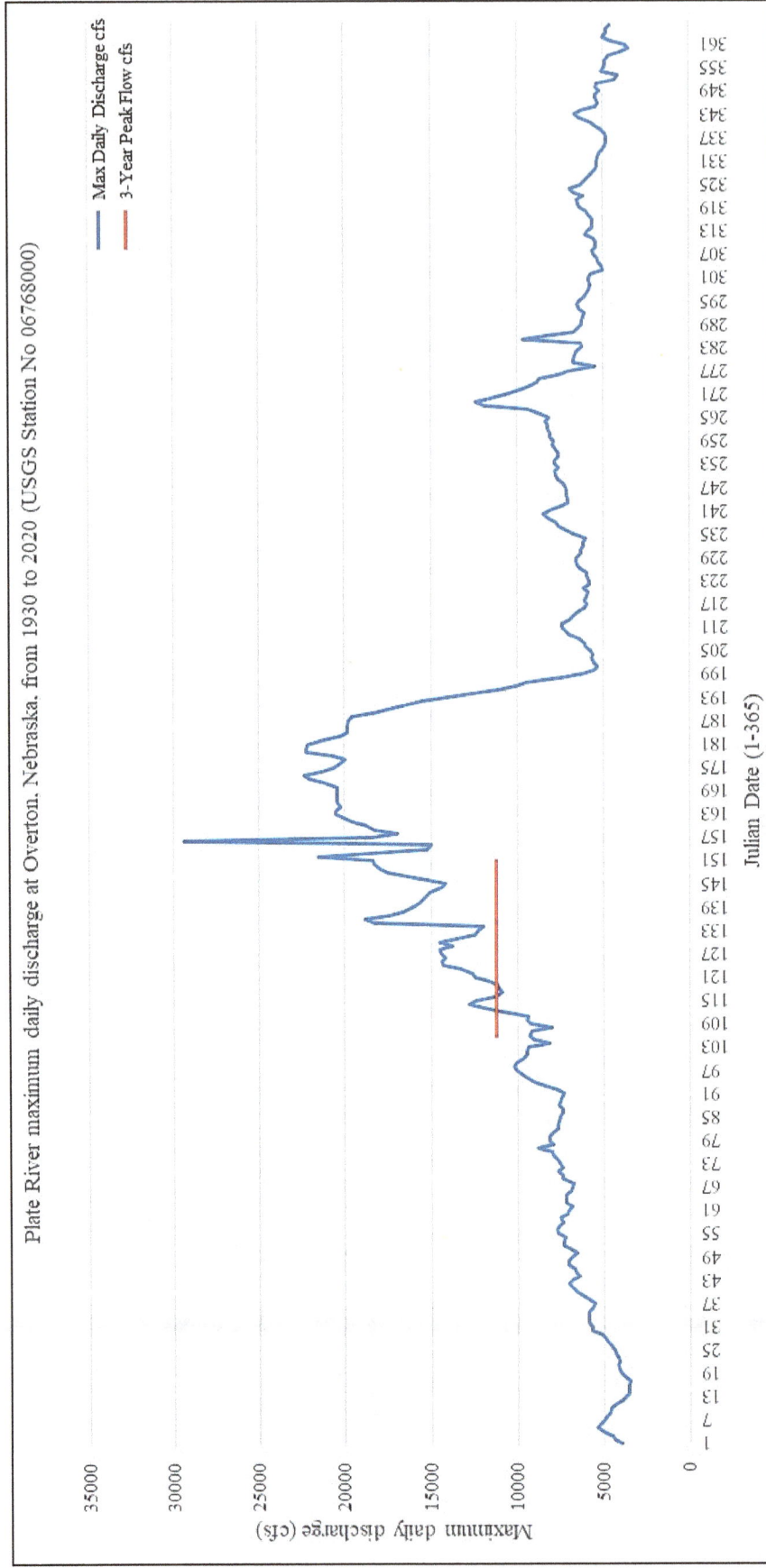

Plate River maximum daily discharge at Overton. Nebraska. from 1930 to 2020 (USGS Station No 06768000)

174

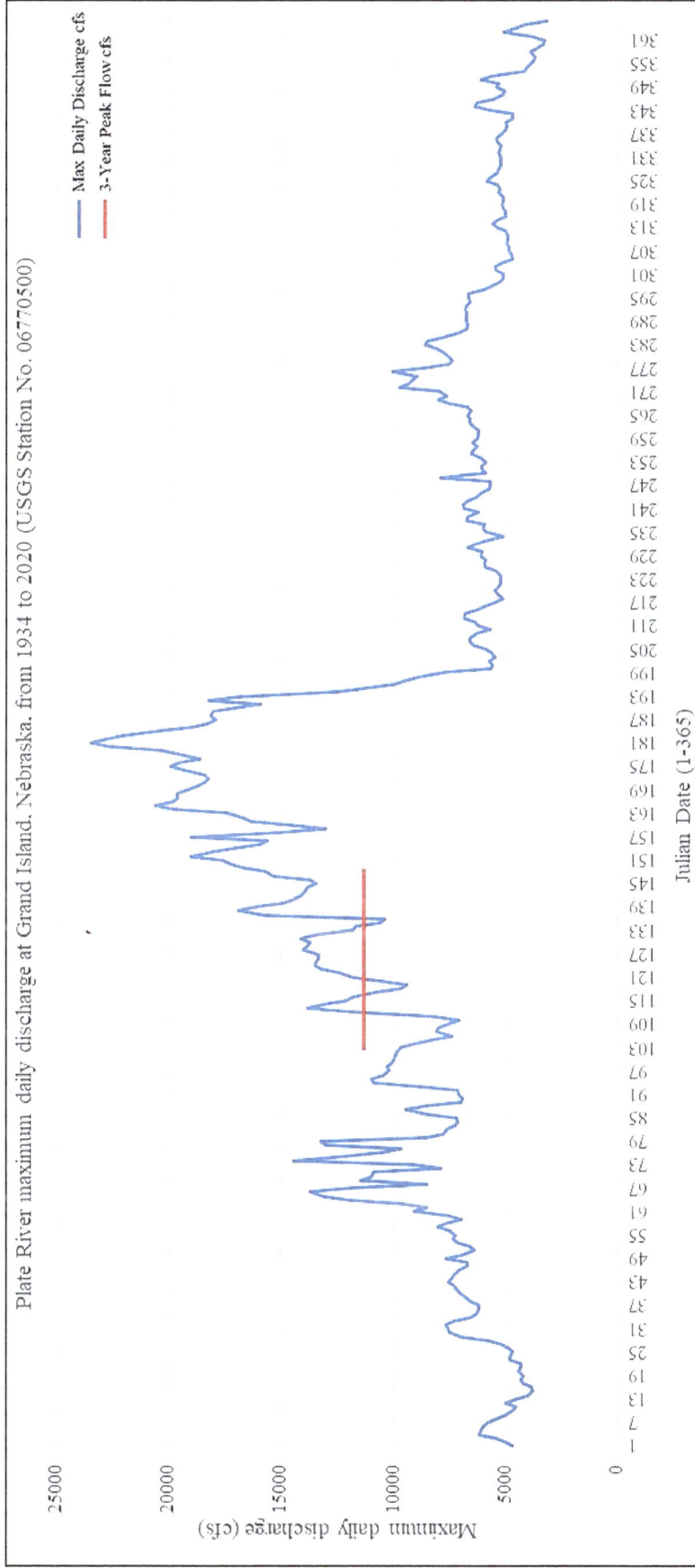

b)

Plate River maximum daily discharge at Grand Island. Nebraska. from 1934 to 2020 (USGS Station No. 06770500)

Max Daily Discharge cfs
3-Year Peak Flow cfs

Maximum daily discharge (cfs)

Julian Date (1-365)

175

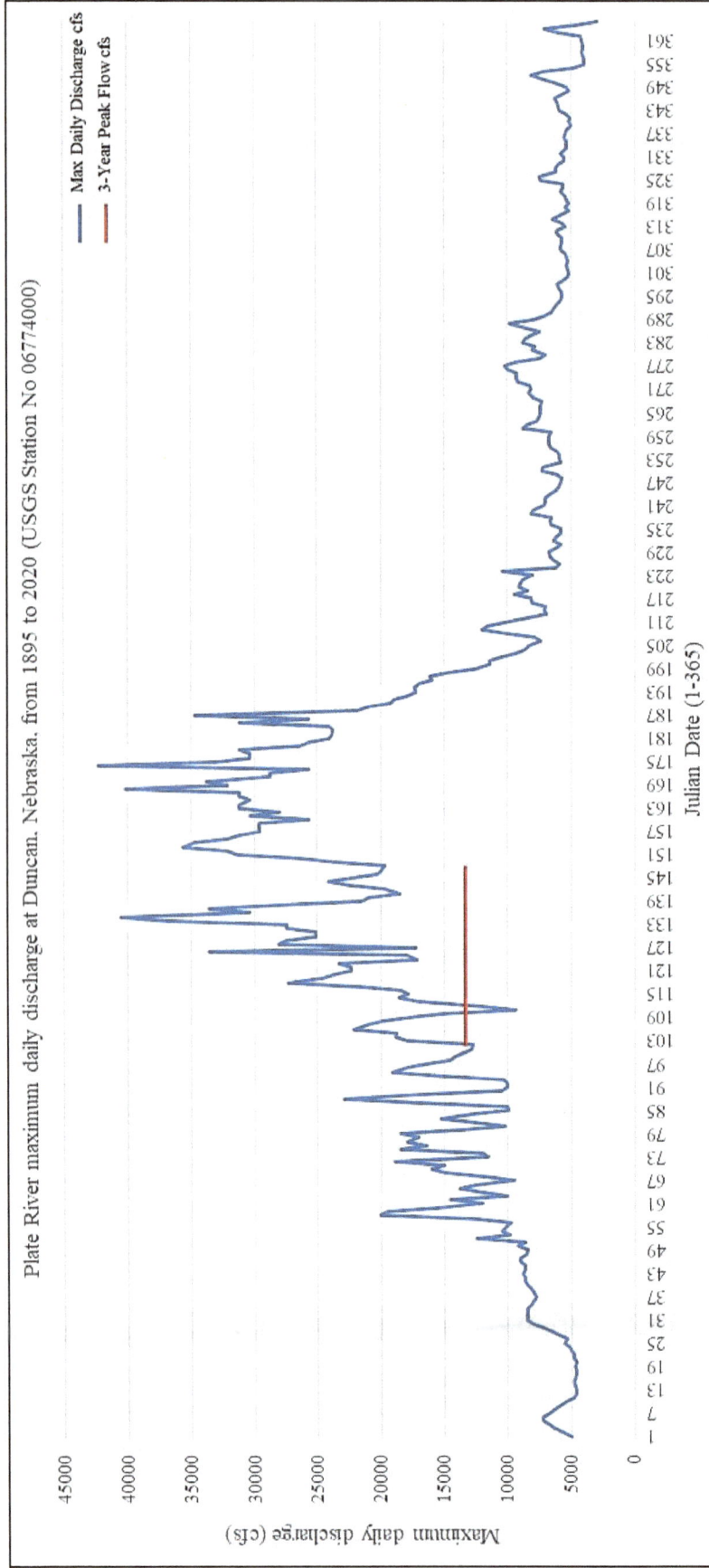

c)

Plate River maximum daily discharge at Duncan. Nebraska. from 1895 to 2020 (USGS Station No 06774000)

Max Daily Discharge cfs
3-Year Peak Flow cfs

Maximum daily discharge (cfs)

Julian Date (1-365)

176

**Figure 3.** Mean annual daily discharge with target flow recommendations to promote long-term ecological function and resilience in the Platte River Valley. Recommendations include minimum flow recommendations for fish communities (orange), Sandhill Cranes (red), Whooping Cranes (purple), wet meadows (black), and seedling germination prevention flows (green).

a)

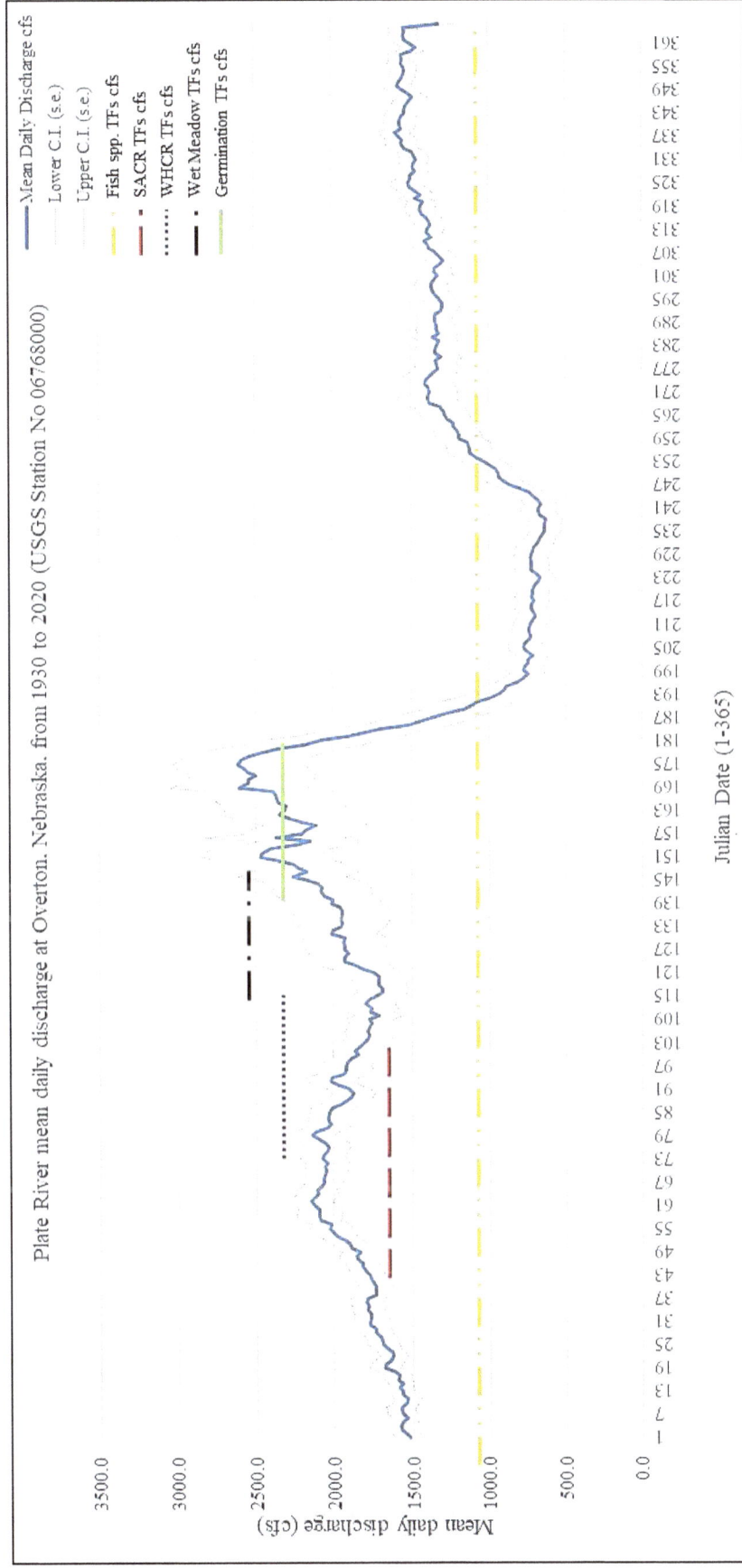

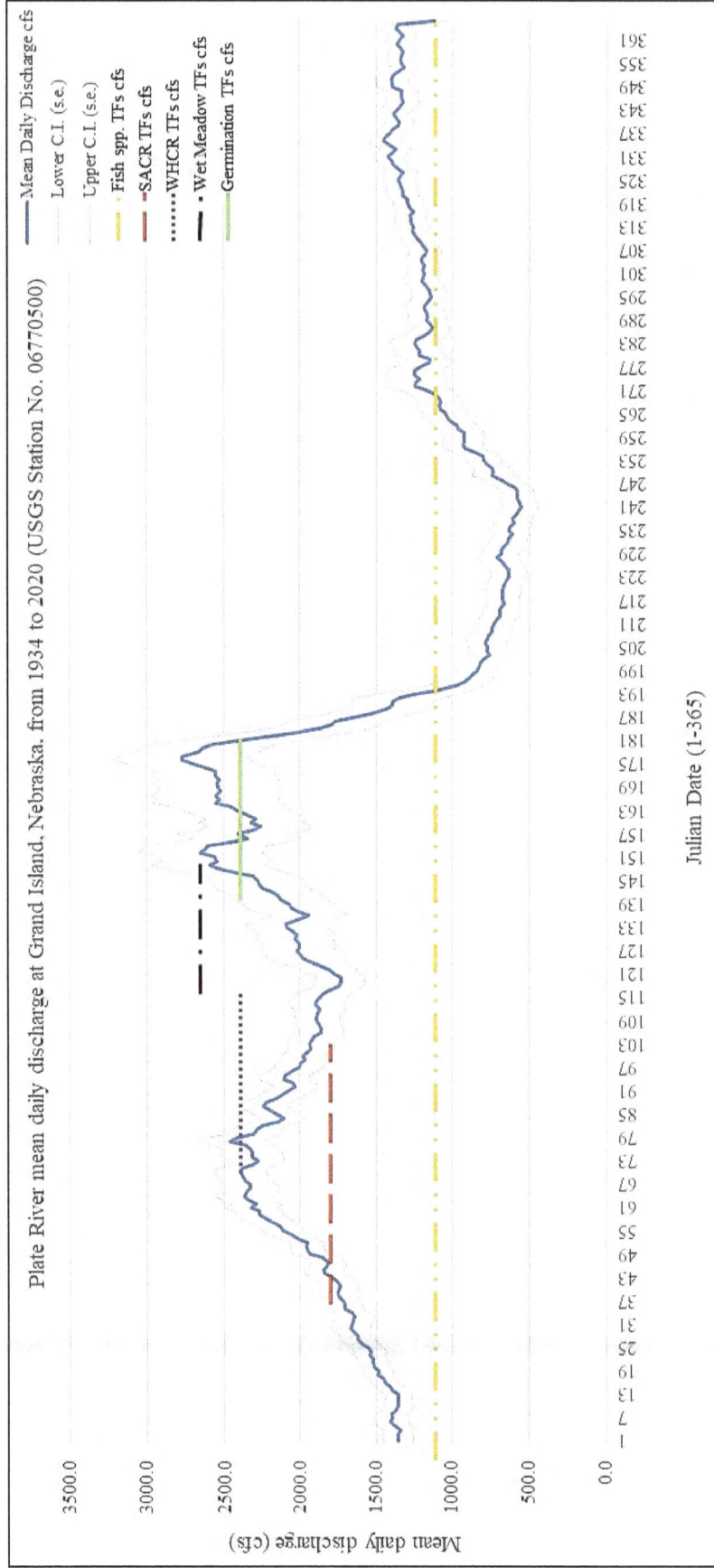

Plate River mean daily discharge at Grand Island, Nebraska. from 1934 to 2020 (USGS Station No. 06770500)

b)

178

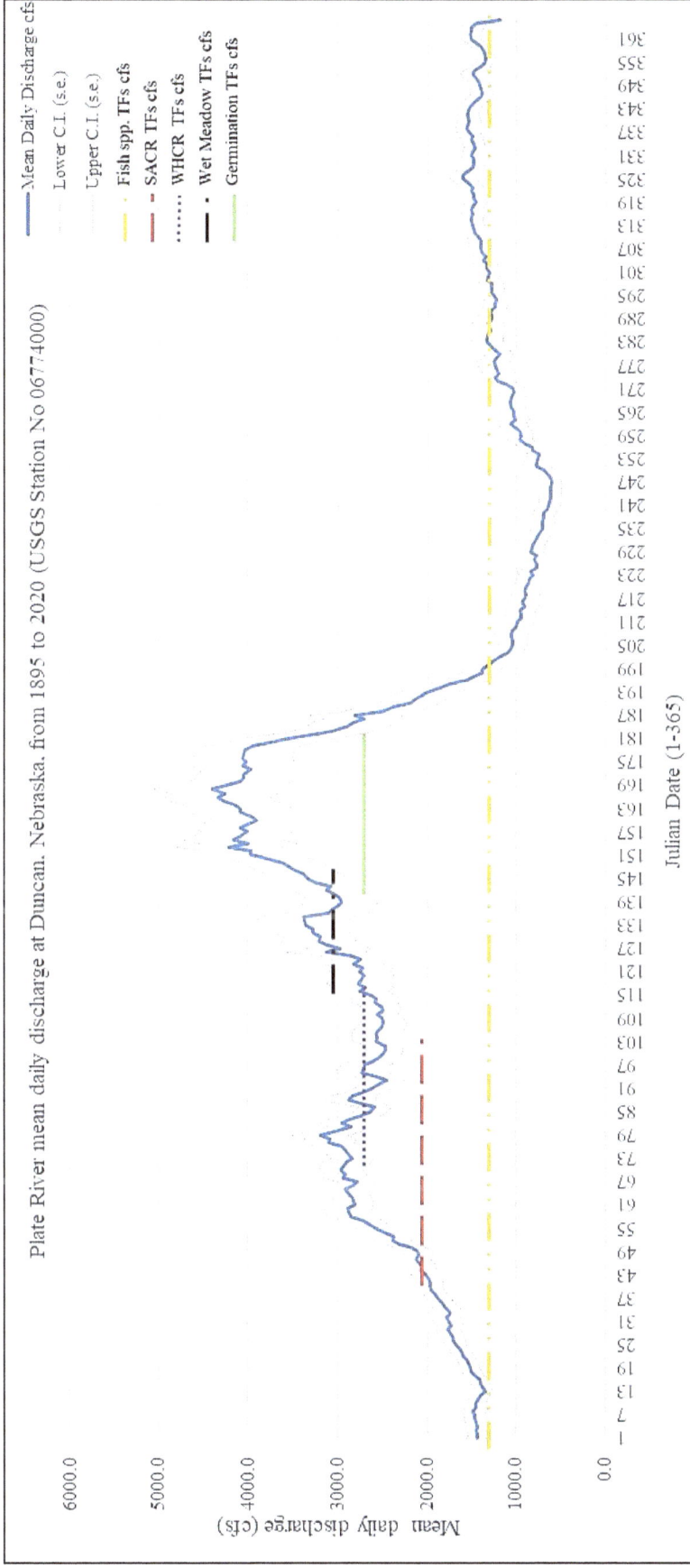

Plate River mean daily discharge at Duncan, Nebraska, from 1895 to 2020 (USGS Station No 06774000)

Legend:
- Mean Daily Discharge cfs
- Lower C.I. (s.e.)
- Upper C.I. (s.e.)
- Fish spp. TFs cfs
- SACR TFs cfs
- WHCR TFs cfs
- Wet Meadow TFs cfs
- Germination TFs cfs

Y-axis: Mean daily discharge (cfs) — 0.0, 1000.0, 2000.0, 3000.0, 4000.0, 5000.0, 6000.0

X-axis: Julian Date (1-365) — 1, 7, 13, 19, 25, 31, 37, 43, 49, 55, 61, 67, 73, 79, 85, 91, 97, 103, 109, 115, 121, 127, 133, 139, 145, 151, 157, 163, 169, 175, 181, 187, 193, 199, 205, 211, 217, 223, 229, 235, 241, 247, 253, 259, 265, 271, 277, 283, 289, 295, 301, 307, 313, 319, 325, 331, 337, 343, 349, 355, 361

c)

179

**Figure 4.** The total number of farming operations per county in the central Platte River Valley along with the number of acres of corn planted by county. Census data starts in 1997 and is every five years, while the agricultural survey data from USDA is every year (NASS 2017).

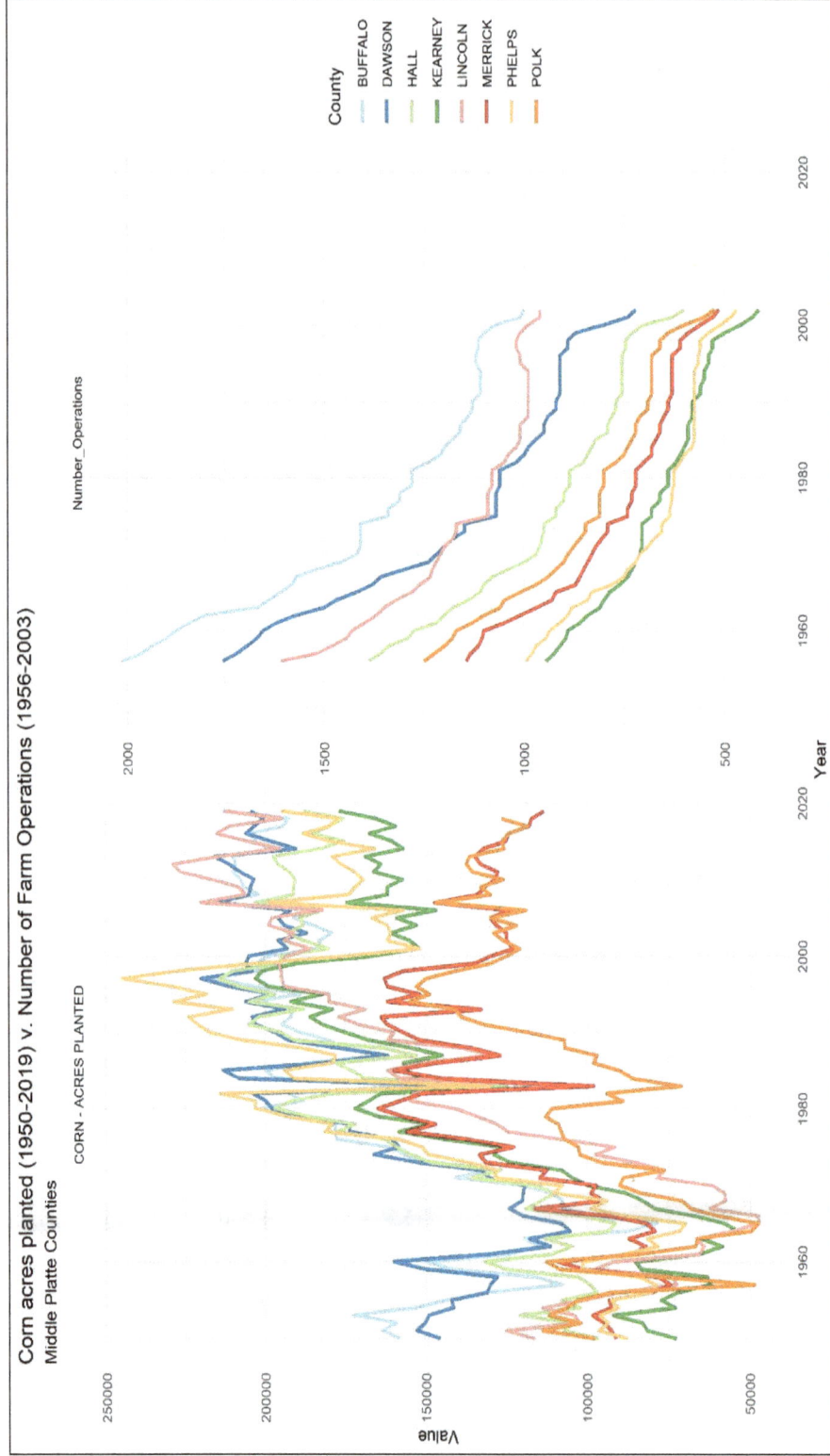

**Figure 5.** Proportional distribution of total crops grown in central Platte River Valley counties from 1960-2018 (NASS 2020)

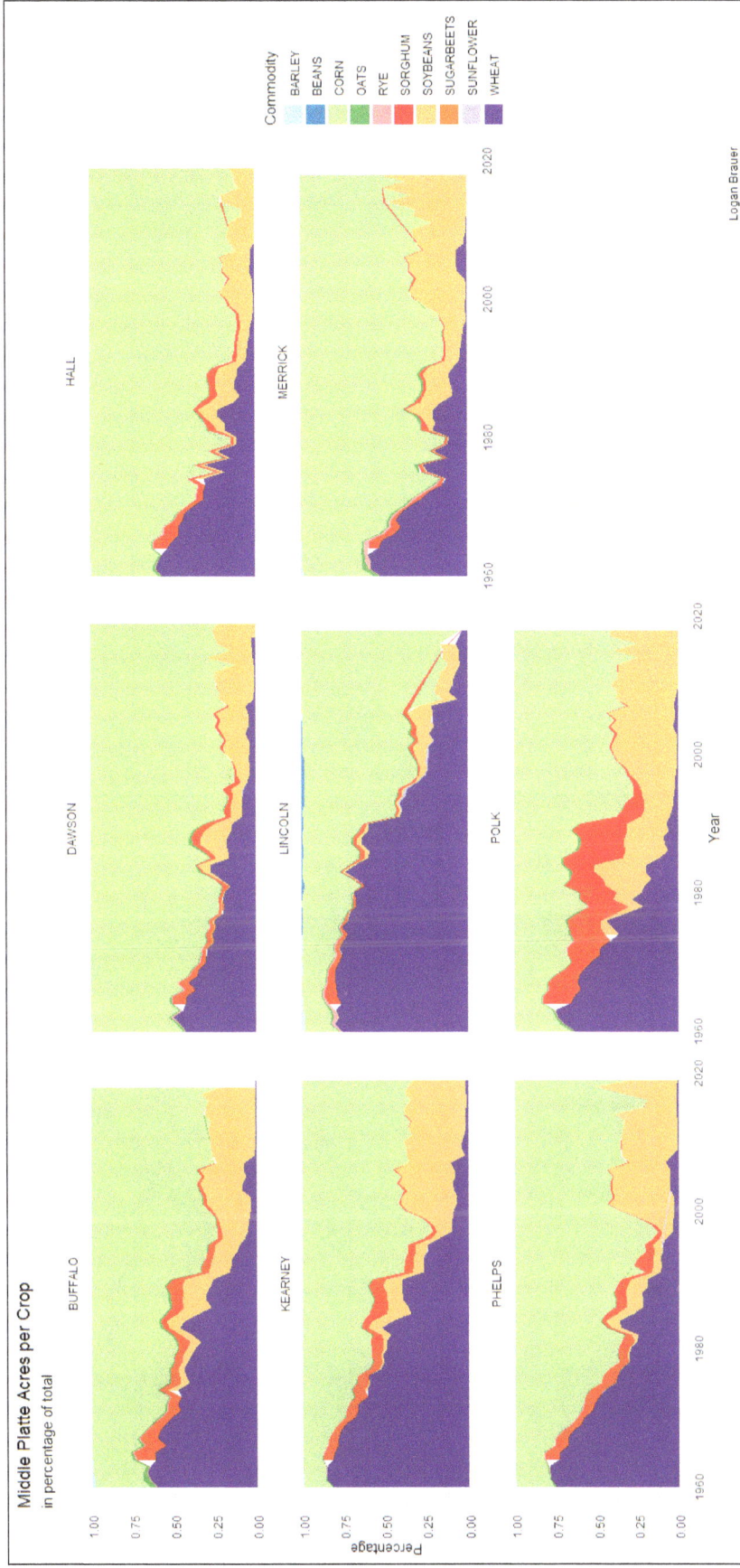

181

**Figure 6.** The use of nitrogen and phosphorus fertilizer in the CPV between 1987-2012 in thousands of pounds (data from Brakebill and Gronberg 2017).

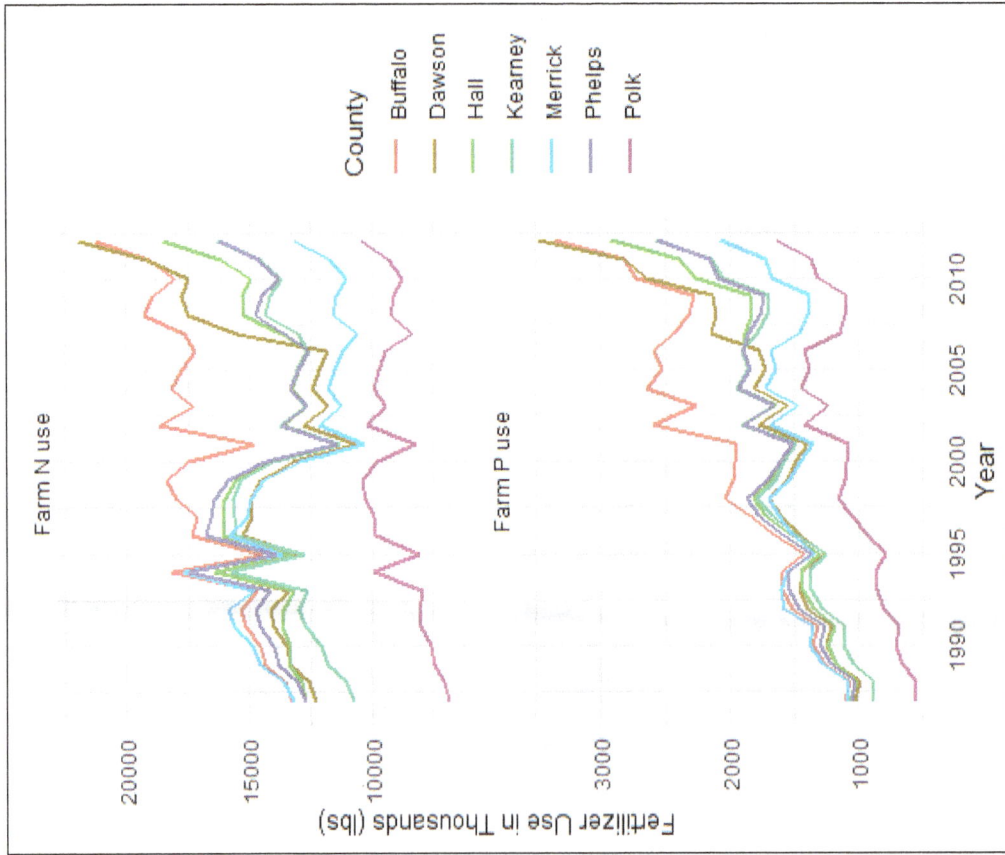

182

**APPENDIX 1.** Vison for an Ecologically Sound Platte River (VESPR) Landscape Design Planning Process Priority Species

| Taxa | Common Name | Scientific Name | Target Habitats Used | General Region | Life History | NGPC Tier | ESA Status | Other Justification |
|------|-------------|-----------------|----------------------|----------------|--------------|-----------|------------|---------------------|
| Amphibia | Blanchard's Cricket Frog | *Acris blanchardi* | Warm-water Slough (permanent)/Braided River | Central, Lower | Resident | 2 | - | - |
| Amphibia | Boreal Chorus Frog | *Pseudacris maculata* | Wet Meadow | Central, Lower | Resident | - | - | Adams et al. 2013 |
| Amphibia | Cope's Grey Treefrog | *Hyla chrysoscelis* | Riparian Woodland/Wet Meadow/Shallow Marsh | Central, Lower | Resident | - | - | Adams et al. 2013 |
| Amphibia | Plains Leopard Frog | *Lithobates blairi* | Warm-water Slough/Braided River | Central, Lower | Resident | - | - | Adams et al. 2013 |
| Aves | American Avocet | *Recurvirostra americana* | Braided River | Central | Migrant | 2 | - | - |
| Aves | American Wigeon | *Anas americana* | Braided River | Central, Lower | Migrant/Wintering | 2 | - | - |
| Aves | Bald Eagle | *Haliaeetus leucocephalus* | Riparian Woodland/Braided River | Central, Lower | Migrant/Resident | 2 | - | - |
| Aves | Baltimore Oriole | *Icterus galbula* | Riparian Woodland | Central, Lower | Breeding | - | - | Rosenberg et al. 2016 |
| Aves | Black Tern | *Chlidonias niger* | Braided River | Central, Lower | Migrant | 1 | - | - |
| Aves | Black-and-white Warbler | *Mniotilta varia* | Riparian Woodland | Central, Lower | Migrant | 2 | - | - |
| Aves | Black-billed Cuckoo | *Coccyzus erythrophthalmus* | Riparian Woodland | Central, Lower | Breeding/Migrant | 1 | - | - |
| Aves | Bobolink | *Dolichonyx oryzivorus* | Wet Meadow/Lowland Tallgrass Prairie | Central, Lower | Breeding/Migrant | - | - | Wilsey et al. 2019 |
| Aves | Canvasback | *Aythya valisineria* | Warm-water Slough (permanent) | Central, Lower | Migrant | 2 | - | - |
| Aves | Dark-eyed Junco | *Junco hyemalis* | Riparian Woodland | Central, Lower | Migrant/Wintering | 2 | - | - |
| Aves | Dickcissel | *Spiza americana* | Lowland Tallgrass Prairie | Central, Lower | Breeding/Migrant | - | - | Rosenberg et al. 2016 |
| Aves | Eastern Meadowlark | *Sturnella magna* | Lowland Tallgrass Prairie/Wet Meadow | Central, Lower | Breeding/Migrant | 2 | - | - |
| Aves | Forster's Tern | *Sterna forsteri* | Braided River | Central, Lower | Migrant | 2 | - | - |
| Aves | Grasshopper Sparrow | *Ammodramus savannarum* | Lowland Tallgrass Prairie | Central, Lower | Breeding/Migrant | - | - | Wilsey et al. 2019 |
| Aves | Greater Prairie-Chicken | *Tympanuchus cupido* | Lowland Tallgrass Prairie | Central | Resident | 2 | - | - |
| Aves | Harris's Sparrow | *Zonotrichia querula* | Lowland Tallgrass Prairie (shrub phase) | Central, Lower | Migrant/Wintering | - | - | Rosenberg et al. 2016 |
| Aves | Henslow's Sparrow | *Ammodramus henslowii* | Lowland Tallgrass Prairie | Central, Lower | Breeding/Migrant | 1 | - | - |
| Aves | Interior Least Tern | *Sternula antillarum athalassos* | Braided River | Central, Lower | Breeding | 1 | Endangered | - |
| Aves | Lesser Scaup | *Aythya affinis* | Warm-water Slough (permanent) | Central, Lower | Migrant | 2 | - | - |
| Aves | Loggerhead Shrike | *Lanius ludovicianus* | Lowland Tallgrass Prairie (shrub phase) | Central, Lower | Breeding/Migrant | 1 | - | - |
| Aves | Marsh Wren | *Cistothorus palustris* | Shallow Marsh | Central, Lower | Breeding/Migrant | 2 | - | - |

| Class | Common Name | Scientific Name | Habitat | Region | Status | No. | Listing | Reference |
|---|---|---|---|---|---|---|---|---|
| Aves | Merlin | Falco columbarius | Lowland Tallgrass Prairie/Wet Meadow/Riparian Woodland | Central, Lower | Migrant/Wintering | 2 | - | - |
| Aves | Northern Bobwhite | Colinus virginianus | Lowland Tallgrass Prairie (shrub phase) | Central, Lower | Resident | - | - | Wilsey et al. 2019 |
| Aves | Northern Pintail | Anas acuta | Braided River | Central, Lower | Migrant/Wintering | 2 | - | - |
| Aves | Pied-billed Grebe | Podilymbus podiceps | Warm-water Slough (permanent) | Central, Lower | Migrant/Breeding | 2 | - | - |
| Aves | Piping Plover | Charadrius melodus | Braided River | Central, Lower | Breeding | 1 | Threatened | - |
| Aves | Prairie Falcon | Falco mexicanus | Lowland Tallgrass Prairie | Central, Lower | Wintering | 2 | - | - |
| Aves | Rose-breasted Grosbeak | Pheucticus ludovicianus | Riparian Woodland | Central, Lower | Breeding/Migrant | - | - | Rosenberg et al. 2016 |
| Aves | Ruby-throated Hummingbird | Archilochus colubris | Riparian Woodland/Lowland Tallgrass Prairie (shrub phase) | Central, Lower | Migrant/Breeding | 2 | - | - |
| Aves | Sandhill Crane | Grus canadensis | Braided River/Wet Meadow/Shallow Marsh | Central | Migrant | 2 | - | - |
| Aves | Savannah Sparrow | Passerculus sandwichensis | Lowland Tallgrass Prairie/Wet Meadow | Central, Lower | Migrant | 2 | - | - |
| Aves | Short-eared Owl | Asio flammeus | Wet Meadow/Lowland Tallgrass Prairie | Central, Lower | Wintering/Resident | 1 | - | - |
| Aves | Swamp Sparrow | Melospiza georgiana | Shallow Marsh | Central, Lower | Migrant/Breeding | 2 | - | - |
| Aves | Upland Sandpiper | Bartramia longicauda | Lowland Tallgrass Prairie | Central, Lower | Breeding/Migrant | - | - | Wilsey et al. 2019 |
| Aves | Vesper Sparrow | Pooecetes gramineus | Lowland Tallgrass/Wet Meadow | Central, Lower | Migrant/Breeding | - | - | Wilsey et al. 2019 |
| Aves | Western Meadowlark | Sturnella neglecta | Lowland Tallgrass Prairie | Central, Lower | Resident | - | - | Wilsey et al. 2019 |
| Aves | Whooping Crane | Grus americana | Braided River/Wet Meadow/Shallow Marsh | Central | Migrant | 1 | Endangered | - |
| Aves | Wood Thrush | Hylocichla mustelina | Riparian Woodland | Lower | Migrant/Breeding | 1 | - | - |
| Aves | Yellow-billed Cuckoo | Coccyzus americanus | Riparian Woodland | Central, Lower | Breeding/Migrant | 2 | - | - |
| Osteichthyes | Blue Sucker | Cycleptus elongatus | Braided River | Lower | Resident | 1 | - | - |
| Osteichthyes | Brassy Minnow | Hybognathus hankinsoni | Warm-water Sloughs | Central, Lower | Resident | - | - | Rondeau et al. 2011 |
| Osteichthyes | Common Shiner | Luxilus cornutus | Braided River | Central, Lower | Resident | 2 | - | - |
| Osteichthyes | Finescale Dace | Chrosomus neogaeus | Braided River | Lower | Resident | 1 | - | - |
| Osteichthyes | Flathead Chub | Platygobio gracilis | Braided River | Lower | Resident | 1 | - | - |
| Osteichthyes | Johnny Darter | Etheostoma nigrum | Warm-water Sloughs | Central, Lower | Resident | - | - | Rohweder 2015 |
| Osteichthyes | Lake Sturgeon | Acipenser fulvescens | Braided River | Lower | Resident | 1 | - | - |
| Osteichthyes | Northern Redbelly Dace | Chrosomus eos | Braided River | Lower | Resident | 1 | - | - |
| Osteichthyes | Pallid Sturgeon | Scaphirhynchus albus | Braided River | Lower | Resident | 1 | Endangered | - |
| Osteichthyes | Plains Minnow | Hybognathus placitus | Braided River | Central, Lower | Resident | 1 | - | - |
| Osteichthyes | Plains Topminnow | Fundulus sciadicus | Warm-water Sloughs | Central, Lower | Resident (endemic) | 1 | - | - |
| Osteichthyes | Sturgeon Chub | Macrhybopsis gelida | Braided River | Lower | Resident | 1 | - | - |
| Osteichthyes | Western Silvery Minnow | Hybognathus argyritis | Braided River | Central, Lower | Resident | 1 | - | - |
| Insecta | Aphrodite Fritillary | Speyeria aphrodite | Lowland Tallgrass Prairie/Wet Meadow | Central, Lower | Resident | 2 | - | - |

| Class | Common Name | Scientific Name | Habitat | Region | Status | Number | State Status | Citation |
|---|---|---|---|---|---|---|---|---|
| Insecta | Iowa Skipper | *Atrytone arogos iowa* | Lowland Tallgrass Prairie | Lower | Resident | 1 | - | - |
| Insecta | Married Underwing | *Catocala nuptialis* | Lowland Tallgrass Prairie | Central, Lower | Resident | 1 | - | - |
| Insecta | Monarch | *Danaus plexippus* | Riparian Woodland/Lowland Tallgrass Prairie | Central, Lower | Migrant | 1 | Candidate | - |
| Insecta | Nebraska (Silver-bordered) Fritillary | *Boloria selene nebraskensis* | Wet Meadow/Shallow Marsh | Central, Lower | Resident | 1 | - | - |
| Insecta | Platte River Caddisfly | *Ironoquia plattensis* | Warm-water Sloughs (semipermanent) | Central | Resident (endemic) | 1 | - | - |
| Insecta | Regal Fritillary | *Speyeria idalia* | Lowland Tallgrass Prairie | Central, Lower | Resident | 1 | Candidate | - |
| Insecta | Smoky-eyed Brown | *Lethe (Satyrodes) eurydice fumosa* | Wet Meadows | Central, Lower | Resident | 1 | - | - |
| Insecta | Southern Plains Bumble Bee | *Bombus fraternus* | Lowland Tallgrass Prairie | Central (confirmed 2020) | Resident | 1 | - | - |
| Insecta | Two-spotted Skipper | *Euphyes bimacula illinois* | Wet Meadow | Central | Resident | 1 | - | - |
| Insecta | Whitney Underwing | *Catocala whitneyi* | Lowland Tallgrass Prairie | Central, Lower | Resident | 1 | - | - |
| Mammalia | Eastern Red Bat | *Lasiurus borealis* | Riparian Woodland | Central, Lower | Breeding/Migrant | 1 | - | - |
| Mammalia | Hoary Bat | *Lasiurus cinereus* | Riparian Woodland | Central, Lower | Breeding/Migrant | 1 | - | - |
| Mammalia | Long-tailed Weasel | *Mustela frenata* | Riparian Woodland/Lowland Tallgrass Prairie | Central, Lower | Resident | 2 | - | - |
| Mammalia | Meadow Jumping Mouse | *Zapus hudsonius* | Wet Meadow/Lowland Tallgrass Prairie | Central, Lower | Resident | - | - | Frey and Malaney 2009 |
| Mammalia | Mountain Lion | *Felis concolor* | Riparian Woodland/Lowland Tallgrass Prairie | Central, Lower | Dispersal | 2 | - | - |
| Mammalia | North American Beaver | *Castor canadensis* | Braided River/Warm-water Slough | Central, Lower | Resident | - | - | Baker and Hill 2003 |
| Mammalia | North American River Otter | *Lontra canadensis* | Braided River/Warm-water Slough | Central, Lower | Resident | - | - | Panella and Wilson 2018 |
| Mammalia | Plains Pocket Mouse | *Perognathus flavescens perniger* | Lowland Tallgrass Prairie (sandy ridge component) | Central | Resident | 1 | - | - |
| Mammalia | Silver-haired Bat | *Lasionycteris noctivagans* | Riparian Woodland | Central, Lower | Migrant/Breeding | 1 | - | - |
| Mollusca | Niobrara Ambersnail | *Oxyloma haydeni* | Braided River | Lower | Resident | 1 | - | - |
| Mollusca | Pimpleback | *Quadrula pustulosa* | Braided River | Lower | Resident | 1 | - | - |
| Reptilia | Blanding's Turtle | *Emydoidea blandingii* | Shallow Marsh/Deep Marsh/Braided River | Lower | Resident | 1 | - | - |
| Reptilia | Lined Snake | *Tropidoclonion lineatum* | Lowland Tallgrass Prairie/Wet Meadow | Central, Lower | Resident | - | - | SD GFP 2014 |
| Reptilia | Northern Prairie Skink | *Plestiodon septentrionalis* | Lowland Tallgrass Prairie | Central, Lower | Resident | - | - | Reeder and Clymer 2015 |
| Reptilia | Red-bellied Snake | *Storeria occipitomaculata* | Riparian Woodland | Central | Resident | 1 | - | - |
| Reptilia | Smooth Green Snake | *Liochlorophis vernalis* | Lowland Tallgrass Prairie | Central | Resident | 2 | - | - |
| Reptilia | Smooth Soft-shelled Turtle | *Apalone mutica* | Braided River/Warm-water Slough | Central, Lower | Resident | 2 | - | - |

185

| | Common Name | Scientific Name | Habitat | Region | Status | | | |
|---|---|---|---|---|---|---|---|---|
| Reptilia | Western Massasauga | *Sistrurus tergeminus* | Wet Meadow/Shallow Marsh/Lowland Tallgrass Prairie | Lower | Resident | 1 | - | - |
| Plantae | Cardinal Flower | *Lobelia cardinalis* | Wet Meadow/Shallow Marsh | Central, Lower | Resident | 2 | - | - |
| Plantae | Smooth False Foxglove | *Agalinis purpurea* | Wet Meadow/Lowland Tallgrass Prairie | Central, Lower | Resident | 2 | - | - |
| Plantae | Western Prairie Fringed Orchid | *Platanthera praeclara* | Wet Meadow/Lowland Tallgrass Prairie | Central, Lower | Resident | 1 | - | - |

APPENDIX 2. Results of cooperative landscape design process including *Future Desired Conditions* (conservation contexts we hope to ultimately observe), *Processes* (biotic or abiotic mechanisms that create landscape patterns), *Drivers* (human influences on processes and the resulting patterns), *Key Audiences* (stakeholders with a vested interest in the management of a relevant resource), *Needed Actions* (measures aimed at achieving a desired outcome via promotion of a "process" or mitigation of a "driver"), *Quantitative Goals* (achievable plans that are based on objective measures), *Confidence* (certainty that meeting the "quantitative goal" would achieve the "desired condition").

| Future Desired Conditions | Processes | Drivers | Key Audiences | Needed Actions | Quantitative Goals | Confidence 1(Low)–5(High) |
|---|---|---|---|---|---|---|
| Increased the extent and resilience of wide and ecologically functional **braided river** habitats for the benefit of waterbirds (e.g., Whooping Crane, Baird's Sandpiper) and other species. | Sustainable **transportation** of a sufficient amount of **sediment** comprised of appropriate grain sizes. | **Dams** - sediment trapping and restriction, reduction in and retiming of river flows. | CNPPID, NPPD, PRRIP, USBR, USFWS | Increased sediment transportation around dams/diversions using bypass systems. Remove dams/diversions that are no longer in use. Ensure new dams/diversions include sediment bypass systems. | 1) Promote installation of a sediment and flow bypass system at the Tri-County Canal Diversion Dam. 2) Restore 400,000 tons of appropriately sized sediment (<0.90 mm diameter) to the Platte River annually between Lexington and Grand Island through augmentation and sediment bypass systems. | 4 |
| | **Peak flows** that replicate the historic ecosystem's structure and function including the periodic scouring of vegetation from the active channel bed, the building and migration of sandbars, and nutrient exchange across riparian wetlands. | **Hydrocycling** - drastic and unnatural fluctuations in streamflow downstream from the hydroplant near Roscoe, Nebraska. | | Sustained base flows that subsists through hydrocycling. | Flatten daily hydrocycling from the hydropower plant to include a sustained base flow of ≥200 cfs for the majority of the year. | 2 |
| | **Base flows** that prevent vegetation establishment within the active river channel during the growing | **Diversions** and **canals** - reduction in sustained and peak river flows, some sediment restriction | CNPPID, Farm, Loc. Land, NEDNR, NRDs, | Limit further diversions of Platte River water. Decommission canals that not functional or no longer in use. | Decommission unused or unfunctional diversion canals (>1,000 in PRV and tributaries) so that there are ≤0 net new canals over the next 50 years. | 3 |

| | | | | |
|---|---|---|---|---|
| season and maintain healthy fish populations of native fish throughout the year. | and removal from active channel. | | | 2 |
| | **Intensive groundwater extraction** - high groundwater demand to support extensive center pivot irrigation during a period of relative water limitation in the CPRV, which is fully or over-appropriated throughout. | NSIA, UNL-NWC | Increase efficiency in agricultural systems through metering. Restrict additional groundwater appropriations in NE within fully appropriated river valleys, including the Platte and its tributaries. | 1) Achieve >90% water meter use on agricultural irrigation wells in the PRV in the next 20 years via grant funding and policy advocacy. 2) Develop policy recommendations that allow actors to temporarily transfer water rights to the river for conservation purposes and share with elected officials. 3) Zero new net appropriations for groundwater extraction from the PRV in the next 50 years. |
| | **Streamflow policies** - largely based on outdated science that recommend peak flows that are insufficient in magnitude and duration to promote essential ecological processes (e.g., river scouring). | NEDNR, NRDs, NWS, PRRIP, USFWS | Update policy recommendations based on a comprehensive review of current science. | Metadata analyses indicate that sustained flows ($\geq$20 days) of $\geq$12,000 cfs (340 cms) at Grand Island, $\geq$11,400 cfs (323 cms) at Overton, and $\geq$13,700 cfs (388 cms) at Duncan, Nebraska, will help maintain functional braided river habitat. | 5 |
| | **Increasing demand by municipalities** - there has been and will continue to be an increased demand for water by growing towns and cities within the PRV for human consumption, maintenance of parks and lawns, industry, and other uses. | CODNR, CWCB, Municipal, NEDNR, SPROWG | Increase efficiency of municipal water users (golf courses, etc.). Educate communities the depend on the Platte River directly or indirectly for water through public outreach efforts and encourage water conservation practices. | 1) Develop information campaign reaching >10,000 people within the next 10 years to promote water conservation. 2) Coordinate with municipalities in the PRV to improve water conservation practices at public parks and golf courses. | 1 |

| Threat | Stakeholders | Strategy | Objectives | |
|---|---|---|---|---|
| **Climate change** - decreasing snowpack and potentially reduced flows in the mid-late summer in the decades ahead. | CNPPID, Cons. Orgs., NEDNR, NRDs, Public, Reg. Univ., State Leg. | Advocate for sustainable management of water resources to increase ecosystem resilience to climate change. Conserve more water in reservoirs near the headwaters to allow for delayed releases to maintain summer base flows in the mainstem Platte River. | Conserve 10% more water in upstream reservoirs for late spring and early summer release. Maintain minimum flows of 1,100 cfs (28 cms) at Overton, 1,160 cfs (33 cms) at Grand Island, and 1,320 cfs (37 cms) at Duncan, Nebraska, to maintain fish communities during summer high temperatures. Depending on conditions, it is likely that larger growing season flows will be necessary to prevent woody encroachment within the active channel bed (1,200-3,000 cfs, 34-85 cms). | 3 |
| **Development/Suburban Sprawl** - increased development of housing, commerce, and intensive agriculture within the floodplain, promoting negative impacts to human communities from natural high flow events. | CBS, Cons. Orgs., Farm, Livestock, Loc. Land, Municipal, NGPC | Coordinate with states, counties, and municipalities to promote zoning policies that limit development in the floodplain. Protect undeveloped tracts adjacent to the Platte River through easement, purchase, and coordination with local landowners (prioritize herbaceous habitats). | 1) Restore >30% of the land within 0.5 miles of the Platte River to wetland or grassland habitat via tree clearing and crop ground restoration. 2) Limit new development within 0.5 miles of the Platte River via coordination with regional land use planning officials and private landowners. | 4 |
| **Bridges and crossings** - sediment transportation and river flows are spatially restricted, increased flooding during high flow events. | CNTY HWYs, CNTY Off., FHA, NDOT, NEDNR, USDOT | Widen bridges and crossings to increase flow conveyance. Prioritize areas that limit our current ability to promote high flow events through Kingsley Dam releases (e.g., North Platte "Choke Point"). | 1) Advocate for 300 m (985 ft) minimum widths for all new and reconstructed bridges on the main channel of the Platte River. 2) Achieve 6,000 cfs (170 cms) capacity at the North Platte Choke Point (i.e., 50% of necessary peak flow at Grand Island) through restoration, engineering, and property acquisition projects. | 4 |

| | Element / Threat | Partners | Objective | Strategies / Actions | Priority |
|---|---|---|---|---|---|
| | Increased spatial extent of **sand and gravel mining operations** - this exposes shallow groundwater to evaporative influences and decreases groundwater levels in the hyporheic zone. | CBS, Cons. Orgs., Gravel, Loc. Land, NDEE, NGPC, USFWS | Reduce incidents of new sand and gravel mining operations in the Platte River floodplain by working with county boards of supervisors, municipalities, and the state to limit the availability of special use permits for mining in lands zoned as agricultural-conservation areas. | 1) Create map of high potential sand and gravel mine locations overlaid with unprotected remnant prairie and wetland habitats. 2) Estimate evaporative losses from sand and gravel mining operations. 3) Prevent new sand and gravel mining in remnant habitats within 800 m of the main channel of the Platte River, in locations zoned as agricultural-conservation areas through coordination with local officials and industry as well as via conservation easements. | 2 |
| | **Exotic/invasive species** - species such as Common Reed (*P. australis*) limit the ability of natural high flows to scour the riverbed and facilitate sandbar migrations. | Cons. Orgs., CWB, Loc. Land, NDA, PVWMA, WCWMA | Coordinated and widespread management of in-channel vegetation encroachment through river disking and herbicide treatments. Build capacity of cooperative invasive/exotic species control programs by garnering a sustainable source of funds. | Develop an annual funding mechanism of $600,000 to contain undesirable species outbreaks in all ecologically important PRV habitats on public, private, or nonprofit lands. | 4 |
| Improved **water quality** in the Platte River and tributaries. | **Filtration** of Platte River flows through functional riparian wetlands. / **Point-source pollution** (e.g., runoff from concentrated animal feeding operations; CAFOs). | NDEE, NRCS, Municipal, Loc. Land, Livestock, Farm, Public, Rec. | Identify and mitigate significant point sources of pollution via coordination with community partners. Advocate for the siting of future CAFOs outside of the floodplain, improve holding pond regulation (e.g., berm height), promote natural buffers. | 1) Promote herbaceous buffers of native vegetation of $\geq$100 m (328 ft) width around CAFOs as well as all waterways. 2) Increase all berms surrounding CAFOs to heights exceeding local flood stage as well as current standard berm heights. 3) Prevent any new CAFOs from being established within the 100-year floodplain of the Platte River. | 4 |

| Goal | Threat | Partners | Strategy | Objective / Metric | Rank |
|---|---|---|---|---|---|
| **Shallow groundwater** levels that sustain riparian wetlands and maintain good water quality in local aquifers for municipalities. | **Non-point-source pollution** (e.g., fertilizer, herbicide, and pesticide runoff from agricultural fields). | | Reduce chemical inputs (fertilizer, herbicide, etc.) to only those necessary by promoting precision agriculture and no-till farming practices in the PRV agricultural community. | 1) Promote herbaceous buffers of native vegetation of >100 m (328 ft) width around all waterways. 2) Support regional precision agriculture efforts to achieve a 50% reduction in fertilizer use and 100% no-till agricultural in the PRV within ≤25 years. | 4 |
| | **Nitrate infiltration** into groundwater supply as a result of intensive groundwater pumping. | | Increase groundwater conservation measures when depths hit a particular threshold preventing nitrate infiltration. | Maintain base flows of >1,100 cfs (>28 cms) in the Platte River even in dry years. Maintain groundwater depths <2 m across all but "sand ridge prairie" habits on functional PRV islands (e.g., Mormon Island, Indian Island, etc.). | 3 |
| Increased the extent and resilience of **seasonal and temporary wetlands** (wet meadow, shallow marsh) for the benefit of waterbirds (e.g., Short-billed Dowitchers), vascular plants (e.g., Cardinal Flower), herpetofauna (e.g., Boreal Chorus Frogs), and other species. | **Agricultural development** - loss of wet meadows as a result of conversion to row crop monocultures. | Cons. Orgs., Loc. Land, NCA, NDA, NGPC, NRCS, Livestock | Develop a coordinated plan to protect remnant seasonal and temporary wetlands via land acquisitions and conservation easements. Work with local farmers to identify agricultural wetlands that are economically unproductive, restore them to native plants, and protect them with easements including upland buffers (i.e., precision agriculture principals). | 1) Restore >30% of the land within 0.5 miles of the Platte River to wetland or grassland habitat via tree clearing and crop ground restoration. 2) Prioritize the protection and restoration of contiguous habitats ≥575 ha (1,420 acres) as well as patches ≥80 ha (~200 acres) within <2 km of larger contiguous wetland/grassland habitats. 3) Restore or protect smaller habitats if they are high quality, relict, facilitate connectivity, or represent unproductive cropland. | 4 |

| Target | Threat | Partners | Strategy | Action | Priority |
|---|---|---|---|---|---|
| River flows that **inundate or saturate wet meadows** for a sustained period in the spring between mid-February to early May through endosaturation. Inundation depths, extents, and durations that vary from year-to-year and maintain wetland dynamism. | **Residential and commercial development** - loss of wet meadow as a result of urban, suburban, and exurban development. | CBS, Cons. Orgs., Farm, Loc. Land, Livestock, NRCS, NGPC | Develop a coordinated plan to protect remnant seasonal and temporary wetlands via land acquisitions and conservation easements. Support working wetlands by connecting ranchers to conservation programs that provide financial support. Work with municipal and county zoning officials to limit development within the floodplain. | In addition to the above goals, identify and contact all private landowners with significant tracts (≥50 ha - 124 ac) of herbaceous wetland/grassland within 800 m of the Platte River and connect them to conservation programs/easement opportunities to support their livelihoods and prevent these habitats from becoming farmed or developed. | 3 |
| Temporal and spatial heterogeneity in vegetation community and limited woody encroachment as a result of **periodic natural disturbances** including fire, grazing, and rest. | **Sand and gravel mining** - loss of wet meadow as a result of conversion to mining operations. This process also results in a lowered water table as shallow groundwater is exposed through excavation and subject to evaporative losses. | CBS, Cons. Orgs, Gravel, Loc. Land, NDEE, NGPC, USFWS | Develop a coordinated plan to protect remnant seasonal and temporary wetlands via land acquisitions and conservation easements. Support working wetlands by connecting ranchers to conservation programs that provide financial support. Work with county boards of supervisors, municipalities, and the state to limit the availability of special use permits for mining in lands zoned as agricultural-conservation areas. | In addition to the above two goals, conduct meetings with officials involved in zoning from all counties along the Platte River. Urge them to limit the availability of special use permits for mining in lands zoned as agricultural-conservation areas along the Platte River based upon the negative impacts on riverine ecosystems. Counties include Lincoln, Dawson, Phelps, Buffalo, Kearney, Hall, Merrick, Hamilton, Platte, Polk, Colfax, Butler, Dodge, Saunders, Douglas, Sarpy, Cass (17 counties). | 2 |
| | **Exotic/invasive species** - species such as Purple loosestrife (*L. salicaria*) and Reed Canary Grass (*P. arundinacea*) are reducing vascular plant diversity and changing the vegetative structure of seasonal and temporary wetlands. | Cons. Orgs., CWB, Loc. Land, NDA, PVWMA, WCWMA | Build capacity of cooperative invasive/exotic species control programs by garnering a sustainable source of funds. Coordinate efforts to efficiently control exotic/invasive species and evaluate the effectiveness of various techniques where uncertainty remains (e.g., Purple Loosestrife). | Develop a funding mechanism of $600,000 USD annually to contain undesirable species outbreaks in the PRV on public, private, or nonprofit owned lands. | 4 |

| Threat | Actors | Strategy | Goal | Priority |
|---|---|---|---|---|
| **Interbasin Transfers** - attempts to siphon off Platte River high flows that sustain wet meadows to provide water for other stressed watersheds (e.g., Republican). | CNPPID, Cons. Orgs., NEDNR, NPPD, NRDs, PRRIP, USBR, USFWS | Advocate against interbasin transfer proposals from the mainstem Platte River and major tributaries through sounds science and legal means if necessary. | No new interbasin transfers from the Platte River or its major tributaries within Nebraska over the next 50 years. | 2 |
| **Groundwater extraction** - intensive pumping during the growing season drastically lowers the groundwater levels altering ephemeral wetland function. | CNPPID, Farm, Loc. Land, NRDs, NEDNR, UNL-NWC | Increase efficiency in agricultural systems through metering. Restrict additional groundwater appropriations in NE within fully appropriated river valleys, including the Platte and its tributaries. Advocate for policies that allow actors to permanently or temporarily transfer water rights to the river for conservation purposes. | 1) Achieve $\geq$90% water meter use on agricultural irrigation wells in the PRV in the next 20 years via grant funding and policy advocacy. 2) Develop policy recommendations that allow actors to temporarily transfer water rights to the river for conservation purposes and share with elected officials. 3) Zero new net appropriations for groundwater extraction from the PRV in the next 50 years. | 2 |
| **Sediment starvation** resulting in **channel incision** where a "sediment hungry" river erodes the channel bed which reduces the water table elevation impacting the hydroregime of temporary and seasonal wetlands. | CNPPID, NPPD, PRRIP, USBR, USFWS | Increase the load of fine sediment carried by the Platte River via augmentation and the installation of sediment bypass systems where appropriate. Continued disking of the river when appropriate to maintain a flat channel bed. | 1) Promote installation of a sediment and flow bypass system at the Tri-County Canal Diversion Dam. 2) Restore 400,000 tons of appropriately sized sediment (<0.90 mm diameter) to the Platte River annually between Lexington and Grand Island through sediment augmentation and bypass systems. 3) Disk the majority of noticeably incising portions of the main channel during low flow years over the next decade (25% of main channel, chiefly Lexington to Grand Island, and the NPRV west of North Platte). | 3 |

| | | | | | |
|---|---|---|---|---|---|
| | **Streamflow policy** that does not consider the hydrological regimes that sustain functional wet meadows. This includes policies that restrict and minimize flood pulse events as well as those that do not include adequate base flow recommendations. | PRRIP, NEDNR, NWS, NRDs, USFWS | Protect elevated spring flows that result in widespread wet meadow inundation as well as base flows that maintain hydrologic connectivity between plant communities and groundwater resources. | Metadata analyses indicate that sustained flows ($\geq$20 days) of $\geq$12,000 cfs (340 cms) at an interval of $\leq$3 years at Grand Island, $\geq$11,400 cfs (323 cms) at Overton, and $\geq$13,700 cfs (388 cms) at Duncan, Nebraska, will help maintain functional braided river habitat and help sustain wet meadows. Annually, May flows should exceed 2,650 cfs (75 cms) at Grand Island (>2,520 cfs at Overton and >3,020 cfs at Duncan), with at least one week of elevated flows between 3,400 cfs (96 cms) and 5,900 cfs (167 cms) for the maintenance of wet meadows and shallow marshes. | 4 |
| | Intensive, repetitive **grazing** and **haying** - applying the same management regimes annually with the expectation of maximizing incomes can lead to a homogenization of the biotic community. | Cons. Orgs., Farm, Livestock, Loc. Land, NCA, NGLC, NRCS, NRDs | Connect ranchers to conservation programs that provide financial support for periodically resting herbaceous wetlands. Provide outreach to interested parties outlining the habitat needs of at-risk species that depend on herbaceous wetlands. | Identify and attempt to contact all private landowners with significant tracts (>50 ha - 124 ac) of herbaceous wetland/grassland within 800 m of the Platte River and connect them with conservation programs or easements (e.g., NRCS) that would allow them to periodically rest their wetlands/grasslands without financial losses. | 4 |

| | | | | | |
|---|---|---|---|---|---|
| Increased the extent and resilience of semi-permanent and perennial **warm-water slough wetlands** for the benefit of waterbirds (e.g., Blue-winged Teal), aquatic mammals (e.g., Northern River Otters), native fishes (e.g., Plains Topminnow), aquatic insects (e.g., Platte River Caddisfly), and other species. | **Sediment starvation resulting in channel incision** where a "sediment hungry" river erodes the channel bed which reduces the water table elevation impacting the hydroregime of warm-water sloughs. | CNPPID, NPPD, PRRIP, USBR, USFWS | Warm-water sloughs present at an appropriate **scale and interconnectedness** to facilitate important ecological processes (e.g., wildlife dispersal, etc.). | 1) Promote installation of a sediment and flow bypass system at the Tri-County Canal Diversion Dam. 2) Restore 400,000 tons of appropriately sized sediment (<0.90 mm diameter) to the Platte River annually between Lexington and Grand Island through sediment augmentation and bypass systems. 3) Disk the majority of noticeably incising portions of the main channel during low flow years over the next decade (25% of main channel, chiefly Lexington to Grand Island, NE). | 3 |
| | Increase the load of fine sediment carried by the Platte River via augmentation and the installation of sediment bypass systems where appropriate. Continued disking of the river when appropriate to maintain a flat channel bed. | | | | |
| River flows that **sustain inundation in warm-water sloughs** throughout the year via endosaturation. Depths should vary from year-to-year to maintain wetland dynamism. | **Streamflow policy** that does not consider the hydrological regimes that sustain functional permanent and semi-permanent sloughs. This includes policies that restrict and minimize flood pulse events as well as those that do not include adequate base flow recommendations. | NEDNR, NRDs, NWS, PRRIP, USFWS | Protect elevated spring flows that promote fluctuation in slough depths and base flows that maintain inundations through most of the growing season. | Annually, May flows should exceed 2,650 cfs (75 cms) at Grand Island (>2,520 cfs at Overton and >3,020 cfs at Duncan), with at least one week of elevated flows between 3,400 cfs (96 cms) and 5,900 cfs (167 cms) for the maintenance of warm-water sloughs. Base flows of 1,100 cfs (28 cms) at Overton, 1,160 cfs (33 cms) at Grand Island, 1,320 cfs (37 cms) at Duncan, 1,800 cfs (51 cms) at North Bend, and 3,700 cfs (105 cms) at Louisville, Nebraska, should be maintained as target flows (even in dry years) to sustain warm-water sloughs. | 4 |

| Desired Condition / Threat | Partners | Strategy | Action | Priority |
|---|---|---|---|---|
| Temporal and spatial heterogeneity in the vegetation community and limited woody encroachment as a result of **periodic natural disturbances** including fire, grazing, and rest within as well as on the margins of warm-water sloughs.<br><br>**Exotic/invasive species** - species such as Common Reed (*P. australis*) and Purple Loosestrife (*L. salicaria*) are reducing vascular plant diversity and changing the vegetative structure of warm-water sloughs. | Cons. Orgs., CWB, Loc. Land, NDA, PVWMA, WCWMA | Build capacity of cooperative invasive/exotic species control programs by garnering a sustainable source of funds. Coordinate efforts to efficiently control exotic/invasive species and evaluate the effectiveness of various techniques where uncertainty remains (e.g., Common Reed). | Develop an annual funding mechanism of $600,000 to contain undesirable species outbreaks in all ecologically important PRV habitats on public, private, or nonprofit lands. | 4 |
| **Precipitation-driven inundation** and high water events facilitated by relatively unimpeded overland flow that carries natural amounts of sediment.<br><br>**Intensive agricultural practices** that promote **wetland sedimentation** as a result of soil erosion; this process reduces wetland functionality and generally increases invasive species cover. | Farm, Loc. Land, NDA, NRDs, NRCS, UNL-NWC | Protect and/or restore buffers surrounding high value warm-water slough wetlands and include upland buffers in all new slough restorations. Promote no-till farming practices in the river valley. | 1) Quantify remaining area of warm-water slough habitat in various reaches of the PRV. 2) Protect, restore, and/or enhance warm-water sloughs and associated grassland buffers (>100 m width) with regionally specific goals after inventory (e.g., restore >2,000 acres in the LPRV). 3) Reach 100% no-till agricultural in the PRV within <25 years. | 3 |
| **Repetitive grazing/management** - intensive annual cattle grazing or a complete lack of grazing or other management can lead to a reduced ecological functionality of warm-water slough wetlands (i.e., erosion, invasive species issues, or woody encroachment). | Farm, Loc. Land, NCA, NDA, NGLC, NRCS, NRDs, UNL-NWC | Connect ranchers to conservation programs that provide financial support for periodically resting wetlands from grazing. Provide outreach to interested parties outlining the habitat needs of at-risk species that depend on warm water slough wetlands. | Identify and attempt to contact all private landowners with significant tracts (>50 ha - 124 ac) of herbaceous wetland/grassland within 800 m of the Platte River and connect them to conservation programs or easements (e.g., NRCS) that would allow them to periodically rest their wetlands/grasslands without financial losses. | 3 |

| | | | | | |
|---|---|---|---|---|---|
| Increased the extent and resilience of **lowland tallgrass prairie** habitats for the benefit of grassland birds (e.g., Henslow's Sparrow), terrestrial insects (e.g., Regal Fritillary), native herpetofauna (e.g., Smooth Greensnake), and other species. | **Agricultural development** - loss of lowland tallgrass prairies as a result of conversion to row crop monocultures. | Cons. Orgs., Loc. Land, NCA, NDA, NGPC, NRCS, Livestock | Develop a coordinated plan to protect remnant lowland tallgrass prairies via land acquisitions and conservation easements. Support working prairies by connecting ranchers to conservation programs that provide financial support. Identify unproductive agricultural areas and connect farmers with resources to convert these areas to native prairie if the landowners desire. | 1) Restore >30% of the land within 0.5 miles of the Platte River to wetland or grassland habitat via tree clearing and crop ground restoration. 2) Prioritize the protection and restoration of contiguous habitats >575 ha (1,420 acres) as well as patches >80 ha (~200 acres) within <2 km of larger contiguous wetland/grassland areas. 3) Restore or protect smaller habitats if they are high quality, relict, facilitate connectivity, or represent unproductive cropland. | 4 |
| River flows that maintain shallow groundwater which **subirrigates** and therefore sustains **lowland tallgrass prairies** during the growing season. | **Residential** and **commercial development** - loss of lowland tallgrass prairies as a result of urban, suburban, and exurban development. | CBS, Cons. Orgs., Farm, Livestock, Loc. Land, NCA, NGPC, NRCS | Develop a coordinated plan to protect remnant lowland tallgrass prairies via land acquisitions and conservation easements. Support working prairies by connecting ranchers to conservation programs that provide financial support. Work with municipal and county zoning officials to limit development within the floodplain. | In addition to the above goals, identify and contact all private landowners with significant tracts (>50 ha – 124 ac) of herbaceous wetland/grassland within 800 m of the Platte River and connect them to conservation programs/easement opportunities to support their livelihoods and prevent grassland habitat from becoming farmed or developed. | 3 |

| Threat / Description | Partners | Action | Additional Action | Priority |
|---|---|---|---|---|
| Dynamic grassland function including temporal and spatial heterogeneity in vegetation structure resulting from **periodic natural disturbances** including fire, grazing, rest, and variation in moisture regime.<br><br>**Sand and gravel mining** - loss of lowland tallgrass prairies as a result of conversion to mining operations. | CBS, Cons. Orgs., Gravel, Loc. Land, NGPC | Develop a coordinated plan to protect remnant lowland tallgrass prairies via land acquisitions and conservation easements. Support working prairies by connecting ranchers to conservation programs that provide financial support. Work with county boards of supervisors, municipalities, and the state to limit the availability of special use permits for mining in lands zoned as agricultural-conservation areas. | In addition to the above two goals, conduct meetings with officials involved in zoning from all counties along the Platte River. Urge them to limit the availability of special use permits for mining in lands zoned as agricultural-conservation areas along the Platte River based upon the negative impacts to riverine ecosystems. Counties include Lincoln, Dawson, Phelps, Buffalo, Kearney, Hall, Merrick, Hamilton, Platte, Polk, Colfax, Butler, Dodge, Saunders, Douglas, Sarpy, Cass (17 counties). | 2 |
| **Exotic/invasive species** - species such as Eastern Redcedar (*J. virginiana*) and Smooth Brome (*B. Inermis*) are reducing vascular plant diversity and changing the vegetative structure of lowland tallgrass prairies. | Cons. Orgs., CWB, Loc. Land, NDA, NRCS, PBAs, PVWMA, WCWMA | Build capacity of cooperative invasive/exotic species control programs by garnering a sustainable source of funds. Coordinate efforts to efficiently control exotic/invasive species and evaluate the effectiveness of various techniques where uncertainty remains (e.g., Eastern Redcedar). | 1) Develop a funding mechanism of $600,000 USD annually to contain undesirable species outbreaks in the PRV on public, private, or nonprofit owned lands. 2) Develop a regularly occurring workshop where individuals/organizations can report on the effectiveness of their exotic/invasive species management efforts (could be linked with future Platte River Basin Ecosystem Symposia). | 4 |
| **Overgrazing** - many remnants are chronically grazed to maximize cattle yields. This promotes exotic and woody species establishment and limits habitat value for a host of native species (e.g., small mammals, breeding birds, etc.). | Cons. Orgs., Loc. Land, Livestock, NCA, NGLC, NRCS, NRDs | Connect ranchers to conservation programs that provide financial support for periodically resting prairies from grazing. Provide outreach to interested parties outlining the habitat needs of at-risk species that depend on lowland tallgrass prairies. | Identify and attempt to contact all private landowners with significant tracts (>50 ha - 124 ac) of herbaceous wetland/grassland within 800 m of the Platte River and connect them to conservation programs or easements (e.g., NRCS) that would allow them to periodically rest their wetlands/grasslands without financial losses. | 4 |

| Threat | Partners | Strategy | Actions | Priority |
|---|---|---|---|---|
| **Misapplication of Herbicide** - a common practice regionally is to spray all thistles (e.g., *Cirsium* spp., *Carduus* spp.) regardless of status (i.e., native or exotic). Even more problematic is the spraying of all "broadleaf weeds" to improve pasture production (e.g., *Verbena* spp., *Gutierrezia* spp., etc.). These practices can severely denude habitat values for pollinators (e.g., Monarch). | CWB, Cons. Orgs., Livestock, Loc. Land, NCA, NDA, NGLC, NRCS, NRDs, PVWMA, WCWMA | Provide outreach outlining the habitat needs of at-risk species that depend on lowland tallgrass prairies (e.g., Monarchs). Provide native forb seed to local landowners who want to plant it. Coordinate with the County Weed Board and others to promote native forbs and improve local knowledge of thistle identification. | 1) Identify and attempt to contact all private landowners with significant tracts (>50 ha - 124 ac) of herbaceous wetland/grassland within 800 m of the Platte River and provide them with accessible information regarding lowland tallgrass prairie species of concern and native forbs (i.e., thistles). 2) Secure grant funding to provide aforementioned landowners with native, local-ecotype forb seed if interested. | 2 |
| **Fire Suppression** - lowland tallgrass prairie is the most fire-dependent priority habitat addressed in our plan. It represents a "disturbance climax" community as woody species readily establish in fire's absence. Current data indicates the need to radically increase the total acres burned annually in NE to maintain prairie habitats in the long-term. | CPNRD, Cons. Orgs., PBAs, USFWS | Support community burn associations and local land owners in burning private lands in the PRV. Coordinate efforts between state, federal, and NGO conservation organizations to get more burning completed on conservation lands. Provide outreach materials about the benefits of fire to landowners. | 1) Achieve $\leq$5-year burn intervals on all state, federal, and conservation organization-owned land where appropriate (grassland, wetland, shrubland, savanna, open woodland, etc.). 2) Contact all prescribed burn associations (PBA) operational in or near the PRV and work to build collective capacity (Buffalo/Sherman PBA, Central Nebraska PBA, Rainwater Basin PBA, and Elkhorn Valley PBA, etc.). | 4 |

**Key Audiences:** Central NE Public Power and Irrigation District (CNPPID), Central Platte Natural Resources District (n.b., Prescribed Burn Task Force; CPNRD), Colorado Dept. of Natural Resources (CODNR), Colorado Water Conservation Board (CWCB), conservation organizations (e.g., Pheasants Forever; Cons. Orgs.), County Boards of Supervisors (n.b., zoning; CBS), County Road/Highway Depts. (CNTY HWYs), County Officials (CNTY Off.), County Weed Boards (e.g., Hall County Weed Board; CWB), farmers (Farm), Federal Highway Administration (FHA), general public (Public), livestock producers (Livestock), local landowners (n.b., easements, Loc. Land), Lower Platte North Natural Resources District (LPNNRD), Lower Platte South Natural Resources District (LPSNRD), Municipalities (e.g., Lincoln Water System; Municipal), National Weather Service (n.b., flood stage designation; NWS), Natural Resources Conservation Service (n.b., Conservation Stewardship Program; NRCS), Natural Resource Districts (n.b., general; NRDs), Nebraska Cattlemen Association (NCA), NE Dept. of Agriculture (n.b., Noxious Weed Program; NDA), NE Dept. of Environment and Energy (NDEE), NE Dept. of Natural Resources (NEDNR), NE Dept. of Transportation (NDOT), NE Game and Parks Commission (NGPC), NE Grazing Lands Coalition (NGLC), NE Public Power District (NPPD), NE State Irrigation Association (NSIA), Platte River Recovery Implementation Program (PRRIP), Platte Valley Weed Management Area (PVWMA), Prescribed Burn Associations (e.g., Buffalo/Sherman PBA; PBAs), recreationists (Rec.), Regional Universities (e.g., Univ. of NE at Kearney; Reg. Univ.), sand and gravel mining industry (e.g., Hooker Bros; Gravel ), South Platte Regional Opportunities Working Group (SPROWG), State legislators (State Leg.), Twin Platte Natural Resources District (TPNRD), University of NE-Lincoln – NE Water Center (UNL-NWC), U.S. Bureau of Reclamation (USBR), U.S. Dept. of Transportation (USDOT), U.S. Fish and Wildlife Service (USFWS), West Central Weed Management Area (WCWMA).

www.ingramcontent.com/pod-product-compliance
Lightning Source LLC
Chambersburg PA
CBHW080612270326
41928CB00016B/3017